SIMPLE LIBRARY CATALOGING

SUSAN GREY AKERS

Fourth edition

Simple library cataloging

AMERICAN LIBRARY ASSOCIATION

Chicago 1954

Fourteenth printing, April 1968

Contents

Introduction

The catalog. A catalog is a record of the material in a library. It answers such questions as: What books have you by Robert Nathan? Have you a copy of *Some Enchanted Evenings?* Have you material on interplanetary voyages? The catalog can also answer questions about the individual author or book, for instance: What is the most recent book in the library by A. J. Cronin? Does Schlesinger's *Rise of Modern America* include illustrations? Who published Anne Terry White's *Prehistoric America?* Besides showing what authors' works are represented in the library, whether or not the library has material on a given subject or contains a particular book, whether or not a certain book has illustrations, and so forth, the catalog may bring out portions of books; for example, there may be a card for *High Tor* in Barrett H. Clark's *Nine Modern American Plays,* and one for material on Christmas in Deming and Bemis' *Pieces for Every Day the Schools Celebrate.*

A given book is represented in the catalog under its author, title, and, if nonfiction—or, in some libraries, even if fiction—under the subject of which it treats. To illustrate: *City Neighbor: the Story of Jane Addams* would have cards under the title, *City Neighbor;* the author, Clara Ingram Judson; and under the subjects ADDAMS, JANE and HULL HOUSE, CHICAGO. Books may also be found under the name of the series, if it is an important subject series, e.g., "American Guide Series." In addition to the cards for specific books there are reference cards referring the reader from the form of the author's name under which he may look to the form used in that catalog:

Struther, Jan, pseud.
    See
Maxtone Graham, Joyce Anstruther.

There are also cards referring the reader from the term or terms under which he may look for material on a subject to the term or terms used in the catalog for that subject:

INTERSTELLAR VOYAGES
See
INTERPLANETARY VOYAGES.

Purpose of this manual. This book has a three-fold purpose: (1) to give to the librarian of the small public, school, college, or special library who lacks professional education and experience under expert guidance the necessary directions for classifying and cataloging a collection of printed and audio-visual materials, that they may be made accessible; (2) to serve as a textbook for short elementary courses in cataloging; and (3) to serve as collateral reading in the earlier parts of the basic cataloging courses. Fundamental rules for classifying and directions for using the Dewey Decimal Classification tables are given. An effort has been made to state the necessary cataloging rules as clearly, simply, and briefly as possible. These rules have been adapted from those in the *A.L.A. Cataloging Rules,* 1949 edition, and *Rules for Descriptive Cataloging in the Library of Congress,* 1949 edition and its supplements.

Order of the chapters. There were three groups of users to be considered in deciding upon the order in which to arrange the chapters: (1) instructors of courses in cataloging; (2) inexperienced librarians with little or no training who study this book alone and follow it through in direct connection with their work; and (3) librarians using the book as a catalog code. The first group is the most diverse and thus was considered least. Cataloging instructors, like instructors in other subjects, vary widely in the order and the method they follow in presenting topics. It is expected, therefore, that they will use the material in whatever order best suits the requirements of their courses. The material has been arranged with reference to the convenience of the second group especially and to some extent to that of the third. It is logical in bringing together closely related topics; e.g., Chapter I treats of classification and Chapter II of subject headings, two allied processes. Then follow the chapters which deal with the headings used as entries; and these chapters in turn are followed by the ones concerned with the actual description of the book in the catalog entry. At the end of the volume are chapters on the use of printed catalog cards, the arrangement of the cards in the catalog, and other subjects not strictly concerned with cataloging processes but essential in the cataloging of a library.

Scope. The following paragraphs summarize the contents of the chapters and indicate the changes made in this edition. It is based on the *A.L.A. Cataloging Rules,* 1949 edition, the *Rules for Descriptive Cataloging in the Library of Congress,* 1949 edition with its supplement, 1949-1951, rules for *Phonorecords,* 1952, and *Motion Pictures and Filmstrips,* 1953; and the sixth edition of the *Sears List of Subject Headings,* edited by Bertha M. Frick. The Standard (15th) Edition Revised of the Dewey Decimal Classification system omits such detailed expansions as that for 630, Agriculture; changes the place of many topics, some quite radically, and is considerably abridged throughout. The chapter on classification discusses some of the differences between the fourteenth and fifteenth editions and their effect on a library.

An entirely new chapter has been added to this edition to treat of the cataloging of the audio-visual materials most commonly found in small general libraries; namely, maps, records, filmstrips, and lantern slides. An appendix of sample catalog cards, with captions pointing out their special features, has also been added. These cards are in addition to typewritten and printed cards in the body of the text.

Recent books have been substituted in many of the examples. As in former editions there is an appendix of definitions of technical terms, almost all of which are taken from the *A.L.A. Glossary of Library Terms;* an appendix of abbreviations, revised to conform with the practice of the new rules for headings and the body of the entry; and an appendix which gives a short bibliography of aids for authors' names, subject headings, filing cards, etc. To these has been added the new appendix of sample catalog cards.

Chapter I defines and describes classification and discusses book numbers. Illustrations are taken from the fourteenth and the fifteenth editions of the Dewey Decimal Classification tables. Chapter II on subject headings has illustrations from the sixth edition of the *Sears List.* Chapters III–V, treating of personal names, anonymous classics and sacred books, and names of organizations are rewritten to incorporate the changes made in the new editions of the catalog rules.

Chapters VI and VII deal respectively with main and added entries. More recent books have been substituted for examples, and a section on cataloging fiction more simply than nonfiction has been added to Chapter VI.

Chapter VIII on cataloging sets, serials, and independent works bound together is much the same as in earlier editions. Chapter IX, on cataloging audio-visual materials, is entirely new. Chapter X, on the use of printed catalog cards, has had few changes. Chapter XI on arranging cards in a dictionary catalog is now based almost entirely on Appendix V, "List of the Rules Recommended to Small Libraries: Comprehensive Example," in the *A.L.A. Rules for Filing Catalog Cards*. Chapter XII, "Related Topics and Miscellaneous Information," remains practically the same.

Two minor changes in the form of the cards have been introduced in this edition: (1) tracing is given in the style used on Library of Congress and Wilson printed catalog cards and is put on the front rather than on the back of the card; and (2) *See* and *See also* are put on a separate line on reference cards, as it is believed that this form will be clearer for the reader and easier for the cataloger.

Acknowledgments. The author wishes to express her appreciation of the kindness of the Library of Congress in granting permission to quote from their catalog rules and to use their printed catalog cards freely as sample cards; to the H. W. Wilson Company for permission to use their printed catalog cards; and to the critics whose replies to a questionnaire were so helpful in deciding certain points about this revision. The author also wishes to record the assistance that she has received from her students during many years in the teaching of cataloging.

Chapel Hill, North Carolina   S. G. A.
September, 1953

chapter I

Classification

Definition. "To classify books is to place them in groups, each group including, as nearly as may be, all the books treating of a given subject, for instance, geology; or all the books, on whatever subject, cast in a particular form, for instance, poetry; or all the books having to do with a particular period of time, for instance, the Middle Ages.... Its purpose is...to make...books more available."[1]

Reasons for classifying. If a miscellaneous collection of books is to be used with ease, it should be arranged in some way. The books could be sorted and put on the shelves in alphabetic order according to their authors or titles. A collection arranged in that way would be many times more useful than a collection without any arrangement. Collections of books, however, are consulted more for material on a given subject than for any other purpose. Readers like to have the books on the same subject together, as they much prefer examining the books to searching a list or a catalog.

Dewey Decimal Classification scheme. If books are to be classified by subject, some scheme or system of classification should be adopted. Melvil Dewey's Decimal Classification is the one most widely used in the United States, and it has been adopted by many libraries in foreign countries. The *A.L.A. Catalogs,* the *Booklist,* the H. W. Wilson Company's Standard Catalogs, and many other library publications use this

---

[1]J. C. Dana, *A Library Primer* (Boston: Library Bureau, 1920), p.98.

classification system. It is published in two forms, the unabridged and the abridged.[2]

This system is called the decimal system because each class may be subdivided into ten divisions, each subdivision into ten further ones, the numbers being considered as decimals, not consecutive numbers. The ten main classes of the system are:

000 General works	500 Pure science
100 Philosophy	600 Applied science
200 Religion	700 Arts and recreation
300 Social sciences	800 Literature
400 Linguistics	900 History

Certain numbers are used for form divisions (i.e. to show in what form the material is written, e.g., a dictionary) as follows:

01 Philosophy Theory Methodology	06 Associations, societies
02 Compends, handbooks, outlines	07 Study and teaching
03 Dictionaries, encyclopedias	08 Collections
04 Essays, addresses, lectures	09 History and general local
05 Periodicals	treatment

Examples of form numbers in different classes:

900 History	700 Arts and recreation
902 An outline of history	703 A dictionary of art
903 A dictionary of history	705 An art periodical

Form divisions always include a zero, but the decimal point may come between the zero and the second figure, e.g., 720.9 (history of architecture—0.9 is the form number which indicates that it is history); 359.09 (history of the Navy); 720.5 (periodical dealing with architecture)—*but* 759.05 (nineteenth century painting, in the Standard (15th) Edition). Form numbers should be used with great care, first making sure that they have not been used for some other purpose. For instance, in European history the numbers .01–.09 are used for period divisions, e.g., 942.01 Anglo-Saxon England to 1066, and .1–.9 for geographic divisions, e.g., 942.1 London.

---

[2]Melvil Dewey, *Decimal Classification and Relativ Index* (Ed. 14, rev. and enl.; Lake Placid Club, N. Y.: Forest Pr., 1942). $15.

Melvil Dewey, *Abridged Decimal Classification and Relativ Index* (Ed. 6; Lake Placid Club, N. Y.: Forest Pr., 1945). $4.

Melvil Dewey, *Decimal Classification* (Standard (15th) ed.; Lake Placid Club, N. Y.: Forest Pr., [c1951]). $18.50.

Melvil Dewey, *Dewey Decimal Classification & Relative Index* (Standard (15th) ed. rev.; Lake Placid Club, N. Y.: Forest Pr., [c1952]). $18.50.

If a miscellaneous collection of books is to be classified according to the decimal system, the books will be grouped according to their subject matter, with, for instance, general books on all or many subjects, e.g., an encyclopedia, in one group; books about philosophy in a second; books about religion in a third; and those about applied science in another. A reader interested in literature will find all the material on literature and all the books of literature, poetry, drama, etc. together on the shelves.

The divisions of the science class, given below, show the principle of subdivision:

500 Pure science	550 Earth sciences
510 Mathematics	560 Paleontology
520 Astronomy	570 Biological sciences
530 Physics	580 Botany
540 Chemistry	590 Zoology

In turn the books on mathematics may be divided as follows:

510 Mathematics	512 Algebra
511 Arithmetic	513 Geometry

In science (500) typical form divisions are:

501 Philosophy, theory, methodology of science
502 Compends, outlines of science
503 Dictionaries, encyclopedias of science
504 Essays, addresses, lectures on science

The books can thus be arranged so that all the outlines on science will be together, all the essays on science; and in similar fashion all the handbooks on engineering, all histories of France will be together.

For the small general library the abridged edition of Dewey is convenient in size, inexpensive, and serves most purposes. Such editions, however, as the Standard (15th) Edition; the abridged editions of former full editions, e.g., the Abridged Edition 6; and the lists of Dewey Decimal Classification numbers found in general books on school or other special libraries, which have a chapter on cataloging and classification, are often unsatisfactory as they offer no place for new subjects and no indication of where they should go. The unabridged editions show broad general subjects and their subdivisions, so that a new subject can be fitted in, in its proper relation to the older subjects.

In a classification system using arabic figures for the symbols of the classes and using the decimal principle for subdivision of those classes, numbers grow in length as the classification is expanded to make a place for divisions of the subject. The library which does not need these subdivisions, simply uses the broad number, omitting any figures at the end which it does not need, e.g., 973 stands for American history, and if the collection is not large enough for period divisions to be required, they are omitted. 973.917 is the number for the period of history when Franklin Delano Roosevelt was President; but the small library with few books on American history may use only 973.9, Twentieth century American history, or 973.91, Early twentieth century American history.

The Standard (15th) Edition of the Decimal Classification is convenient in size and has conventionalized spelling throughout. The terminology has been modernized. The extensive expansions for medicine (610); engineering (620); agriculture (630); and special numbers for individual authors have been omitted. These changes are all advantageous for the small general library. The sixth edition of the *Standard Catalog for High School Libraries,* 1952, and the eighth edition of the *Children's Catalog,* 1951, and their supplements use the Standard (15th) Edition.

On the other hand there are some features of the Standard (15th) Edition, which need to be carefully considered before a decision to adopt it is made. In some instances the general number has been omitted and the more specific number is not clear unless the classifier is familiar with the system and knows what the general class is, or has an earlier edition to which to refer. For instance, the Standard (15th) Edition gives 681.1 Horology, but does not give 681 Fine mechanism, Instruments of precision, Watch and clock making; 659.1 Advertising, publicity, and public relations is given, but not 659 Advertising. Form numbers are given in three different ways: page lv, which is referred to throughout the tables lists them correctly: 01, 02, 03, etc. For the science class (500) the user of the tables is referred to the form divisions 1-9 on page lv; but for mathematics (510), a division of science, the reference is to form divisions .1-.9 on page lv. These variations are confusing.

One of the important features of the Dewey Decimal Classification system has been its relative index. A relative index as defined by Mr. Haykin is an index "which will show under each entry the different senses in which the term is used and the diverse aspects of the subject with their appropriate places in the classification system."[3] The index to the Standard (15th) Edition does not do this though the Standard (15th) Edition Revised does it in some of its index entries. The examples given below are taken from the indexes to four editions of the Decimal Classification:

Edition 14

Beverages
  alcoholic temperance   178
  and nutrition physiology 612.3931-2
  chemic technology   663
  cookery   641.87
  hygiene   613.3
  state inspection   614.34
  see also Drinks

Abridged...Edition 6

Beverages
  adulterations   614.3
  alcoholic temperance   178
  chemic technology   663
  cookery   641
  hygiene   613.3

Standard (15th) Edition

Beverages   663
  Public health control   614.3

Standard (15th) Edition Revised

Beverages   663
  (Public health control) 614.3

Edition 14

Restoration
  1660 English history   942.066
  furniture fine arts   749.222
  Japanese history   952.022

Abridged...Edition 6

Restoration
  of art objects   708
    paintings   751
      photographic negatives
        and prints   770
  1660 English history   942.06

Standard (15th) Edition

Restoration (no entry in Index)

Standard (15th) Edition Revised

Restoration   942.06
  furniture   749.22
  (Judaism)   296.3
  of art objects   708
    See also specific fields of art
  of paintings   751

Larger subjects must occasionally be subordinated to smaller ones in an index. For instance, the place in United States history of the Federal party must be shown in an index by an entry for United States history under the smaller subject Federal party. The Index to the

[3]D. J. Haykin, *Subject Headings: A Practical Guide* (Washington: Govt. Print. Off., 1951), p.2.

Standard (15th) Edition Revised uses parentheses around the subordinated larger subject:

> Federal party
> (U.S. history)

The new library, which is being classified for the first time, decides on a classification system and follows it. New editions of the adopted system always bring up problems due to changes, but the Standard (15th) Edition offers more such problems than other editions. Some examples of the radical changes in numbers are listed below:

	Edition 14	Standard (15th) Edition
Commercial geography	380.9	911.3
Professional and business ethics	174	610, 340, etc., with the profession
International ethics	172.4	177
Family relations, customs and manners	392.3	301.42

How to classify. The book which is to be classified should be carefully examined to see *what it is about, what the author's purpose was in writing it, what class of readers will find it most useful.* To do this, read the title page, preface, all or part of the introduction, look over the table of contents (as this spreads out before the examiner the skeleton of the book), and read parts of the book itself. Having determined to what class the book belongs, e.g., history, turn to the table for that class —in this case 900. An examination of the table shows that 900 is divided according to place and time. Such questions arise as: What country or section of a country is the book about? Does it cover the entire history of that country or section or only a specific period? Of course, if it covers the entire world from the creation to the present time, it goes in the general number for history, 909. But if the book is limited to United States history, it will go in 973, the figure 9 indicating that it is history, 7 that it is limited geographically to North America, and 3 that it is further confined to the United States. The 900 class, which includes history, travel, and biography, is a good one with which to begin the study of classification. It is readily determined whether or not a book treats of history, travel, or biography; and, if it is history, the country and period of time covered are clearly indicated.

If the book is one of pure literature, the first deciding factor is the nationality of the author; the second, the literary form. Thus Masefield's poems are put with other books of English literature and in the section for poetry, 821. A book on the theory of electricity would go in the main class, science, the division for physics, and the section on electricity, 537.

The figures are the symbol of the class; e.g., 620 represents engineering and all general books on engineering would be so marked. If a book is on a specific kind of engineering, the third figure changes to show that fact, e.g., 621, Mechanical engineering. Having discovered what a book is about and its place in the classification scheme, one puts the number representing that subject in the system (the notation) in the book and on its cover, so that all books may be kept together on the shelves in the order of their classes.

General rules for classifying. Sayers gives the following general rules for classifying:

1 Class a book first according to its subject, and then by the form in which the subject is presented, except in generalia and in pure literature where form is paramount.
2 In determining the subject consider the predominant tendency or obvious purpose of a book, and its author's intention in writing it.
3 When a book appears to belong equally to two places in the classification make a decision as to the one in which it is to go.
4 When a book deals with two (or three) divisions of a subject, place it in the one which appears to be the most important; or, if the parts seem of equal importance, in the one first treated. When more than two (or three) divisions of the subject are dealt with, place the book in the general heading which contains all or the majority of them.
5 When a subject arises for which no place is provided in the scheme of classification, find the heading to which it seems to be most nearly allied and make a place for it there.
6 Place a book in the most specific head that will contain it.
7 Avoid placings which are in the nature of criticism. Pros and cons of any subject go together.
8 Index all decisions, or new headings, which are not already included in the index to the scheme; that is to say, make your index exactly represent your practice.
9 Finally (to repeat), *place a book where you think it will be most useful; and always have a reason for placing it there.*[4]

To illustrate the application of the first of these rules for classifying:

[4]W. C. B. Sayers, *An Introduction to Library Classification* (8th ed.; London: Grafton, 1950), p.167-68.

Grove's *Dictionary of Music and Musicians* would be given the Dewey Decimal Classification number 780.3; 78 shows that it treats of music, 0.3 that it is in the form of a dictionary. Masefield's poems would be given the number 821, 8 showing that it is pure literature, 2 that it is by an Englishman, and 1 that it is poetry. The literary form here determines its symbol, not the subject matter.

Rules number 3, 4, and 9 may be illustrated by a single group of books. *Reptiles and Amphibians; an Illustrated Natural History,* as the title indicates, deals with reptiles and amphibians, represented in the tables by two numbers, 597.6 Batrachia (amphibia) and 598.1 Reptiles. The *Standard Catalog for High School Libraries* gives this book the number 598.1 Reptiles, "where it will be most useful," thus deciding which heading should prevail. In this connection it should be added that in the dictionary catalog there will be entries for this book under both subjects, namely, BATRACHIA and REPTILES, so that it can be easily found by readers desiring material on either subject.

M. W. Jernigan's *American Colonies, 1492-1750* covers two periods of American history according to the divisions in Dewey, 973.1, the period of discovery and exploration, and 973.2, the colonial period. The emphasis is on the colonial period, the earlier material being given as background for it; therefore it will be more useful and will be in accordance with the emphasis and purpose of the author to place it in colonial history, 973.2.

Occasionally a book comes up for classification which deals with an entirely new subject, one for which there is no place in the Dewey Decimal Classification table. Representative of such subjects are the terms *guided missiles, geopolitics, sulfanilamide* and many others. Frank Xavier Ross' *Guided Missiles; Rockets & Torpedoes,* published by Lothrop in 1951 and S. B. Jones and M. F. Murphy's *Geography and World Affairs,* published by Rand McNally in 1950 are illustrations.

The sixth abridged edition of the Dewey Decimal Classification, 1945, does not include the terms *guided missiles, geopolitics, radio broadcasting,* and *sulfanilamide* in its index or tables. The fourteenth edition of the unabridged Dewey has only Radio broadcasting—advertising, and Sulfanilamid—pharmacy. The Standard (15th) Edition index has Guided missiles, 623.451; Geopolitics, 320.1; and Radio broadcasting, 384.5; Sulfanilamide, 615, is found only in the Revised Index of the Standard (15th) Edition.

If the library uses the abridged edition of Dewey or the fourteenth unabridged edition, where shall the books on guided missiles be classified? In rule number 5 Sayers states that if there is no place for a subject of which a book treats, the heading to which it is most nearly related should be determined and a place made for it there. The Abridged Edition 6 includes in its index:

Projectiles
    ordnance engineering   623
    physics   531

The tables give: 623 Military and naval engineering; 531 Physics—mechanics. If the book which is being classified treats the subject from the point of view of physics it should go in 531; if from the point of view of military and naval engineering it should go in 623, even though this puts it with material on the general subject. The fourteenth unabridged edition index gives:

Projectiles
    ordnance   623.451
    physics   531.55

Again the question arises, is this book on the theoretical side or the practical? 531.55 is to be used for material on mechanics—gravity—projectiles and 623.451 for artillery projectiles. The term *guided missiles* should be added, in its correct alphabetic place, to the index of the edition of the tables which the library owns. It may also be added in the tables, e.g., 623 Military and naval engineering—guided missiles, in the abridged edition, and 623.451 Artillery projectiles—guided missiles, in the fourteenth edition.

Applying rule number 6, one would give James Truslow Adams' *Provincial Society, 1690-1763* the classification number 973.2, the number for colonial history of the United States, not 973, the general number for United States history.

Books which would come under rule number 7 are quite rare. For instance, the early books on Christian Science were placed in 615 with books on therapeutics. This classifying was according to the classifier's personal view of the subject. A place has since been made for Christian Science in class 200, religion.

When ready to classify a collection of books, first sort them by general groups, then examine those in each group carefully and see precisely what they are about. This is much easier than taking books as they come and switching one's thoughts from science to religion, to drama, to railroading, and so forth. The rules for classifying quoted from Sayers will be found very helpful. But one learns to classify by classifying. Keep in mind the purpose of classifying; namely, "to make books more available" to the readers for whose benefit classification is used. Be as consistent as possible; in deciding upon a certain class for a certain book, see what other books are in that class. In her pamphlet, *Classification,* Bacon says: "Concrete well-defined subjects should be more closely classified than abstract ones."[5]

Changes from the Dewey Decimal Classification. Bacon's pamphlet points out further:

> Some deviations from the D.C. [Decimal Classification] tables may often be employed to advantage, e.g., public libraries generally disregard the classification in fiction and arrange all fiction printed in English, whether original or translation, in a single group, alphabetically by authors...The average public library will find it best to arrange individual biography alphabetically by subject in a single group, marked either B or 92...Almost every library will find lives of artists and musicians more useful classed in art and music [e.g., Anne Leslie's *Rodin, Immortal Peasant* in 735 and David Ewen's *Living Musicians* in 780.92]. Collective biography should be classified according to the D.C. divisions 920–928, or [preferably] arranged alphabetically by authors in a single group under 920, just as in any part of the classification the subdivisions may be disregarded and the material collected under the general number.[6]

Since these or other changes in the tables are inevitable in every library, it is most important that each library, no matter how small, have an official copy of the adopted classification table annotated to show the practice of that particular library. For instance, if the library uses 92 for individual biography, it is necessary to cross out the letter B suggested as an alternative for 92 for individual biography. If this is done no one will forget and use B for the biography of an individual. The library which uses the fifteenth edition will need to indicate in which cases it is following the recommendation that another number be used. For instance: 172.4 "It is recommended that International Ethics be classified in 177." The sentence could be crossed out and "See 177" be written in after 172.4; then no one would forget and use 172.4.

---

[5]Corinne Bacon, *Classification* (rev. ed.; Chicago: A.L.A., 1925), p.21.
[6]*Ibid.,* p.19.

The *Standard (15th) Edition Revised Relative Index* gives the entry: Travel, 900; History, 900; Geography, 910. The tables give: 910 Geography; 913–919 Regional geography; 900 History—political, social, cultural; 940 European history. The fourteenth edition index has: Geography—descriptive, 910; History, 900; Travels, 910; the tables give: 900 History in general; 910 Geography, travels, description; 914–919 is subdivided like 940–999. Whenever these main geographic headings occur they may be subdivided exactly like History. The *Standard Catalog for High School Libraries,* sixth edition, has:

910 Geography

Books on description and travel of the various countries have been transferred to the history and civilization classification, 930–999, in accordance with a decision of the Dewey Decimal Committee

The *Children's Catalog,* eighth edition revised, has:

914–919 Description and Travel

Books on description and travel of various countries formerly classified 914-919 and subdivisions have been changed to be with the history of the various countries in 940–999

The newly established library will probably wish to follow this trend and put books which are strictly geography in 914–919 and all others, whether history or description, in 940–999. The library with a considerable collection classified in 914–919 Description and travel and 940–999 History may write in its copy of the Dewey Decimal Classification that 914–919 is for geography, description, and travel, 940–999 for history, and continue to classify as formerly.

Classification aids and how to use them. The *Booklist, Book Review Digest, A.L.A. Catalogs* and the Wilson Standard Catalog series and their supplements give among other items the suggested classification number for each book listed. The *Guidepost* of the Public Library of Cincinnati; The *Wisconsin Library Bulletin,* which contains in each number lists of current books; the North Carolina State Board of Education, Division of Textbooks', *Library Book Catalogue,* a classified list for elementary and high school libraries; and the Oregon State Library's *List of Books for School Libraries* are examples of bulletins which give the decimal classification numbers.

The use of these and other aids may show complete agreement or considerable variation as to the number for the book. The *Book Review*

Digest, 1952, lists H. L. Ewbank and S. P. Lawton's *Broadcasting: Radio and Television* and gives as the classification numbers 792.93 and 791.4. The *Standard Catalog for Public Libraries, 1952 Supplement,* lists this book and gives as the suggested classification number 792.94, and the *Booklist* gives 384. Which of these numbers should the library use? Is it a difference of opinion among the classifiers who assigned the numbers, variations in the editions of the *Dewey Decimal Classification,* or both? Pertinent entries from the tables and indexes of the various editions still in use follow:

Edition 14

Tables

384	Telegraf Cable Telefone
.5	Radio Wireless
791.4	Panoramas Magic lanterns Moving pictures Radio
792	Theater Stage Dramatic art
.9	Other

Index

Broadcasting	
radio	621.384193
Radio	
broadcasts, types of	621.3841938
. . . .	
recreation	791.4
. . . .	
television electrical engineering	621.38853
Television	
recreation	791.4

Abridged...Edition 6

Tables

384	Telegraph Cable Telephone Radio Television
791.4	Panoramas Magic lanterns Moving pictures Radio
792	Dramatic art Theater Stage

Index

Radio	
recreation	791.4
television	621.388
. . . .	

Television
   recreation   791.4

Standard (15th) Edition

Tables

384	Communication
384.5	Radiocommunication
	For Radio engineering and broadcasting, see 621.384
.55	Television Communication
	For Television engineering and broadcasting, see 621.388
791	Shows
792.93	Moving Picture Production
792.94	Radio Show Production
792.95	Television Show Production

Index		Index (Relative Index volume)	
Broadcasting		Broadcasting	
radio	621.3849	radio	384.5
television	621.3889	television	384.55
....		....	
Radio		Radio	621.384
show production	792.94	play production	792.94
....		....	
Television		Television	
show production	792.95	play production	792.95

To sum up for the book by Ewbank and Lawton: the aids suggest 791.4, which would place it with material in the general field of public entertainment—moving pictures and radio; or 792, with material on dramatic art, plays; or 384, with material on radio and television as a means of communication, as shown by the quotations from the decimal classification tables and indexes. 621.38 and its subdivisions, which the indexes bring out, is the number for electric communication. The book describes radio and television systems and discusses in detail the preparation, rehearsal, and production of programs to be put on by radio and television. Two out of the three aids consulted give 792 or a division under it, hence that would seem to be the better number, using 792.9, as it covers both radio and television, unless the library uses the Abridged Edition 6, in which case it would use 792. There is a difference of opinion among the classifiers and there are differences in expansion in the different editions of the Decimal Classification system.

Another aid for users of the Dewey Decimal Classification system is *Sears List of Subject Headings,* sixth edition, by Bertha M. Frick.[7] On pages 428-430 are found:

Radio	621.384
Radio advertising	659.1
Radio and music	780
Radio broadcasting	621.384
Radio in aeronautics	621.384

Ewbank and Lawton's book on broadcasting would have as subject headings: Radio broadcasting (which in the *Sears List,* sixth edition, is followed by suggested number 621.384) and Television broadcasting (suggested number, 621.388). In general, however, the usage of the Standard Catalogs of the H. W. Wilson Company as regards Decimal Classification numbers is followed in the *Sears List of Subject Headings.*

These aids and others will be found very useful as a check on one's classification and may suggest more desirable classification numbers when the specific topic is not included in the index to the tables. If one is continually in agreement with the aids, presumably one knows how to classify. In case of doubt always consult the aids. But having consulted the aids, be sure to consult the particular library's collection and see that the number suggested is in accordance with its practice and is the best place for the given book in that library.

An aid may change its policy as the *Booklist* has done in regard to the use of 810 and 820. At one time all literary works of American or English authors were put together, and 821 English poetry was used for both American and British poetry in the *Booklist.* The sixth edition of the *Standard Catalog for High School Libraries* states that "Books on the Federal Bureau of Investigation are now classified 353.5; Secret Service of the Treasury Department 353.2." Both were formerly classified in 351.74. If a library is to adopt such a change in policy, all of the books and records involved should have the classification numbers changed, while a bibliography such as the *Booklist* may ignore earlier volumes and simply be consistent in present and future issues. It is a

[7]B. M. Frick, *Sears List of Subject Headings* (6th ed.; N. Y.: Wilson, 1950).

saving in time for the library to make the change when the aid first makes it. Otherwise, for instance, the library using the *Standard Catalog* series in its cataloging must assign different class numbers to all books issued after a change is made, and, if Wilson cards are used, must change the numbers on the cards.

Shelf arrangement of books within a class. In many libraries, especially in small public libraries but also in schools and colleges, the books of fiction have an F, Fic, or no symbol at all on the spine of the book and on the catalog cards to show the location of the books on the shelves. All fiction printed in English is shelved together, regardless of the language in which it was originally written. Some libraries use SC (Story Collections) to designate the books of short stories and shelve them immediately following the books of fiction. Juvenile fiction is usually designated in public libraries by marking it with a plus sign or a J. E is similarly used for Easy Books for children in the first to third grades. Easy books, because of their size and shape, may be kept on specially built shelves and are arranged alphabetically by author, but as a rule no attempt is made to keep the works of an author in alphabetical order by title; and, if two authors have the same surname, no special effort is made to keep their works separated on the shelves.

In the case of nonfiction, however, library practice will be found to vary. Many libraries use book numbers as well as classification numbers; many do not. Book numbers make it possible to keep the books within a class—i.e., those having the same content and therefore the same classification symbol—in exact order with little difficulty.

Individual biography, whether or not book numbers are used, is arranged by the name of the person written about, not the biographer, so that all of the biographies of one person will come together on the shelf. If book numbers are not used, individual biographies should have the name of the person written about underscored on the spine of the book for convenience in shelving. It should be added where it does not appear; for example, Eaton's *Leader by Destiny* should have "Washington" written on the spine and be shelved under Washington's name.

The name by which a book is to be shelved should be underscored on the back in the case of books with editors, translators, and joint authors when there may be any doubt as to the choice of name. If fiction is published anonymously, but the author is known and his books are entered in the catalog under his name, the name should be added to the spine of the book. When a book is published under a pseudonym and is cataloged and consequently shelved under the real name, the name under which it is to be shelved should be underscored or added to the cover.

Book numbers. A book number is a combination of letters and figures taken from an alphabetic order table, e.g., the Cutter-Sanborn table.[8] The basic elements of the book number system now commonly used are as Barden states:

1 An *initial letter* followed by figures to represent a name. This provides an alphabetic arrangement.
2 The *figures* arranged *as decimals* to make possible the insertion of a new name between any two combinations already used.[9]

For example, Miles 645, Millikan 654, Mills 657; or better, if just two figures are used: Miles 64, Millikan 65, but Mills 657, since it must be distinguished from Millikan if the titles being cataloged have the same classification number. If the book by Millikan is classified in 530 and the one by Mills in 591.5, however, M65 may be used for both, since the classification numbers differ.

If the books in the collection of individual biography are classified in 92 and arranged by the name of the subject of the biography, many book numbers may begin with the same initial letter or letters. To illustrate: Agassiz, A262; Allen, A425; Arliss, A724; or shortening them to two figures: A26, A42, and A72. Thus they may be distinguished with three symbols. By adding the initial letter of the biographer's name, one may readily differentiate several biographies of the same person and arrange them in alphabetical order by author: e.g., Goss' biography of Johann Sebastian Bach would have the book number 92 and Wheeler and Deucher's 92; Dan Beard's auto-
$$\text{B11G} \qquad\qquad\qquad\qquad \text{B11W}$$
biography 92 and Clemens and Sibley's biography of Beard 92. Note
$$\text{B36} \qquad\qquad\qquad\qquad\qquad\qquad \text{B36C}$$
that the autobiography has no letter added after the number B36 and would stand before the other biographies.

Many small libraries have found the first letter of the author's surname a satisfactory substitute for book numbers and use it for both fiction and nonfiction. Thus Stevenson's *Treasure Island* might be

---

[8]C. A. Cutter, *Alphabetic order table, altered and fitted with three figures* by Kate E. Sanborn.
[9]B. R. Barden, *Book Numbers; a Manual for Students* (Chicago: A.L.A., 1937), p.7.

marked $\frac{F}{S}$ on the back, this same symbol being used on the catalog cards to show the location of the book. P. F. Ashton's *Everyone Can Paint Fabrics* would be 745.5.

$$\frac{A}{}$$

The system of using the initial letter only sometimes breaks down in the class of individual biography if there are many cases of persons with the same surname or surnames beginning with the same letter or letters. To illustrate, Franklin D. Roosevelt's biographies would be marked 92 and if there were several biographies the author's initial letter would be added to distinguish them, e.g., $\frac{92}{RL}$ for Ludwig's life of Roosevelt. Suppose the library having this book adds Eleanor Roosevelt's autobiography, *This Is My Story*. An *o* may be added to the *R* either in the call number for biographies of Franklin D. Roosevelt or, better, to the number for biographies of Eleanor Roosevelt. As there are likely to be more biographies of Franklin D. Roosevelt, it may be well to keep the shorter designation for them even though the arrangement on the shelves would not be strictly alphabetical. The book numbers may be $\frac{92}{Ro}$ for *This Is My Story* and $\frac{92}{RL}$ for Ludwig's *Roosevelt; a Study in Fortune and Power;* or both may be $\frac{92}{R}$ the order of the books being only approximately alphabetical within a class. Another illustration may be drawn from the Adams: Henry Adams' *Letters (1892–1918);* Mrs. Henry Adams' *Letters, 1865–1883;* and J. C. Miller's *Sam Adams: Pioneer in Propaganda.* They could all be assigned the number 92; or (in order) $\frac{92}{A}$, $\frac{92}{A1}$, and $\frac{92}{A2}$. If the Cutter-Sanborn tables are used, the books present no problem if three figures are used; they are $\frac{92}{A213}$, $\frac{92}{A215}$, and $\frac{92}{A217}$ respectively. There are not likely to be many such cases in the average small general library. Cutter-Sanborn numbers may be used for individual biography, and the initial letter used in other classes.

Barden states that book numbers in addition to class numbers are needed—

1 To arrange books in order on the shelves.
2 To provide a brief and accurate call number for each book.

3 To locate a particular book on the shelf.
4 To provide a symbol for charging books to borrowers.
5 To facilitate the return of books to the shelves.
6 To assist in quick identification of a book when inventories are taken.[10]

Fargo[11] in a brief discussion of book numbers says that their value is a moot question in the larger high school libraries; that school librarians frequently compromise and use just the initial letter of the author's surname instead of a book number. She points out that the difficulty comes when a library has several general histories of the United States by authors whose surnames begin with the same letter. The *Standard Catalog for High School Libraries,* sixth edition, 1952, lists general histories, all classified in 973, by Baker, Bassett, Beard, Benét, and Butcher. The initial of the author's name, B, would not be of much help in arranging these books on the shelf.

Tomlinson points out that if book numbers are omitted, time is saved in the work room; but as much or more time may be lost in shelving books and in locating books on the shelves.[12] On the other side of the argument Brown writes: "In small village and town libraries and perhaps in small school libraries I should not recommend Cutter numbers."[13] And Douglas recommends that the small school library, especially where a teacher-librarian is in charge, use only the initial of the author's surname.[14]

Miss Brown and Mrs. Douglas were writing about the very small library, but Miss Latimer, writing about the Children's Department of the Public Library of the District of Columbia in 1932, lists among labor savers the doing away with book numbers on all juvenile nonfiction except collective biography and collective poetry, adding, "The pages report shelving no harder even in the transition period."[15]

To sum up this discussion: Adopt a policy regarding the use of book numbers and adhere to it. If the library has book numbers, continue them, studying their advantages and disadvantages. If it does not have them, continue without them unless certain that they would improve the service to the public. In case of a new library or one previously uncataloged and unclassified, go over the arguments for and against book

[10]Barden, *op. cit.,* p.9.
[11]L. F. Fargo, *The Library in the School* (4th ed.; Chicago: A.L.A., 1947), p.279.
[12]A. L. Tomlinson, "Are Cutter Numbers Doomed?" *Library Journal,* 57:292, March 15, 1932.
[13]Zaidee Brown, "More about Cutter Numbers," *Library Journal,* 57:437, May 1, 1932.
[14]M. P. Douglas, *Teacher-Librarian's Handbook* (2d ed.; Chicago: A.L.A., 1949), p.38-39.
[15]L. P. Latimer, "Labor Saving," *Library Journal,* 57:647, August 1932.

numbers in this and other manuals, make your decision, and stand by it. Unless the book collection includes many different editions which may be difficult to distinguish without book numbers or many books by the same author in the same class, it would seem unnecessary to have them.

Book numbers from the Cutter-Sanborn alphabetic order table are given on the sample cards for nonfiction in this book. Librarians deciding not to use book numbers have simply to omit them from their cards and follow the sample cards in all other respects.

chapter II

Choice of
subject headings

Introduction. This chapter deals with the problem of determining of what subject a book treats and the topic or topics under which it should be listed in the catalog. The forms of the subject card and the subject analytical card[1] are discussed in a later chapter. Some libraries find that subject entries for certain types of fiction serve a real purpose and improve the service of the library. If sea stories and detective stories, to take two of the best-known examples, are entered in the catalog under the headings SEA STORIES, and MYSTERY AND DETECTIVE STORIES, respectively, as well as under author and title, time will be saved both for the public and the library staff—though the time saved by the staff in serving the public may possibly be counterbalanced by the time spent in assigning those subjects and in making those extra cards.

School libraries will find subject cards for fiction almost as useful as those for nonfiction. Both the *Standard Catalog for High School Libraries* and the *Children's Catalog* indicate subject headings for most of the books of fiction. For example, Carl Daniel Lane's *The Fire Raft* has listed below the description of the book: STEAMBOATS—FICTION. Douglas Warner Gorsline's *Farm Boy* has: FARM LIFE—FICTION. These are suggested subject headings under which to list these books in the catalog. On the other hand, it is not advisable to try to find subjects for all books of fiction. The *Standard Catalog for High School Libraries*

---

[1] An analytical entry is made for a portion of a book; e.g., a card with the heading AIR CONDITIONING would be made for pages 1279-1312 of F. D. Graham's *Audels Handy Book of Practical Electricity,* while a subject card under ELECTRIC ENGINEERING. HANDBOOKS, MANUALS, ETC. would be made for the entire book.

does not suggest any subjects for Dorothy Gilman Butters' *Ragamuffin Alley;* nor does the *Children's Catalog* give any for Bunyan's *Pilgrim's Progress.* Make subject cards for the catalog for fiction and nonfiction if the book gives definite information on a given subject.

Subject treated. To determine the subject of a book requires such a careful examination of its contents as is described on page 10 in discussing "How to classify." For this reason the subject headings should be determined and assigned at the same time as the classification number; otherwise examining the book and determining what it is about has to be done twice. The two topics are separated in this manual because, since both classification and subject headings are difficult, it is better to take them up separately until each one is clearly understood. Furthermore, in organizing or reorganizing a library it is frequently best to classify the books, make a shelf list,[2] and later catalog the collection.

Review the directions given in Chapter I: Read the title page, look over the table of contents carefully, read the preface, read or look through the introduction, and dip into the book itself in several places. This scrutiny will show what the book is about and what the author's purpose was in writing it. Such an examination may bring out the fact that the book treats of one subject, of several distinct phases of a subject, or of two or more subjects. No matter of how many subjects a book may treat, it can be classified in only one place and stand on the shelves in only one place; but it may be entered in the catalog under as many subject headings as are necessary. If the book treats of one subject, it requires only one subject heading; e.g., Bassett's *A Short History of the United States* deals with the general subject and would be entered in the catalog only under the heading U. S. HISTORY.

On the other hand, Norman V. Carlisle's *Your Career in Chemistry* needs to be brought out under three subjects, CHEMISTRY, TECHNICAL; CHEMISTS; and VOCATIONAL GUIDANCE. Similarly Alfred P. Morgan's *Home Electrical Repairs* treats of both electric apparatus and appliances and of electric wiring and should be represented in the catalog by two subject cards, one under ELECTRIC APPARATUS AND APPLIANCES, DOMESTIC and one under ELECTRIC WIRING. Another type of book has one general topic and includes a number of specific topics, e.g., Carroll A. Fenton

---

[2]The shelf list, which will be discussed in detail in a later chapter, is a brief record of the books in a library.

and Mildred A. Fenton's *Mountains*. The general subject is mountains, and a card will be made for the catalog with that word as the heading. But the book will be much more useful in the children's library if it is also entered in the catalog under the special topics with which it deals, e.g., pages 23–36 are on volcanoes, pages 83–98 on glaciers, pages 99–111 on trees, pages 112-122 on botany, and pages 123-135 on animals. Subject analytical cards should be made for each of these topics, or as many of them as the library is likely to have calls for. This depends upon the other material available on the subject and the special interests of the library's readers.

Fenton and Fenton's *Mountains* illustrates another point about added entries. The title of this book is *Mountains* and the subject treated is mountains, so the subject heading would be MOUNTAINS. It is unnecessary to have the same book entered in the catalog twice under the same word; but if only a title card is made it will file at the end of all the cards for the material about mountains even though the author's name begins with F; hence the rule, if the first word or words of the title and the subject are the same do *not* make a title card.

Thus the book is examined, the subject of which it treats determined, and one or more subject cards are made for the catalog. Whether these cards are general subject entries or subject analytical entries for a particular portion of the book depends upon whether two or more subjects are discussed together throughout the book or each subject is discussed separately.

Selecting subject headings. When deciding upon the heading for a subject entry, choose that heading which most truly represents the contents of the book or a certain part of the book, that is, the most specific subject or subjects possible. For example, if a book is about trees—how to identify them, their uses for ornamentation—select the specific term TREES. The subject heading BOTANY includes the subject heading TREES, but it obviously includes a great deal more, and this book tells of no other plant than the tree. The subject heading FORESTS AND FORESTRY would be used for a book which treats of trees as they grow in forests, how to care for and preserve forests, but not for a book which treats of trees as individual varieties, trees as an ornament for lawns and streets, and the like. It would not, therefore, be a suitable heading for this book. Likewise, Fabre's *The Life of the Fly* would have the specific heading FLIES, and not the general one INSECTS. Of two equally correct and specific headings, such as BIRDS and ORNITHOLOGY, the choice depends upon the type of library, and a cross reference[3] may be made from the one not chosen. In a public or a school library, choose the heading BIRDS as the term commonly used by the readers. In a special ornithological library, use the heading ORNITHOLOGY, for the users of such a library are quite familiar with the scientific term.

Consider opposite terms such as *temperance* and *intemperance*. A book on one of these subjects necessarily includes material on the other. Choose one, e.g., TEMPERANCE, and put all the material under it, referring from the other term.

Select as many subject headings as are necessary to cover the contents of the book, but do not multiply them unnecessarily. Test each heading by asking whether or not a patron would be glad to be given the book or books listed under the given heading if he were looking for material on the topic used as heading. It would be an unusual book which would need more than three or four subject headings, and one or two will cover most books. In the case of subject analytical entries, however, very many may be needed for certain kinds of books. In the *Children's Catalog,* eighth edition, 1951, Nellie Van de G. Sanchez' *Stories of the States; Tales of Early Exploration and Settlement,* revised edition, 1951, has the general subject headings, SEALS (NUMISMATICS) and U. S. HISTORY, and 57 subject analytical entries, e.g., ALABAMA, *pages 3–8.* But, as is explained in more detail in a later chapter, it is not desirable to analyze books already indexed in books available in the library. The usefulness of such books as Cutts' *Scenes & Characters of the Middle Ages,* which is not analyzed in any of the Wilson Standard Catalogs, would be greatly increased, however, by having subject analytical entries made for each of the groups described, e.g., KNIGHTS AND KNIGHTHOOD, PILGRIMS AND PILGRIMAGES.

Another example of the kind and number of subject headings may be illustrated by Percy Boynton's *America in Contemporary Fiction,* which is about American fiction and American authors. The *Standard Catalog for High School Libraries, 1938-1941 Supplement,* lists this book and suggests as subject headings: AMERICAN FICTION—HISTORY AND CRITICISM and AUTHORS, AMERICAN (10 biography anals). If the library owns this catalog, the librarian will not need to make these ten analytics, since the reader can refer to the printed book catalog to find

[3]A cross reference directs the reader from one heading to another.

references on individual authors. The two subject cards, however, are necessary. First the suggested headings should be checked with the *Sears List of Subject Headings,* if it is the list adopted by the library, to see if they are authorized. AMERICAN FICTION, as a subject heading, is found in its alphabetical place; below it the heading AMERICAN LITERA-TURE; and below that the form subheading HISTORY AND CRITICISM. The form subheads used under literature may also be used under the head-ings for the different types of literature, so for this book the heading AMERICAN FICTION—HISTORY AND CRITICISM may be used. The heading AUTHORS, AMERICAN is also found in the *Sears List* and below it: *x* AMERICAN AUTHORS. So a second subject card should be made with the heading AUTHORS, AMERICAN, and a reference card should be made, reading:

> AMERICAN AUTHORS
> See
> AUTHORS, AMERICAN.

Why use the terms AMERICAN FICTION, AMERICAN LITERATURE, etc., but AUTHORS, AMERICAN? The aids and the lists agree that it is important to bring all material in the catalog together under AUTHORS, then separate it according to nationality, e.g., AUTHORS, AMERICAN; AUTHORS, ENGLISH; while with terms *literature, poetry, fiction,* etc., it is more use-ful to put the national adjective first and bring together everything on the literature of one country, as AMERICAN DRAMA, AMERICAN FICTION, AMERICAN LITERATURE. Among these headings in the catalog will be the reference from AMERICAN AUTHORS.

Besides subject entries for books and parts of books, subject cards may be made to call attention to an entire group of books. One method is suggested in Mrs. Douglas' *Teacher-Librarian's Handbook*[4] and is now in use in some school libraries and children's departments of public libraries. By means of this scheme one subject card may serve for all the general books on a given subject, by simply referring the reader to the books on the shelves by classification number, and to the shelf list to find the books which may be temporarily out of the library. This practice serves the reader quite satisfactorily in a small library, where he makes his choice from the books on the shelves and uses the catalog only to see that there are books on the subject and where they are. Also the librarian's time is saved and space is saved in the catalog.

---

[4]M. P. Douglas, *The Teacher-Librarian's Handbook* (2d ed.; Chicago: A.L.A., 1949), p.75.

1 General subject entry for all of the books in a subject class

```
629.13    AIRPLANES.

          Books about airplanes will be found on the
       shelves under 629.13.

          For a complete author list of the books in the
       library on airplanes, consult the shelf list under
       629.13.



                         O
```

If the library has books with chapters on airplanes not indexed in the *Standard Catalog for High School Libraries, Standard Catalog for Public Libraries,* or *Children's Catalog* and their supplements, or if the library does not have these aids, subject analytical cards for the catalog should be made for this material. Chapter VII (pages 103–07) gives details as to how to make these cards. Card 1 should be filed in the catalog before these subject analytical cards and should include as a third paragraph: "For parts of books on airplanes see the cards following this one."

Subdivisions of a subject. Some subjects need to be subdivided to be exact. Most subjects can be divided by either: (1) phase, (2) form, (3) geographical area, or (4) period of time. For instance, the subject heading BIRDS would be used for a general book on that subject. But if a given book is limited to the protection of birds or the migration of birds, the general subject heading BIRDS can be limited by adding a phase subdivision, e.g., BIRDS. PROTECTION; BIRDS. MIGRATION. If, however, the book is not a book about birds but a list of books about birds, the form subhead BIBLIOGRAPHY should be added and the heading becomes BIRDS. BIBLIOGRAPHY. Or the book may be on birds of the United States, and the heading may be limited by geographical area to BIRDS. U. S.

For some subjects, notably history, next in importance to the geographical area is the period of time covered. For a general history in which there is no geographical limitation, the period of time covered is the significant item. For Hayes, Moon and Wayland's *World History,* which covers all countries and all periods up to 1950, the subject heading would be WORLD HISTORY. But a history which, though covering all lands, stops at the beginning of the Middle Ages would have the subject heading HISTORY, ANCIENT. A general history of the United States, however, would have the subject heading U. S.   HISTORY. A time subhead may be added, e.g., U. S. HISTORY. REVOLUTION, or U. S. HISTORY.   1898– . The use of subheads depends upon whether or not the book is limited to one phase, period of time, etc., and the amount of material on that subject which the library has or expects to have.

If the collection contains only a few (e.g., five) books treating of United States history, they may as well all have the same subject heading, namely, U. S.   HISTORY. The larger library may have a dozen or more books, e.g.: three general works covering the history of the United States from the Revolution to the present time; two books dealing exclusively with the period of the Revolution; one on the Civil War period; two on the history of the period since 1898. It would be well to group them in the catalog under such headings as U. S.   HISTORY; U. S.   HISTORY. REVOLUTION; U. S. HISTORY. CIVIL WAR; U. S. HISTORY.   1898– .

To sum up this matter of the choice of subject headings: use the term or terms which most clearly describe the contents of the book. "In choosing between synonymous headings prefer the one that—(a) is most familiar to the class of people who consult the library; (b) is most used in other catalogs; (c) has fewest meanings other than the sense in which it is to be employed; (d) brings the subject into the neighborhood of other related subjects."[5]

Form headings. A subject heading, as noted before, is the word or words used to describe the content of the book; thus Peterson's *How to Know the Birds* will have the subject headings BIRDS. Novels do not usually have a definite subject and are read for their style, characterizations, etc., rather than for information. This is also true of poems and plays. They have author and title entries in the catalog but seldom

---

[5]C. A. Cutter, *Rules for a Dictionary Catalog* (4th ed. rewritten; Washington: Govt. Print. Off., 1904), sect. 169.

2 General subject entry for all of the books in one or more classes

```
AMERICAN POETRY.  COLLECTIONS.

    Books of poetry by individual American poets
will be found on the shelves under 811.

    Collections of poetry by several American poets
will be found on the shelves under 811.08.

    For a complete list of books in the library con-
taining poetry by individual American poets, consult
the shelf list under 811; for collections by several
American poets, 811.08.
```

subject entries. The heading POETRY is not used for a book of poems, but for a book *about* poetry; e.g., Max Eastman's *Enjoyment of Poetry* requires POETRY as a subject heading. The literary works of an individual are represented in the catalog under his name and under the title if distinctive. Whoever wishes to read Edwin Arlington Robinson's *Nicodemus* will look under Robinson or *Nicodemus;* and his collected poems will be found only under Robinson, not under POETRY. It is, however, worthwhile and practical to bring together in the catalog collections of poems, essays, or dramas of three or more authors. This is done by adding a form subhead to the heading. Thus the heading POETRY or AMERICAN POETRY is used for books about poetry; while the headings POETRY. COLLECTIONS or AMERICAN POETRY. COLLECTIONS are used for such works as Untermeyer's *Modern American Poetry*. These latter headings, POETRY. COLLECTIONS and AMERICAN POETRY. COLLECTIONS are called form headings, as they refer to the form in which the material is written, not to its content.

Form cards similar to card 2 might take the place of the form heading POETRY. COLLECTIONS and AMERICAN POETRY. COLLECTIONS and direct the reader to books on the shelves. If this practice is adopted, similar cards would be made for ENGLISH POETRY. COLLECTIONS; AMERICAN DRAMA. COLLECTIONS; ENGLISH DRAMA. COLLECTIONS; etc.

Lists of subject headings. Next in importance to choosing the right subject heading for a given book is to use the same wording for all the subject headings for books or parts of books on the same subject, so that they may be brought together in the catalog. To do this it is essential to have a carefully worked-out list of subject headings from which to choose and to check it to show which headings have been used.

There are available two very good lists: for small public and high school libraries, *Sears List of Subject Headings,*[6] and for elementary and junior high school libraries and for the children's books of the public library, Rue and LaPlante's *Subject Headings for Children's Materials.*[7]

Names of persons and of organizations are the subject headings for material about the person or the organization. The form of the name to be used for the subject heading is determined from the rules in Chapter III for persons and the rules in Chapter V for organizations. For instance, Hesketh Pearson's *Dizzy, the Life & Personality of Benjamin Disraeli* would have as its subject heading DISRAELI, BENJAMIN; and a history of Yale University would have as its subject heading YALE UNIVERSITY. This type of heading is not found in the printed lists of subject headings.

How to use lists of subject headings. Determine what the book is about; then look in the list of subject headings adopted by the library for a suitable heading which expresses the content of the book.

On examining the list itself or the accompanying reproduction of pages 13 and 137, one should note that the headings are listed in alphabetical order and that some are in boldface type. Those in boldface type are followed by the Dewey Decimal Classification number for material on that subject, e.g., AIR DEFENSES with the numbers 355.23 and 623.38.

Note that just below the heading AIR DEFENSES is a paragraph beginning "Use for..." This type of explanatory note is given below some of the headings to explain for what kind of material they are to be used. Following this note the words *see also* introduce one or more suggested headings that may be better for the book in hand than the first subject heading looked up. If that is the case, turn to AIR RAID SHELTERS or BLACKOUTS IN WAR in their alphabetical places in the list. But if AIR DEFENSES is the better term, use it. Note that the next line

---

[6]B. M. Frick, *Sears List of Subject Headings* (6th ed.; N. Y.: Wilson, 1950), $4. 7th ed., 1954, $4.
[7]Eloise Rue and Effie LaPlante, *Subject Headings for Children's Materials.* (Chicago: A.L.A., 1952), $6.

Sears List of Subject Headings, Pages 13 and 137–38

Air conditioning   697
    See also Refrigeration and refrigerating
       machinery; Ventilation
    xx Refrigeration and refrigerating ma-
       chinery; Ventilation
✓ Air defenses   355.23; 623.38
    Use for works on civilian defense
       against air attack. Works on mili-
       tary defense against air raids are
       entered under Aeronautics, Military.
       General works on civilian defense
       are entered under Civilian defense
    See also Air raid shelters; Blackouts in
       war
    x Air raids—Protective measures; Air
       warfare; Defenses, Air
    xx Aeronautics, Military; Civilian defense
Air engines   621.4; 387.7
    See also Compressed air
    x Caloric engines; Hot air engines
    xx Compressed air; Engines   — Air flow
✓Air freight. *See* Aeronautics, Commercial
Air lines   629.13
    Use for works dealing with systems of
       aerial transportation and with com-
       panies engaged in this business.
       Works dealing with the routes
       along which the planes are flown
       are entered under Airways
    See also Airways
    xx Aeronautics, Commercial; Airways

Court and courtiers
    Use as a subdivision under names of
       countries, states, etc.
✓Court life. *See* Courts and courtiers
Court martial. *See* Courts martial and
       courts of inquiry
Courtesy   395; 177
    See also Conduct of life; Etiquet
    x Manners; Politeness
    xx Conduct of life; Ethics; Etiquet
✓Courtiers. *See* Courts and courtiers
Courts (Use geog. subdiv.)   351.9
    See also Courts martial and courts of
       inquiry; Judges; Jury; Justice, Ad-
       ministration of; Juvenile courts
    xx Judges; Justice, Administration of;
       Law
✓Courts and courtiers   909 (930-999 in spe-
       cific countries)
    See also Kings and rulers; Queens; also
       names of countries, states, etc. with
       the subdivision *Court and courtiers,*
       e.g. Spain—Court and courtiers
    x Court life; Courtiers
    xx Kings and rulers; Manners and cus-
       toms; Queens
Courts martial and courts of inquiry   344
    See also Military law
    x Court martial
    xx Courts; Military law; Trials
Covenanters   274.1; 941
    xx Church of Scotland

begins with *x;* this means that a *see* cross reference should probably be made from the term AIR RAIDS—PROTECTIVE MEASURES, AIR WARFARE, and DEFENSES, AIR to the one chosen, AIR DEFENSES. A *see* reference is a reference from a heading which is not used in the catalog to a heading that is used.

Below "*x* Air raids—Protective measures" is a line beginning *xx* AERONAUTICS, MILITARY; CIVILIAN DEFENSE. This is to suggest related terms, which if also used as subject headings in this catalog, should have cross references made from them to this heading, so that attention may be called to all related subjects. Such a reference from one heading that is used to another that is used is called a *see also* reference. Richard E. Holmes' *Air Conditioning in Summer and Winter* would have a subject entry in the catalog under AIR CONDITIONING and there would be a *see also* reference from related headings, for instance, VENTILATION, *see also* AIR CONDITIONING, if there were other books in the catalog under VENTILATION.

This same page from the *Sears List* gives "Air freight" in its alphabetical place, but it is in light face type and is followed by the phrase: *See* AERONAUTICS, COMMERCIAL. This means that this list recommends that the term "Air freight" not be used, but any material on that subject be entered in the catalog under AERONAUTICS, COMMERCIAL. On page 6 is found listed AERONAUTICS, COMMERCIAL 629.13; 387.7 and below that "*x* Air cargo; Air freight..." Terms followed by *see* are not to be used as headings. The Preface to the *Sears List* explains what subjects have been included, what omitted, and the provision for references. Preceding the list of headings is a short list of form divisions which may be used under any subject.

The *Sears List of Subject Headings* contains a section, "Practical Suggestions for the Beginner in Subject Heading Work," by Minnie E. Sears, revised by Bertha M. Frick, which will be found very helpful. The librarian who has a copy of this list may well pass over the directions given here.

Rue and LaPlante's *Subject Headings for Children's Materials* is designed for materials in elementary and junior high school libraries and children's departments of public libraries. The form is somewhat similar to that of the *Sears List*. It gives terms suitable for use as subject headings, sometimes with explanatory notes; includes suggested related headings and suggested *see* and *see also* references. Preceding the list of subject headings are some suggestions for the use of the list and four lists of subdivisions, which may be used as form subdivisions under the terms in the main alphabetical list of subject headings or as subdivisions under countries, states, and cities. This list does not include any personal names, but does include many geographic names not ordinarily found in a subject headings list, because they are names frequently used in children's catalogs.

Subject cross references. In deciding upon subject headings, as explained before (pages 26-29), sometimes it is found that there are two or more different terms that might be used for the same subject. For example, which is better, AVIATION or AERONAUTICS? MARIONETTES or PUPPETS AND PUPPET PLAYS? POTTERY or CERAMICS? COUNSELING or GUIDANCE. Pages 26–27 give four criteria on which of two synonymous headings to choose. Unless there is some very good reason for not doing so, one should always use the heading given in the subject headings list adopted by the library. If one looks up these groups of terms, he will see that Sears gives AERONAUTICS, COUNSELING, PUPPETS AND PUPPET PLAYS, and POTTERY, but some persons who will use the catalog will undoubtedly look under the terms AVIATION, GUIDANCE, MARIONETTES, and CERAMICS. When they find nothing, will they think of the other terms? They may not. Therefore, adopt one of these terms and refer from the other; e.g., use POTTERY and refer from CERAMICS. The lists of subject headings not only suggest subject headings to be used but list synonymous and related terms from which it is wise to refer.

Some librarians do not consider *see also* references necessary for the small library's catalog and do not make them. Other librarians feel that they are needed especially in the small catalog, since the collection is limited, and that all material on related subjects should be brought to the inquirer's attention.

Notice that the *see also* card is made precisely like the *see* card except for the words *see also*. Detailed directions for making cross reference cards are given on page 30. Most *see* references are made at the time that the subject heading to which they refer is first used, since they are synonyms for the headings decided upon. One should avoid making too many references for the small catalog. It is not desirable to make *see* references from terms not in the vocabulary of the public; for example, one would not refer from NECROMANCY to MAGIC unless the public using the library in question might be likely to look under the

3 See reference card

```
        AVIATORS
          See
   AIR PILOTS.
```

4 See also reference card

```
        JUSTICE, ADMINISTRATION OF
             See also
   COURTS.
   CRIME AND CRIMINALS.
```

term *necromancy*. One need not make a card DUNGEONS, *see* PRISONS if the book to be entered under PRISONS has nothing in it on dungeons.

Before making *see also*'s one should consider the following questions:

> Does the catalog have material under the term referred from?
> Is the term suggested for a reference one which anyone is likely to use?
> Is there material in the book on the topic that this reference term suggests? For example, does the book on pantomimes have anything on the ballet? If it has, make a reference from BALLET.

It is true that after a reference is once made from one subject to another, there is no way of telling which of the books treat of that phase of the subject except by examining the books in question. That does not matter, however. To go back again to the example given above—if there is a card in the catalog which reads BALLET, *see also* PANTOMIMES the reader turns to PANTOMIMES and there among the several books on the subject finds upon examination one or more which contain something on the ballet, and he is satisfied. But if, on the other hand, he turns to the subject PANTOMIMES and finds a few books, none of which has the slightest reference to the ballet, he may lose faith in the catalog.

Thus a catalog may be made much more useful by the wise and restricted use of the suggested *see* and *see also* references, since the first

5 General reference card

```
    MANNERS AND CUSTOMS
        See also Names of countries, cities, etc.
    with the subdivision SOCIAL LIFE AND CUSTOMS, e. g.,
    U. S.  SOCIAL LIFE AND CUSTOMS
```

subject the reader thinks of may not be exactly what he desires. References, especially *see also* references, should be made sparingly, as nothing is more annoying than to turn card after card and find only, *see* so and so, or *see also* so and so.

Another and a slightly different kind of reference is the so-called general reference card. In the *Sears List,* page 317, in the list of *see also*'s under MANNERS AND CUSTOMS is found: "...and names of countries, cities, etc. with the subdivision *Social life and customs,* e.g., U. S.—SOCIAL LIFE AND CUSTOMS." This sort of reference is very useful in a catalog and saves much duplication, as otherwise it would be necessary to list on a reference card a heading for each individual country with the subdivision SOCIAL LIFE AND CUSTOMS.

Keep down the number of cross references. Be absolutely sure that no reference refers to a heading not in the catalog. See the first restriction given above. Do not make a *see also* reference from a subject on which there is no material, but wait until there is material on that subject. On the other hand one may make temporary *see* references. For example, in order that the reader may have the suggestion and find the small amount of material on the ballet that is included in the book on pantomime, one may make a temporary card, BALLET, *see* PANTOMIMES. Later, if there is a card with the heading BALLET, this reference card may be changed to read "see also."

Other aids for subject headings. Appendix IV contains information on where to find lists of subject headings for special subjects. Even small public libraries and school libraries will have books and parts of books treating of a subject not included in the *Sears List* or Rue and LaPlante's list. This is especially true of the new subjects which are constantly developing, e.g., psychometrics and social planning. The subject headings used in general and special periodical indexes, bibliogra-

phies of special subjects, and the terms in general and special encyclopedias will be found very helpful in determining the wording for such
headings. First be sure no term in the regular list meets the need, then
look in the authorities mentioned for the best possible term.

At the end of this manual is found a list of aids some of which
include headings for the newest subjects. An authoritative checked list
either in book or card form is absolutely necessary. Great care should
be taken in the use of indexes coming out at regular intervals, e.g., the
Booklist, since these lists can best serve their purpose by changing their
headings to suit the latest development of subjects. If a heading in a
catalog is changed, all the cards with that heading should be changed.

To illustrate how the aids may vary, take the subject *airplanes.* Since
1935 the *Booklist,* which follows Library of Congress practice, has
used the term AEROPLANES as a subject heading; the *Standard Catalog
for Public Libraries,* 1949 edition, on the other hand, uses AEROPLANES
as a *see* reference to the heading AIRPLANES, as both the *Cumulative
Book Index,* 1933–52, and the *Standard Catalog for High School
Libraries* in all of its editions do. Another example is the use of the
terms *aviators* and *air pilots.* The *Cumulative Book Index* since 1928
has used AVIATORS with a *see* reference from AIR PILOTS. But the *Standard
Catalog for High School Libraries,* sixth edition, 1952, uses AIR PILOTS
with a *see* reference from AVIATORS.

Checking lists of subject headings for tracing. When a heading is
decided upon for the first time, it is checked in the list of subject headings
to show that it has been adopted for entry. Note the check mark (✔)
before AIR DEFENSES and before COURTS AND COURTIERS on the reproduced
page from Sears (page 33). In this way the librarian can tell which
subject headings have been used without referring to the catalog. This
is a great convenience, and care should be taken that each subject heading is checked the first time it is used. In cases where there is no suitable
heading in the adopted list and a heading is selected from some other
source, this heading is written in the printed list of subject headings
in its alphabetical place. The sample page from Sears shows the subject heading AIR FLOW—used in the *Cumulative Book Index,* 1950—
written in.

As subject headings used for the catalog are checked in the list, so
also should subject references used in the catalog be recorded. This
shows the librarian which of the references have already been made.

If it is decided to discontinue a heading in the catalog, this checked list will be a guide in removing the references to that heading.

The rule is: Mark with a check (✔) at the left the subject heading used and the references which have been made to it; turn to each reference in its regular alphabetical place and check it and the subject heading used. The checks on the page reproduced from Sears indicate that there are entries in the catalog under AIR DEFENSES and COURTS AND COURTIERS and that a reference has been made from AIR FREIGHT to AERO-NAUTICS, COMMERCIAL and from COURT LIFE and COURTIERS to COURTS AND COURTIERS.

To summarize: In making subject entries for a catalog use the headings and the references suggested in the list of subject headings selected and keep it carefully checked for all terms used.

Subject authority file. Instead of checking a printed list of subject headings the special library for which there is no suitable printed list or the general library may have a subject authority file on cards. In this file there is one card for each subject used in the catalog and on this card is a record of all references made to that subject. If the subject is not taken from the adopted list of subject headings, the source is given on this card. There is also a card corresponding to each reference card in the catalog. Cards 6, 7, and 8 are sample subject authority cards.

Reference cards, the second kind of card to be made for the subject authority file, are just like the *see* and *see also* reference cards for the catalog, given on page 36, except that the subject headings are not in full capitals. Subject headings in the card catalog need to be distinguished in some way from other headings for the convenience of the readers. In some catalogs red ink is used for these headings; in other

6 Subject authority card

```
Air pilots.

          Refer from
     x Airplanes.  Pilots.
     x Aviators
     x Pilots, Airplane
    xx Aeronautics
    xx Aeronautics.  Biography.
```

7 Subject authority card with explanation of spacing

```
Air pilots. ← - - - - 2nd line, 2nd space from left edge

        Refer from←4th line, 12th space from left edge
   x Airplanes.  Pilots
   ↕ ↑ - - - - - - - 5th line, 6th space from left edge
     ↓ - - - - - - - 5th line, 8th space from left edge




                        O
```

8 Subject authority card showing source of heading

```
Space stations (proposed)    (R. G. 1953)
```

catalogs full capitals are used. As the subject authority file is only for the use of the librarian, the terms are given with only the first letter of each heading or subheading capitalized. Cards 9 and 10 are sample reference cards for the subject authority file.

Card 11 shows the exact location on the card of the heading referred from, in this example AVIATORS, the word *See*, and the heading referred to, AIR PILOTS. If the heading referred from cannot all be written on one line, it would be continued on the line below, beginning on the fourteenth space from the left. *See* or *See also* begins on the line below the heading referred from and on the fourteenth space. Similarly the heading referred to, if very long, would be continued on the line below, beginning on the twelfth space from the left. This arrangement makes the first word of each heading stand out.

The advantages of a subject authority file on cards are: (1) It saves adding to a printed list the headings chosen from other sources. (2) It

9 See reference card for subject authority file

```
                    Aviators
                      See
              Air pilots.
```

10 See also reference card for subject authority file

```
              Aeronautics, Commercial
                    See also
              Air mail service.
              Air lines.
```

11 See reference card with explanation of spacing

```
              - - - - - - - 4th line, 12th space from left
              |                       edge
              ↓
              Aviators
                    See ← -   5th line, 14th space from left edge
              Air pilots. ← - - - 6th line, 8th space from left
                                        edge




                            ◯
```

avoids transferring the checks when a new edition of the adopted list comes out. (3) It gives space in the proper alphabetical place for new subjects to be added. (4) It is always up to date.

chapter III

Choice of
personal names

Introduction. Offhand it seems simple to make catalog cards for books, and it is not difficult if one knows how to meet the problems which are presented. Even in cataloging the smallest collection, it will soon be discovered that all authors do not have simple names, such as George Bernard Shaw; and even if they have, they may publish one book as Bernard Shaw, another as George Bernard Shaw, and a third as G. Bernard Shaw. In that case the obvious thing to do in order that all cards for books by or about the same author may stand together in the catalog is to find out the author's full name—George Bernard Shaw—and use that form consistently.

An investigation of any miscellaneous group of books shows quite a variety of kinds of names, but further study shows a limited number of types of names, thus indicating the possibility of introducing a system. The names may be complicated, but librarians have sought to simplify the task of locating them in the catalog by framing rules to cover the points most often met.

There are two general rules about names: (1) List a person under the best-known form of his name, putting the surname first, then the given name. (2) *Always use the same form* of a name.

Personal names fall into the following groups: simple surnames, compound surnames, surnames with prefixes, noblemen with both family name and title, married women's names, pseudonyms, and forenames only.

RULES FOR NAMES AS HEADINGS

Simple surnames with one or more given names (A.L.A. 1949.37, adapted; 40B)[1] "Enter...under the family name followed by the fore-names."

> Adams, James Truslow.
> Morgan, Alfred Powell.
> Harris, Joel Chandler.
> Milne, Alan Alexander.

"Unused given names, middle as well as first names, are as a rule to be omitted in author headings, especially in the case of living authors..." Refer from full name if anyone is likely to look under it, especially if the first name has been omitted.

> Full name: Joseph Hilaire Pierre Belloc
> Name used: Hilaire Belloc
> Full name: Herbert Sebastian Agar
> Name used: Herbert Agar
> Full name: Basil Kingsley Martin
> Name used: Kingsley Martin

Compound surnames (A.L.A. 1949.38) "In general enter compound surnames under the first part of the name and refer from the other parts."

> Lloyd George, David.
> Langdon-Davies, John.
> Mendelssohn-Bartholdy, Felix.

References should be made from the other part if it is at all likely that anyone would look under it, e.g.:

> George, David Lloyd
>   See
> Lloyd George, David.

Surnames with prefixes (A.L.A. 1949.39) "Enter under the prefix in all languages surnames with attributive prefixes such as A', Ap, Fitz, M', Mac, Mc, O', Saint, San, etc."

> MacDowell, Edward Alexander.
> Saint-Exupéry, Antoine de.

"Names beginning with a preposition, an article, a preposition and an

---

[1]American Library Association, Division of Cataloging and Classification, *A.L.A. Cataloging Rules for Author and Title Entries* (2d ed., ed. by Clara Beetle; Chicago: A.L.A., 1949). The parenthetical citation is to rules 37 and 40B.

article, or a contraction of the two are entered under the prefix, or the part of the name following the prefix variously in different languages.

"When the bearer of a name with a prefix has changed his citizenship, enter according to the rules for the language of the country adopted.

"Exception is to be made in any case where established usage...is contrary to the prescribed rule."

1. "Enter under the prefix and refer from the part following the prefix:"

   a. "English names."

   > De Quincey, Thomas.
   > De Voto, Bernard Augustine.
   > De la Mare, Walter John.
   > La Farge, Oliver.

   b. "French names when the prefix consists of an article or the contraction of a preposition and an article."

   > Du Chaillu, Paul Belloni.

   c. "Italian names when the prefix consists simply of an article."

   > La Guardia, Fiorello Henry.

   d. "Scandinavian names of romance origin *(a)* all Swedish names, and *(b)* Danish and Norwegian names when the prefix consists of or contains an article."

   > De la Gardie, Magnus Gabriel, *grefve.*
   > La Cour, Jens Lassen.

   e. "In all languages when the prefix and name are written as one word."

   > Debussy, Achille Claude.
   > Delacroix, Eugène.
   > Lafayette, Marquis de.

"Since such names occur sometimes as separate words, make reference from the component parts."

> Delacroix, Eugène.
> *Refer from:* Croix, Eugène de la;   La Croix, Eugène de.

2. "Enter under the part of the name following the prefix in all cases not specified above and refer from name beginning with the prefix:"

   a. "French names when the prefix consists of a preposition."

   > Ronsard, Pierre de.

"In French names containing a preposition and an article (not a contraction of the two) the article precedes and the preposition follows the name."

> Le Bédollière, Émile Gigault de.
> La Fontaine, Jean de.

b. "Italian names when the prefix consists of or contains a preposition."

> Annunzio, Gabriele d'
>   *Refer from:* D'Annunzio, Gabriele.

c. "Dutch and Flemish names."

> Van Loon, Hendrik Willem. (He was born in Holland, but lived in the United States many years.)
> Gogh, Vincent van.

But: "In Dutch names the prefix *de* has the same significance as *van* and follows the forename."

> Helm, Cornelis de.

d. "German names."

> Goethe, Johann Wolfgang von.

e. "Scandinavian names when the prefix consists of the preposition *av (af)* or the German equivalent *von*."

> Linné, Carl von

f. "Spanish and Portuguese names. With very rare exceptions, Spanish and Portuguese names are entered under the part of the name following the prefix."

> Cervantes Saavédra, Miguel de.
> Gama, Vasco da.

Titles of address (A.L.A. 1949.41B) "Omit from the heading titles of address (Miss, Mr., Mrs., Frau, Mme., etc.); minor ecclesiastical titles (abbé, archdeacon, dean, rabbi, reverend, etc.); governmental titles below the highest rank (vice-president, senator, governor, etc.); military and naval titles; academic and professional titles. Make exceptions ...when [title is] needed as an aid in identification."

Noblemen with family name and title (A.L.A. 1949.57) "Enter a nobleman under his latest title unless he is decidedly better known by an earlier title or by the family name." When necessary, "refer from the name not adopted as entry word."

Duke   Wellington, Arthur Wellesley, *1st duke of.*
                Refer from: Wellesley, Arthur, *1st duke of Wellington.*

Earl   Chesterfield, Philip Dormer Stanhope, *4th earl of.*
                Refer from: Stanhope, Philip Dormer, *4th earl of Chesterfield.*

Viscount   Grey of Falloden, Edward Grey, *1st viscount.*
                Refer from: Grey, Edward, *1st viscount Grey of Falloden.*

Baron   Beaverbrook, William Maxwell Aitken, *baron.*
             Dunsany, Edward John Moreton Drax Plunkett, *18th baron.*
             (No references are necessary in these cases as they are known only as Beaverbrook and Dunsany.)

Baronet   Scott, Sir Walter, *bart.*

Better known by the family name
             Bacon, Francis, *viscount St. Albans.*
             Buchan, John, *1st baron Tweedsmuir.*

"The titles of address *Lord* and *Lady* are commonly applied to all members of the English peerage except dukes and duchesses. In the heading the appropriate title is substituted." For example, Lord Dunsany becomes:

Dunsany, Edward John Moreton Drax Plunkett, *18th baron.*

The names of titled persons of other countries are written in a similar way, e.g.: Hugo, Victor Marie, *comte;* Tolstoi, Lev Nikolaevich, *graf*— or in this case the entire name may be anglicized: Tolstoy, Leo, *count.*

Married women's names (A.L.A. 1949.46) "Enter a married woman under her latest name unless...she has consistently written under another name. The heading is to consist of (a) husband's surname, (b) her own [given names], and (c) her maiden name, when known, in parentheses." In accordance with the rule given on page 45 the title *Mrs.* is to be omitted unless needed as an aid in identification. Refer from any other names or forms of name under which she may be known.

Buck, Pearl (Sydenstricker). (She is now Mrs. Richard J. Walsh, but Buck is the name she has used in all of her writing.)
Earhart, Amelia. (She always wrote under her maiden name.)
Rawlings, Marjorie (Kinnan). (Latest form of name.)

Pseudonyms (A.L.A. 1949.30, adapted) "Enter works published under pseudonym under the author's real name when known..." Refer from pseudonym. Include the pseudonym, followed by the abbreviation, *pseud.,* in the title if entry is under the real name. Enter under pseudonym when real name is unknown or when the pseudonym has been fixed in literary history, e.g., enter under Sand, George, *pseud.*, and refer from Dudevant, Mme.

> Hannay, James Owen
> > *Refer from:* Birmingham, A., *pseud.*
> Russell, George William
> > *Refer from:* A. E., *pseud.*
> Eliot, George, *pseud.*
> > *Refer from:* Cross, Marian Evans

Entry under forename (A.L.A. 1949.43;61) "Sovereigns, ruling princes, saints, and other persons known by their forenames only are entered under forename. Add titles of nobility in English. Add any epithet, byname or adjective of origin, nationality, etc., by which the person is usually known."

> Patrick, Saint
> George VI, *King of Great Britain.*
> Albert, *consort of Victoria, Queen of Great Britain.*
> Albert I, *Prince of Monaco.*
> George, *Duke of Kent.*
> > *Refer from:* Kent, George, *Duke of.*

"Enter medieval authors under the given name...include in the heading any epithet or byname denoting place of origin, domicile, occupation, or distinguishing characteristic by which the individual is known. Refer from...any other names by which the author is known..."

> Geoffrey of Monmouth.

Works which have been abridged, retold, etc. Two books about King Arthur for young people illustrate how a title page may leave one in doubt about the correct entry.

The
Boy's King Arthur
Sir Thomas Malory's History
of
King Arthur and His Knights of the Round Table
Edited For Boys
by
Sidney Lanier
Illustrated by N. C. Wyeth
New York
Charles Scribner's Sons
1923

Close examination of this book and its title page shows that it is Malory's book, edited and with an explanatory introduction to make it clear to readers. It is therefore entered in the catalog under Malory with an added entry for Lanier.

The Book of King Arthur
And His
Noble Knights
Stories from Sir Thomas Malory's Morte Darthur
By
Mary Macleod
Introduction by John W. Hales
Illustrations from Drawings by A. G. Walker, Sculptor

New York
Frederick A. Stokes Company
Publishers

A work similar to *The Boy's King Arthur* is *The Book of King Arthur,* by Mary Macleod. Miss Macleod has selected certain stories from Malory and reworded them to suit her young readers. It is neither Malory's language nor his selection; therefore the main entry for the catalog would be under Macleod with added entry under Malory. It is not known just when Malory was born or died, so that if the library's policy is to give author's dates, the closest approximation to the real date is given, in this instance the century in which he lived. Note that on the Macleod card (Card 26, Appendix I), since the date of birth is not known, the abbreviation *d.* is given preceding the date of her death. For children's classics the earliest copyright date is given rather than the latest, as it is nearer the date of writing of the book.

Lamb's *Tales from Shakespeare* is cataloged in the same way, the main entry under Lamb, the adapter, with an added entry under Shakespeare.

Another type of book which is sometimes puzzling is selections from an individual work of an author. Hill's translation of a selection of *The Canterbury Tales* is an example. In some titles *selected* is used in the sense that the selections included are taken from all the works of an author rather than from a single work. In either case the treatment is the same. The main entry is made under the author's name and the translator's or editor's name is included in the entry. An added entry would be made for the editor or the translator; for this book, Frank Ernest Hill.

The Canterbury Tales
The Prologue and Four Tales with the
Book of the Duchess and Six Lyrics
By Geoffrey Chaucer
Translated into Modern English Verse by
Frank Ernest Hill
Illustrated by Hermann Rosse

Longmans, Green and Company
London: New York: Toronto
1930

Compiler or editor as author. *Nine Modern American Plays* consists of nine well-known plays written by different authors and edited by Barrett H. Clark. "Enter under the compiler or editor, individual or corporate, a collection of independent works by various authors, artists, composers, etc., issued with a collective title, except...if the work of the editor or editing body seems to be but slight and their names do not appear prominently in the publication, or if there are frequent changes of editor, enter under title. Make added entry under editor." (A.L.A. 1949.5A)

The main entry for *Nine Modern American Plays* would be under the editor since he is considered the author of the volume, and the abbreviation *ed.* would be added one space after the comma following his name. If no dates are given, thirteen spaces are left before the abbreviation *ed.* so that the dates may be filled in later if found. If only the date of birth is given, six spaces are left before *ed.* for the date of death, e.g., 1904–   ed.

A similar work is Roe's *Nineteenth Century English Prose.* The title page reads:

Nineteenth Century English Prose
Early Essayists
Lamb, Hazlitt, Hunt
DeQuincey, Macaulay
Edited with Introduction
By
Frederick William Roe
Junior Dean and Associate Professor of English
The University of Wisconsin

New York
Harcourt, Brace, and Company
1923

Should this be entered under Lamb, the first author mentioned on the title page, or under Roe, the editor? Since Roe's name is prominent on the title page as is Clark's on the title page of *Nine Modern American Plays* this book would be entered under Roe. The contents would indicate which essays were included and who was the author of each.

Dramatization. "Enter a dramatization based on a novel, legend, poem, or other literary form under the playwright with added entry under the author and title of the work upon which the dramatization is based." (A.L.A. 1949.23A) For example, *Junior Miss,* a play by Jerome Chodorov and Joseph Fields based on the book by Sally Benson, would be entered under Chodorov, with added entry under Benson (Card 27, Appendix I).

* * *

Conclusions regarding choice of personal names. It will be seen from these rules that nearly all authors' names will fall into one of the preceding groups. Sometimes the rule is not absolutely definite. The rule regarding noblemen's names includes the phrase "better known," and most of the rules conclude with "...refer from the other parts," or "...refer from the name not adopted as entry word." It is believed that the illustrations will make the meaning clear, as in most instances the form of the reference is indicated. The better known form would be the one used on the title pages of the author's books, the one given in most biographical dictionaries, encyclopedias, the *Booklist,* and other standard authorities. It is necessary to consult only one reliable aid for each name provided that aid gives full name and does not suggest other forms. If other forms are indicated, the librarian should consult several aids before deciding on the form for the catalog.

Where one form is as well known as the other, choose one and always use it. A few authors use their real names for one type of writing and a pseudonym or pseudonyms for other types. Ray Stannard Baker wrote under his own name except when writing his popular essays, *Adventures in Contentment, Adventures in Friendship,* etc., for which he used the pseudonym David Grayson. In some libraries his books are entered in the catalog under both his real name and his pseudonym, his essays under Grayson, his other works under Baker, and *see also* cross references are made from one to the other. But for the small library it would seem better to put all his works under his own name and refer from Grayson, David, *pseud.*

There may be cases where the librarian does not know whether the name is real or a pseudonym. Consider it a real name. If later it proves to be a pseudonym, add the abbreviation *pseud.* to the name as given in the catalog and make a reference from the real name, unless it is decided to change the entry to the real name.

Some libraries find it very useful to have authors' dates of birth and death included in the heading on the catalog card:

Cather, Willa Sibert, 1876–1947.
Bennett, Arnold, 1867–1931.

In a number of schools the pupils are required to know the dates of birth and death of the authors on whose works they report. Where bibliographical tools are few, it is convenient for both pupils and librarians to have these dates on the catalog cards. The librarian, in looking up the forms of the name for the heading in the catalog, may note the dates if they are given and include them in the heading. If the dates are not readily found, they may be omitted and added later. Dates are essential for the identification of different authors whose names are the same.

Authority file for names. Many librarians find it convenient to have an authority file for the names used in their catalogs. The librarian may decide to enter all of Elizabeth Janet Gray's books under Vining, Elizabeth Gray. A card would then be made using the adopted form as heading. It would be followed by the title of one of her books to identify the author, by a list of the authorities consulted in deciding on that form, and by a note indicating a reference from Gray. After an author's name has been established, all that is necessary when a book is added is to look in the authority file for names, note the form adopted, be sure it is the same person, and use that form for the new title.

The items and form for the cards in this file may be described as follows: (1) The heading on the name authority card is the one adopted for the catalog. (2) The title is that of the first book by that author cataloged for that library and serves to identify him. (3) The date is the copyright date (if no copyright date, the imprint or some other date) of that book, as found on the back of the title page, preceded by the word "copyright" and given on the card as [c1952]. (4) The abbreviations are for the bibliographical and biographical aids in which the

12 Name authority card for person as author

```
    Vining, Elizabeth (Gray) 1902-
          Windows for the Crown Prince.      ⌐c1952⌐

  ntd C. B. I. 1943-1948 (Gray, Elizabeth Janet (Mrs. Mor-
        gan Vining))
  nt Bklist v. 48



                    x Gray, Elizabeth Janet
                    x Vining, Mrs. Morgan
                         O
```

librarian looked. (5) An *n* to the left of the abbreviation for the name of an aid means that the author's name was found in that aid; a *t* means that the title was found. (6) If the author's dates of birth and death are included in the heading, a *d* may be added to indicate that the date or dates were found. (7) If the form of the name in the aid differs from that given in the heading on this card, or if the date differs, the variant form is put in parentheses after the abbreviation for the aid. (8) If references are made from other forms of the name, they are indicated on the line or lines directly above the hole in the card, preceded by an *x,* the symbol for a *see* reference.

If the name is not that of the author of the book, but the subject or the illustrator, for example, it is given above the author's name and is indented farther to the right. To the left of the author's name is given an abbreviation which stands for the relation of the name in the heading to the book. The form is shown in Card 13, the authority card for Henry Hudson, subject of James Maurice Scott's biography. The abbreviation *subj.* indicates that Hudson is the subject of this book. The remainder of the card would have exactly the same form as the card for Vining. The aids would be those consulted for Hudson. There would be another authority card for the heading Scott, James Maurice, the same form as Card 12.

13 Name authority card for person as added entry

```
              Hudson, Henry, d. 1611.
   subj. Scott, James Maurice, 1906-
              Hudson of Hudson's Bay.      1951.

     n Amer. ency. 1951 ed.
   ntd Std. cat. for h.s. libs. 6th ed.
    nd Webster's dict. (? - 1611)
```

The name authority file should have an authority card for every name used as a heading in the catalog whether as author, subject, illustrator, or in any other capacity.

When to have authority files for names. If the library uses printed cards, which are discussed in Chapter X, and is able to get them for practically all of its books, it is best to use the form of the name given on the printed card; thus an authority file for names would be unnecessary, though the librarian may find it useful to order an extra printed card and use it as an authority card. If a special library's collection, however, is of such a nature as to include many works by authors with complicated names—foreign names, for instance—and there are no printed cards for many of them, a name authority file will be found to save time. It records, once for all, the form of name to be used, the information obtained in establishing the form of name, and the references to it which have been filed in the catalog.

If the library is small and the catalog is near the desk, a name authority file is not necessary; the catalog itself may be the authority file. One drawback to this arrangement is that when references are made from other forms of the name than that adopted, either a special file of name references must be maintained or these references must be noted on the first main card for that author; when that card is withdrawn, the tracing of the references must be transferred to another main card, and so on.

The value of an authority file for names depends upon: (1) whether or not the names to be entered are so complicated that any one of a number of different forms might be used; (2) whether there are one or more references from other forms to be recorded; (3) the distance from the desk of the librarian to the catalog; (4) whether or not printed cards are used.

chapter IV

Anonymous classics
and other title entries

ANONYMOUS WORKS

Anonymous works are those whose authors are not known, or, at least, are not given in the book. There may be: (1) no indication of authorship; (2) a descriptive or generic word or phrase preceded by an article, e.g., "by 'the soldier'"; (3) the title of another of the writer's works, e.g., "by the author of..."; or (4) initials, which may or may not be those of the author's name. If the author uses a specific word or phrase with or without a definite article, this word or phrase is treated as a pseudonym. (Based on A.L.A. 1949.32)

General rule (A.L.A. 1949.32 modified) "Enter works published anonymously under author when known. Make added entry under title and added entry or reference under any phrase used instead of the author's name."

> The log-cabin lady.
> The way to life, by 'the soldier.'
> *Make added entry under:* The soldier.
> Griffith, Hubert Freeling.
> R. A. F. occasions, by H. G.
> *Refer from:* G., H.; H. G.

ANONYMOUS CLASSICS

"An anonymous classic is a work of unknown or doubtful authorship, commonly designated by title, which may have appeared in the course of time in many editions, versions, and/or translations...The

term includes:...poems, epics, romances, tales, plays, chronicles,...
sacred literature..." (A.L.A. 1949.33)

General rule (A.L.A. 1949.33A) "Enter editions of anonymous
classics and their translations under a uniform heading consisting of
the traditional or conventional title of the work in the language of the
original version when known. However, prefer entry under the English
form, if the classic is known equally well in many languages."

> Mother Goose.
>> The little Mother Goose.
>
> Arabian nights.
>> The Arabian nights entertainments.
>
> Chanson de Roland.
>> The song of Roland.

Refer from forms not chosen for entry.

> Song of Roland
>> See
>
> Chanson de Roland.
>> Roland
>>> See
>
> Chanson de Roland.

The following list, based on various codes and aids, gives some headings commonly used:

Arabian nights.	Grail.	Njals saga.
Arthur, King.	Kalevala.	Reynard the Fox.
Beowulf.	Mabinogion.	Robin Hood.
Cid Campeador.	Mother Goose.	Chanson de Roland.
Cuchulain.	Nibelungenlied.	Seven sages.

The title page of *The Arabian Nights* as reproduced and the main
card for an anonymous classic illustrate the rule.

The
Arabian Nights
Based on the Translation
From the Arabic By
Edward William Lane
Selected, Edited, and Arranged
For Young People By
Frances Jenkins Olcott
Illustrations and
Decorations By
Monro S. Orr
New York
Henry Holt and Company

Arabian nights is the form given in the list of commonly used headings for anonymous classics on page 56 and is in accordance with the rule given there. These headings take the place of an author and are in the position of the author's name on the card.

The entering of anonymous classics under the name of the person who retells the story is explained in Chapter III. For instance, James Baldwin's *Story of Roland* has the main entry under Baldwin, but has an added entry under "Chanson de Roland." Likewise Eleanor Hull's *Boys' Cuchulain; Heroic Legends of Ireland* may be entered under Hull as in the *Children's Catalog,* but with an added entry under Cuchulain.

Bible (A.L.A. 1949.34) "Enter the Bible or any part of it...under the word BIBLE. Include as subheading...*Old Testament,...New Testament,* the name of the book or group of books...Refer...from the names of individual books to the heading under which they appear in the catalog."

> Bible.
>> The Holy Bible Containing the Old and New Testaments.
> Bible.   Old Testament.
>> *Refer from:* Old Testament.
> Bible.   New Testament.
>> *Refer from:* New Testament.
> Bible.   Old Testament.   Psalms.
>> *Refer from:* Psalms.
> Bible.   New Testament.   Gospels.
>> *Refer from:* Gospels.
> Bible.   New Testament.   John.
>> *Refer from:* John.

The sacred literature of any other religion is entered in a similar way under a uniform heading.

OTHER TYPES OF TITLE ENTRIES

Periodicals. "Enter a periodical under its latest title. [Use hanging indention. Capitalize the initial article, if there is one, and the word following it.] Make a reference or an added entry for any earlier title or titles under which the periodical may have been issued....A periodical issued by a society, institution, or government body is ordinarily to be entered under its title (especially if this is distinctive in character) with added entry for the issuing body...." (A.L.A. 1949.5C(1))

> The Atlantic monthly.

"If the title of a periodical occurs in different forms on the title-page, covers, captions, etc., prefer the title-page form and refer when necessary from other forms. If the covers, etc., have a fuller title than the title-page, it may be desirable to use the fuller title..." (A.L.A. 1941.214a(1))[1]

"When the title of a periodical begins with the initials of the name of a corporate body, enter under the initials and make added entry or reference under the name of the body for which they stand." (A.L.A. 1949.5C(1))

> S. A. E. journal.
>> *Refer from:* Society of Automotive Engineers, Inc. (Or make an added entry for the society.)

Almanacs, yearbooks, etc. (A.L.A. 1949.5D) "Enter almanacs, general yearbooks and similar serial publications under title."

> The Statesman's yearbook.
> The World almanac.

Encyclopedias and dictionaries (A.L.A. 1949.5B) "Enter encyclopedias and dictionaries under title unless decidedly better known by the name of their editors. In either case make added entry under the form not chosen for main entry, and for the publisher if the work is likely to be referred to by his name."

> Compton's pictured encyclopedia and fact-index.
> Encyclopedia Americana.
> The World book encyclopedia.

Composite works (A.L.A. 1949.4A(1;2)) "Enter a work produced by the collaboration of two or more authors, in which the contribution of each forms a distinct part or section of a planned whole, under the author chiefly responsible for it....If a corporate body is considered to be chiefly responsible for the work, make an added entry for at least the first personal author mentioned on the title page."

> Coyle, David Cushman, 1887–
>> The American way, by David Cushman Coyle; together with three additional discussions by Carl Dreher, Carl Landauer [and] Gerald W. Johnson...

Examination of this book shows a half title for each part with the title and author of that part, e.g.:

---

[1]American Library Association. Catalog Code Revision Committee, *A.L.A. Catalog Rules; Author and Title Entries; prepared with the collaboration of a Committee of the (British) Library Association.* (Prelim. American 2d ed.; Chicago: A.L.A., 1941).

THE AMERICAN WAY
A VOICE FROM THE LEFT
by
Carl Dreher

But "if origin, chief interest, or responsibility is not clearly identified with or attributable to any one of the contributors, enter under the first-named author if there are not more than three and the title of the whole work is applicable to each of the contributions with added entry for the other authors. Otherwise, enter under title, with added entry for the first author mentioned and for as many others as the individual case warrants."

> I'll take my stand; the South and the agrarian tradition, by twelve southerners. Harper, 1930.
>
> 359 p.
>
> Contents.—Introduction; a statement of principles.—Reconstructed but unregenerate, by J. C. Ransom.—A mirror for artists, by D. Davidson.—The irrepressible conflict, by F. C. Owsley.—...

Since no author is mentioned on the title page it is not necessary to make an added entry for the author first listed in the contents.

Compilations without an editor. When a compilation has no editor, how is it entered?

The
Patriotic
Anthology
Introduced by
Carl Van Doren

Doubleday, Doran and Company, Inc.
Garden City, N. Y., 1941

Following the second part of the rule given above, *The Patriotic Anthology* would have its main entry under title. Hanging indention is used; i.e., the title begins where the author's surname would ordinarily stand and the succeeding lines begin at second indention. This arrangement makes the first word of the title stand out clearly on the card and is the form to be followed whenever there is no author, editor, compiler, or the like, to be used as author. "If the first word of a title used as main entry is an article, capitalize the following word, except in the entry of anonymous works, which theoretically are only temporarily main entries." (A.L.A. 1949. Appendix III, E11) With anonymous books, however, since it is expected that the author will be identified at some time, the title of the book begins on the fifth line at the second indention as usual. When the author's name is found it is added to the card in the usual place and the note: "Pub. anonymously," is added to the card.

Name authority cards. Name authority cards are made for anonymous classics and sacred books. They are similar in form to those for personal names, but omit title and date, used for personal authors for identification of the author.

In the smaller, general libraries name authority cards are not necessary for individual books, periodicals, almanacs, encyclopedias, etc., entered under title.

14 Name authority card for anonymous classic

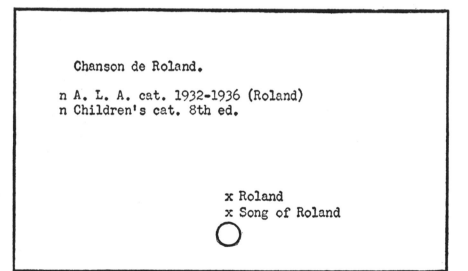

Chanson de Roland.

n A. L. A. cat. 1932-1936 (Roland)
n Children's cat. 8th ed.

                    x Roland
                    x Song of Roland

chapter V

Names of organizations

Introduction. In Chapter III various types of authors' names are considered, but in every instance the author is a person. There is a kind of publication for whose contents no person is primarily responsible, namely, the publications of societies and institutions, and the official publications of countries, states, cities, and towns. Examples of such publications are: *Annual Report of the Board of Regents of the Smithsonian Institution; Journal of the National Education Association of the United States; Annual Report of the Los Angeles Public Library; Collections of the State Historical Society of Wisconsin; Official Guide Book, the World's Fair of 1940 in New York; Handbook of the Layton Art Gallery*. Are not the Smithsonian Institution, National Education Association of the United States, Los Angeles Public Library, State Historical Society of Wisconsin, World's Fair of 1940 in New York, and the Layton Art Gallery the authors of these publications? Since this is so, the works are cataloged under their authors' names just as are other works.

As personal authors, upon close observation, group themselves into certain classes—simple surnames, compound surnames, names with prefixes—so these names of organizations may be grouped by class. The four major divisions are: government agencies, societies, institutions (establishments), and miscellaneous bodies not falling under the other three classifications.

GOVERNMENT PUBLICATIONS

"Governments and their agencies...are to be regarded as the authors of publications for which they, as corporate bodies, are responsible....

Periodicals are entered according to the general rule (A.L.A. 1949.5c) even though issued by governments." (A.L.A. 1949.71)

General rule (A.L.A. 1949.72) "Enter under countries or nations, states, cities, towns, and other government districts, official publications issued by them or by their authority." "Enter publications emanating from the various agencies of government under the names of the agencies (legislative bodies, courts, executive departments, bureaus, etc.) as subheadings (under country, or other jurisdiction) in the latest form in the vernacular. Refer from variant forms."

> U.S.   Dept. of State.[1]

"Use for a subheading the name of the office rather than the title of the officer except where the title of the officer is the only name of the office."

>> Virginia.   Auditor of Public Accounts. (In this case there is no department, office, or other subdivision.)

Legislative bodies (A.L.A. 1949.74) "Enter the proceedings of sessions, debates, reports, etc. (but not 'acts' or laws), of legislative bodies under the name of the government with the name of the body as subheading, subdivided as needed by date of session and/or branch, committee, or other subordinate entity. In the case of the United States Congress, when dates are given, give also the number of the Congress and the session."

>> U.S.   83d Cong. 1st. sess. 1953.
>>   Congressional record, proceedings and debates of the 83d Congress, 1st session.   1953.

Executive departments, etc. (A.L.A. 1949.75) "Enter bureaus or offices subordinate to an executive department, ministry or secretariat directly under the name of the jurisdiction, not as a subheading under the department, ministry or secretariat."

>> U.S.   Bureau of the Census.
>>   *Refer from:* U.S.   Dept. of Commerce.   Bureau of the Census.

"Divisions, regional offices and other units of departments, bureaus, commissions, etc., subordinate to [them] ... are usually entered ... as subheadings ..."

---

[1]For convenience in locating cards in the catalog the distinctive word in the subdivision under the name of a country, state, city, or other government district; or of a society, institution, or other body is underscored.

U.S.   Forest Service.   Forest Products Laboratory.
U.S.   Forest Service.   Pacific Northwest Region.
U.S.   Bureau of Foreign and Domestic Commerce.   Office of Business Economics.

"Enter under the department or other government agency administrative reports which are prepared by an official as a part of his routine duty." An added entry for the official is unnecessary.

U.S.   Federal Housing Administration.
   Annual report.
U.S.   Bonneville Power Administration.
   Annual report.

"Enter under personal author scientific papers, addresses, and other publications, not administrative or routine in character, but which are issued officially by the department to which the author is attached. Make added entry under the department."

Acheson, Dean Gooderham, 1893–
   The peace the world wants. 1950 (U.S.   Dept. of State.   Publication 3977)

"Enter under the writer reports made to a department or other government agency by a person who is not an official, with added entry under the department or agency."

Government commissions and committees (A.L.A. 1949.81) "Enter reports and recommendations of official commissions and committees, whether permanent or temporary, under the name of the country or other jurisdiction, with the name of the commission or committee as a subheading, directly under country or under the appointing department, legislative body, etc. Refer from the name of the commission or committee."

U.S.   Interstate Commerce Commission.
U.S.   Commission on Organization of the Executive Branch of the Government.
U.S.   National Committee on Wood Utilization.

For certain types of government publications there is no department, office, etc., responsible. Examples of such publications are: laws, decrees; constitutions and official drafts of proposed constitutions; single treaties, conventions, executive agreements, and other exchanges of notes having the effect of treaties. In order to have a uniform heading for such publications which will bring them together in the catalog, they are entered under the country or state with a form subheading. Examples of such headings and the specific rules which govern them are given under: *Modern laws; Constitutions;* and *Treaties.*

Modern laws (A.L.A. 1949.84) "Enter laws, decrees, and other acts having the force of law under the country, state, or other jurisdiction with the form subheading LAWS, STATUTES, ETC."

> U.S.   Laws, Statutes, etc.

Constitutions (A.L.A. 1949.85) "Enter constitutions and official drafts of proposed constitutions, under the name of the country or state with the form subheading CONSTITUTION..."

> U.S.   Constitution.
> California.   Constitution.

Treaties (A.L.A. 1949.88) "Enter single treaties, conventions, executive agreements, and other exchanges of notes having the effect of treaties, under the party named first on the title page, with the form subheading TREATIES, ETC. followed by inclusive dates of reign or administration and the name of the executive incumbent in the year of signing."

> U.S.   Treaties, etc. 1945–1953 (Truman)

SOCIETY PUBLICATIONS

"A society is an organization of persons associated together for the promotion of common purposes or objects, such as research, business, recreation, etc.

"Included in the rules for societies are academies, learned societies, associations, and societies of all kinds, scientific, technical, educational, benevolent, moral, etc., even when strictly local or named from a country, state, province, or city; also clubs, guilds, orders of knighthood, secret societies, Greek letter fraternities, Young Men's and Young Women's Christian Associations, affiliated societies, political parties, religious sects, etc., as distinguished from institutions (establishments). (A.L.A. 1949, p.148)

"...societies are to be regarded as the authors of publications for which they...are responsible. Such material as...proceedings and reports of societies...is entered under the heading for the corporate body, even though the name of the individual preparing it is given." (A.L.A. 1949.71)

General rule (A.L.A. 1949.91) "Enter a society under the first word (not an article...) of its latest corporate name, with reference from any other name by which it is known, and from the place where its headquarters are established." Use the article as first word if necessary for clearness, but disregard it in filing.

> American Council on Education.
> American Iron and Steel Institute, New York.
> > *Refer from:* New York.   American Iron and Steel Institute.

Change of name (A.L.A. 1949.91A) "When a society has changed its name, enter under the latest form, with references from earlier forms."

> Congress of Industrial Organizations.
> American Library Association.   Editorial Committee.   Subcommittee on Inexpensive Books for Boys and Girls.
> > *Refer from:* American Library Association.   Section for Library Work With Children. Book Evaluation Committee.

"When two or more societies which have had an independent existence unite to form a new society, enter each under its own name up to the time of union, with *see also* references to and from the new body."

> National Society for the Prevention of Blindness. (Present name, adopted 1927.)
> National Committee for the Prevention of Blindness. (Formed by union of 3 and 4 in 1915; use for its publications, 1915 to 1927.)
> American Association for the Conservation of Vision. (Use for its publications until it united with 4 in 1915 to form 2.)
> New York State Committee for the Prevention of Blindness. (Use for its publications until it united with 3 in 1915 to form 2.)

American state historical and agricultural societies (A.L.A. 1949.105) "Enter American state historical and agricultural societies under the name of the state whether or not it is the first word of the name of the society. If the corporate name begins with the name of the state, the corporate form is to be followed; if not, the name of the state is to be followed by a period."

> Pennsylvania.   Historical Society.
> > *Refer from:* Historical Society of Pennsylvania.

PUBLICATIONS OF INSTITUTIONS

"Institutions (establishments) are entities whose functions require a plant with buildings, apparatus, etc., as distinguished from bodies, organized groups of persons such as societies, associations, etc., whose duties may be performed equally well in one place or another. The necessity of having a permanent material equipment tends to identify the institution with a locality....

"Included in the rules for institutions are colleges, universities, schools, libraries, museums, galleries, radio stations, observatories, laboratories, churches, monasteries, convents, hospitals, asylums, prisons, theaters, buildings, etc...." (A.L.A. 1949, p.148)

"...institutions...are to be regarded as the authors of publications for which they...are responsible. Such material as...official catalogs of libraries and museums; reports of institutions...is entered under the heading for the corporate body, even though the name of the individual preparing it is given...." (A.L.A. 1949.71) Prefer entry under personal author for monographic works of individuals issued by institutions when these are not clearly official or routine in character.

General rule (A.L.A. 1949.92) "Enter an institution (using the latest name) under the name of the place in which it is located."

> Chicago. Public Library.
> Chicago. Natural History Museum.
> New York. Museum of Modern Art.

"Enter an institution of the United States or of the British Empire whose name begins with a proper noun or a proper adjective under the first word of its name and [when necessary] refer from the place where it is located. Add the name of the place to the heading if it does not occur in the name of the institution unless the institution is so well known as to make the addition of the place unnecessary...."

> Corcoran Gallery of Art, Washington, D. C.
> > *Refer from:* Washington, D. C. Corcoran Gallery of Art; Smithsonian Institution.

"Initials of personal names occurring at the beginning of the name of an institution are omitted, but forenames when given in full are included."

> Enoch Pratt Free Library, Baltimore.
> > *Refer from:* Pratt Free Library, Baltimore; Baltimore. Enoch Pratt Free Library.

Institutions forming an integral part of a larger organization (A.L.A. 1949.102) "Enter the various faculties, colleges, professional schools, laboratories, libraries, chapels, museums, observatories, hospitals, shops, etc., which form an integral part of a university or other institution under the larger institution with the name of the particular entity as subheading."

> Chicago. University. Industrial Relations Center.
> California. University. Library.

Exception: "Exception may be made in the case of an observatory which is much more likely to be looked for under its own name than under that of the place or of the institution of which it forms a part."

> Lick Observatory.
>> *Refer from:* California. University. Lick Observatory; Mt. Hamilton, Calif. Lick Observatory.

State and provincial institutions (U̅. S. and Canada) (A.L.A. 1949.104) "Enter state and provincial institutions of the United States and Canada under the name of the state or province. The name of the state or province is to be followed by a period and the next word capitalized."

> California. University.
> Manitoba. University.

Agricultural experiment stations (A.L.A. 1949.106) "Enter agricultural experiment stations of the United States under the name of the state or territory in which they are organized. Include in the heading the name of the place where the station is located. Refer from the university or college of which the station may form a department, from the name of the station, if it is at all distinctive, and from the name of the place where it is located."

> New York. Agricultural Experiment Station, Ithaca.
>> *Refer from:* Ithaca, N.Y. Agricultural Experiment Station; Cornell University. Agricultural Experiment Station.

Churches not organized within national bounds (A.L.A. 1949.115) "For...all churches not organized as corporate bodies within national bounds, adopt the most commonly accepted English form of name as the official entry, and use this form for all subject headings."

> Catholic Church.
> Moravian Church.

PUBLICATIONS OF MISCELLANEOUS BODIES

The term *miscellaneous bodies* includes: "conferences, congresses, exhibitions, and other occasional meetings; firms, and other business concerns; committees and classes of citizens not belonging to any body or organization; foundations and endowments; parks, cemeteries, etc." (A.L.A. 1949, p.199)

National congresses (A.L.A. 1949.134) "Enter national congresses under the vernacular form of the name."

> National Congress of Parents and Teachers.

Institutes, conferences, conventions, etc. (A.L.A. 1949.135) "Enter institutes, meetings, conferences, etc., under the name of the meeting, except when they are meetings of the members of a society or other body and have no distinctive name of their own."

> Pacific Northwest Regional Planning Conference.

"If the institute or meeting is held at some institution (college, university, etc.) add the name of the institution to the heading."

> Conference on the Fine Arts, State University Teachers College, New Paltz, N. Y., 1952.

"Care should be taken not to confuse with such conferences, the 'institutes,' 'workshops,' etc., which are departments or seminars in departments of academic institutions, and which are entered as such."

> North Carolina.   University.   Institute for Social Science Research.

Exhibitions, etc. (A.L.A. 1949.136) "Enter general exhibitions, fairs, bazaars, etc., under the name of the place where they are held, and refer from the official title and any other names by which the exhibition is generally known."

> New York.   World's Fair, 1939–1940.
> *Refer from:* World's Fair, New York.

"Enter exhibitions, fairs, bazaars, etc., held by or under the auspices of some society or institution or in connection with an international or other congress...under the name of the body or congress, with reference from the name of the place and from the name of the exhibition when this is at all distinctive."

> Arts Council of Great Britain.
> Art treasures from Vienna; an exhibition held at the Tate Gallery.

Commissions and committees (A.L.A. 1949.139) "Enter autonomous commissions and committees, international, national or local, under their names, adding the place of headquarters only when necessary for identification."

> Committee for Industrial Organization.
> Committee for Kentucky.

"Enter commissions, committees and delegations appointed by corporate bodies to perform particular functions, either permanent or temporary, as a subheading under the name of the appointing body, with references as required."

> Methodist Church (United States)   Commission on Chaplains.

"Enter joint commissions, committees or boards of two or more governments or organizations under their own names, with references for each of the governments or bodies. The references may be either *see* or *see also* references depending upon the wording of the name of the committee."

> Joint Commission on Rural Reconstruction in China (U. S. and China).
> Joint Committee of the North Carolina English Teachers Association and
>   the North Carolina Library Association.

Boards, trustees, etc. (A.L.A. 1949.142) "Enter bodies whose legal names begin with such words as Board, Corporation, Trustees, under the names of the institutions or bodies over which they exercise supervision."

> Smithsonian Institution. *Not:* Board of Regents of the Smithsonian Institution.

Foundations, endowments, funds (A.L.A. 1949.143) "Enter foundations and endowments, funds, etc., under their names...initials of forenames and abbreviations of titles may be omitted...Refer from place and from the exact name if not used as the heading."

> Rockefeller Foundation.
> Kellogg Foundation, Battle Creek, Mich.
>   *Refer from:* W. K. Kellogg Foundation; Kellogg (W. K.) Foundation.

Firms, business corporations, etc. (A.L.A. 1949.144) "Enter firms, business corporations (including those owned by governments), hotels [which, while they may be considered as institutions, are better treated as firms], railway companies, etc., under the corporate name. The terms incorporated (inc.), limited (ltd.), etc., or their equivalents if included in the corporate name are to be retained. Add the place in the heading for firms located in one city only, but not for those with branches."

> Pennsylvania Railroad Company.
> Rand, McNally and Company.

"If the name begins with the forename or initials of a personal name, enter under surname, giving forenames or initials according to the usage of the firm or corporation. If the inversion brings them *within* the corporate name, inclose them within parentheses rather than commas."

> Hammond (C. S.) and Company, Inc.

"Exception: Entry under forename may be preferred in a few cases, favoring customary use."

> Marshall Field and Company.
> *Refer from:* Field (Marshall) and Company.

GEOGRAPHIC HEADINGS

Further rules regarding geographical headings properly belong here, as many corporate bodies are entered under place.

Language of heading (A.L.A. 1949.150) "Give countries, self-governing dominions, colonies and protectorates in the conventional English form."

> Canada.
> French West Africa.
> Mexico.

Cities and towns (A.L.A. 1949.153) "When used as entry word, cities and towns in the United States and Canada are followed by the name of the state or province, in accepted abbreviated form."

> Richmond, Calif. Chamber of Commerce.

"Cities and towns other than those in the United States and Canada are followed by the name of the country (not by the name of the province or smaller division) or region."

> Richmond, Eng.

"Exception: Enter largest or best-known city of its name, in America or elsewhere, without further designation."

> Richmond. John Marshall High School.
> Richmond, Calif. Chamber of Commerce.

Counties (A.L.A. 1949.152) "Counties in the United States and Canada when used as entry word are followed by the name of the state or province, elsewhere by the name of the country, in accepted abbreviated form."

> Jefferson Co., Ala.
> Meath, Ire. (County)

States, provinces, etc. (A.L.A. 1949.51) "The states of the United States and the provinces of Canada and the more familiar foreign states, provinces and 'départements,' do not require the addition of the name of the country."

> Texas.   State Board of Education.
> British Columbia.   Dept. of Education.

Political division in heading (A.L.A. 1949.154) "When different units have the same name, distinguish them by adding the particular designation in parentheses, preferably in English."

> New York (City)
> New York (State)

* * *

Conclusions regarding choice of name of organization. As indicated on page 61 and in the preceding rules, all corporate authors are divided into four groups: governments, societies, institutions, and miscellaneous bodies. Note that these authors consist of the place *and* the name of the organization, *or* the name of the organization *with* or *without* the place.

In deciding upon the form of the entry for an organization it is necessary to consider whether it is a government, society, institution, or some other body or organization. The statements in this chapter as to what each group includes will help one in determining what the organization is. Take for example: *"Directory of Manufacturers, the State of Washington, May 1952.* Compiled cooperatively by The Division of Industrial Research and The Bureau of Economic and Business Research. The State College of Washington, Pullman, Washington." Who is the author? What form of the name is to be used? See rule under *State and provincial institutions (U.S. and Canada),* page 67. The title page identifies the Division and Bureau which compiled this work cooperatively, and the imprint gives The State College of Washington. Looking in Patterson's *American Educational Directory, 1952,* we find

Washington; under that, Pullman, Whitman County; then State College of Washington. And in L. L. Tucker's *Author Headings for the Official Publications of the State of Washington* is found: Washington (State)   State college, Pullman. In this instance it is necessary to add in parentheses "State" to distinguish it from Washington, D. C. Following this rule the heading would be: Washington (State)   State College, Pullman. The state of Washington has three colleges of education besides the State College and the University, hence the name of the place is added, as "State College" is not a distinctive name. Application of the rule on page 67, *Institutions forming an integral part of a larger organization,* gives as the heading for the *Directory of Manufacturers:*

> Washington (State)   State College, Pullman. Division of <u>Industrial</u> Research.

An added entry may be made under:

> Washington (State)   State College, Pullman. Bureau of <u>Economic</u> and Business Research.

Another illustration is: *"Weeds of California,* by W. W. Robbins, Margaret K. Bellue, Walter S. Ball. For sale by Printing Division (Documents Section) Sacramento." Printed at the top of the page bearing the Foreword is "State of California, Department of Agriculture," and on the spine of the book, "1951." Should this book be entered in the catalog under Robbins, the first author on the title page, or under: California.   State Department of Agriculture, with an added entry under Robbins? The title page states that Robbins is Professor of Botany and Botanist in the Experiment Station, University of California, and this information is confirmed in his biographical sketch in *Who's Who in America,* 1952-1953. The *Cumulative Book Index,* April, 1953, lists under Robbins, Wilfred William: *Weed Control; a Textbook and Manual,* a 1952 publication of McGraw-Hill. Mr. Robbins is of sufficient importance to be listed in *Who's Who in America* and has had published a book on weed control.

On page 63, "Enter under personal author scientific papers, addresses, and other publications, not administrative or routine in character, but which are issued officially by the department to which the author is attached. Make added entry under the department." This publication fits nicely under this rule and should be entered in the catalog under: Robbins, Wilfred William, 1884-1952; with an added entry under: California. State Department of California. The California *Blue Book,* 1950, lists the State Department of Agriculture as one of the executive departments of the state, and the form given here would come under the *General Rule* on page 62: "Enter under countries or nations, states...official publications issued by them..." and: "Enter publications emanating from the various agencies of government under the names of the agencies (legislative bodies, courts, executive departments, bureaus, etc.)..."

To cite another example the *Annual Report of the International Health Division of the Rockefeller Foundation* would come under the term "Miscellaneous bodies" which includes "...foundations and endowments, etc." and the rule which reads: "Enter foundations and endowments, funds, etc. under their names." This report would be cataloged under the Rockefeller Foundation, with the International Health Division as a subdivision of the heading; in this way the cataloger would bring together in the catalog all of the publications of the Rockefeller Foundation and under that all of those of the International Health Division.

> Rockefeller Foundation. International Health Division.

There may be a reference *from* New York (City) Rockefeller Foundation *to* Rockefeller Foundation.

15 Name authority card for an organization

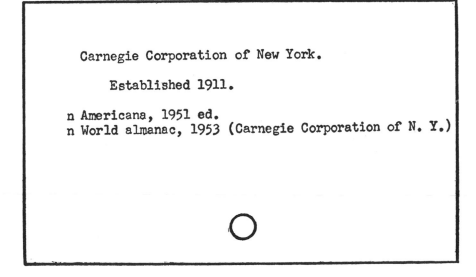

In determining the heading to be used for the publication of an organization one consults the cataloging rules and library aids. An authority card may be made if it is considered desirable to have a permanent record of the form adopted and the aids consulted (see Card 15).

chapter VI

Main catalog entries

Introduction. Up to this point the reader has been concerned with the contents of the book and how books of similar content may be grouped together; the forms of personal names and names of organizations, with reference to the choice of proper headings for catalog entries. This chapter discusses the items about the book to be put on the unit catalog card.

The catalog is expected to answer such questions as: What books by Archibald MacLeish are in the library? Has the library a copy of *Treasure Island?* What material has the library on air conditioning? These questions can be answered by consulting the catalog for the author's name, the title, or the subject heading and noting the call numbers in order to locate the books on the shelves.

Besides these types, however, such questions are asked as: What is the latest book in the library by Marjorie Rawlings? Has the library the one-volume edition of *The Science of Life* by H. G. Wells, Julian S. Huxley, G. P. Wells? What books has the library with illustrations by Kurt Wiese? When and by whom was the first edition of Robinson's *Collected Poems* published? In deciding upon what to include in the description of the book in the catalog entry consider the items given for books in such aids as the Standard Catalog series of the H. W. Wilson Company. Remember that where the shelves are open to the readers, little time is spent at the catalog looking at the cards. On the other hand, even in the smallest library the catalog may be called upon to answer some question about a book which is out in circulation; and in looking for material on a subject the reader will sometimes examine all the cards before going to the shelves, considering the author, publisher, date, and size of the book as indicated by the number of pages.

Cataloging a book. The first step in cataloging a book is to examine the title page, the *official page* from which the librarian gets most of the information for the catalog entry. Besides the author and the title, the title page often gives the author's degrees and other information, yet this information on the catalog card would not be of sufficient value to warrant the space it would take. The title page may also give a statement about the edition—as second edition or revised edition—and may specify how the book is illustrated. Then there is the imprint, that is, place of publication, publisher, and date of publication, given at the bottom of the title page. The librarian should examine not only the title page for the items mentioned but also the pages preceding the title page and the cover to see if the book belongs to a series, e.g., "The Rivers of America"; the back of the title page for the copyright date; the preface for further information regarding the edition; the table of contents for the list of works if the book includes a number of separate works, e.g., plays; the book itself: (1) for the collation—that is, the number of pages or volumes and illustrations and (2) for bibliographies, appendixes containing material of special value and other special features which should be brought out in notes.

Take, for instance, Elizabeth Vining's *Windows for the Crown Prince:*

WINDOWS

for the

CROWN PRINCE

By Elizabeth Gray Vining

"We want you to open windows
on to a wider world for our Crown
Prince."

—VISCOUNT MATSUDAIRA

J. B. LIPPINCOTT COMPANY
PHILADELPHIA AND NEW YORK

On the back of the title page is found:

COPYRIGHT, 1952, By

ELIZABETH GRAY VINING

PRINTED IN THE
UNITED STATES OF AMERICA

FIRST EDITION

16 Main entry for nonfiction with person as author

```
952
V78    Vining, Elizabeth (Gray) 1902-
          Windows for the Crown Prince.    ⌜1st ed.⌝
       Lippincott ⌜c1952⌝
          320 p.  illus.




       1. Akihito, Crown Prince of Japan, 1933-
       2. Japan.  Social life and customs.  3. Education.
       Japan.  I. Title.
                              O
```

Examination of the book shows that it has 320 pages and is illustrated, including portraits. After the cataloger has examined the book, the next step is to assign the classification number and the subject headings. Chapter I describes the process of classifying and gives directions for doing it. Chapter II does the same for subject headings. The classification number, 952, should be written in pencil in the upper left-hand corner of the page following the title page about an inch from the top of the page and from the hinge. Here it will be easy to locate, and if the book is rebound it will not be cut off in the trimming nor hidden by the sewing.

The author card for the book would include: the classification number, book number if book numbers are used in the library, author and her dates (if dates are used), title, publisher, copyright date[1] the total number of pages, information about the illustrations.

In some books part of the title of the book, of the author's name, or the place of publication or publisher's name spreads over two pages, facing each other. This is called a "double title page" or a "double-spread title page." The necessary information for the catalog entry is taken from both pages. No mention of this type of title page is needed in the catalog entry. An example of a double title page is given.

---

[1]See p.85 for information regarding dates of books.

A Girl   Grows Up
BY RUTH FEDDER
NEW EDITION   Psychologist, Bucks County Schools
Completely Revised and   Bucks County, Pennsylvania
Enlarged

Drawings by Roberta Paflin

(P I C T U R E)

Whittlesey House, NEW YORK: TORONTO
McGRAW-HILL BOOK COMPANY, INC.

Indention and spacing on cards. Before discussing the place and the order of the items given in the catalog entry it is necessary to explain the indentions and spacing commonly used on catalog cards. The purpose of indention and spacing is to emphasize the different groups of information and to give special prominence to certain words, e.g., the author's surname.

Cards 7 and 11 in Chapter II show the indentions and spacing used on subject authority and cross reference cards. The sample name authority cards, numbers 12–15 in Chapters III–V, show the indention and the spacing recommended for these types of cards, but do not indicate the specific lines and spaces. They are, in general, the same as for the catalog cards given in this and subsequent chapters. Card 17 is a skeleton card with indentions and spacing indicated to make clear the

17 Skeleton card showing location of the different items

use in this textbook of the terms first, second, and third indention. This card also shows the relative location on the card of the call number, author, title, imprint, collation, series note, and other notes.

Call number	Classification number, 3rd line, 2nd space from left edge of card. Book number 4th line, 2nd space from left edge of card.
Author	4th line, *1st indention* (8th space from left edge of card). If author's name runs over, the succeeding line begins at *3rd indention* (14th space from left edge of card).
Title	Line below author, *2nd indention* (12th space from left edge of card). If title runs over, the succeeding line begins at 1st indention.
Edition	3rd space after period following title.
Imprint	5th space after period following title *or edition statement,* if there is space; if not, at 1st indention. If the imprint runs over, the succeeding line begins at 1st indention.
Collation	Line below imprint, 2nd indention; if it runs over, the succeeding line begins at 1st indention. There are two spaces between the subgroups giving the pages and the illustrations.
Series note	5th space after collation if there is space; if not, on the next line at 1st indention. If the series note runs over, the succeeding line begins at 1st indention.
Notes	One line is skipped before the first note. Notes begin at 2nd indention, the succeeding line at 1st indention. Each note forms a separate paragraph.
Contents	In paragraph form beginning at 2nd indention, the succeeding line at 1st indention.

RULES FOR CATALOGING

Call number. The call number is the classification symbol and the book number or initial of the author's surname; e.g., 952 is the call

V78

number for Elizabeth Vining's book. Other illustrations of call numbers are: 92   973 or if the author's initial letter only is used: 92   973.

C87   B31   C   B

This combination of figures and letters, which is necessary to direct the reader to the shelves, is given on the catalog cards, on the spine of the book, and on the book card. Some librarians put this number on the catalog cards in red to make it more conspicuous.

Author. Chapter III explains how to determine the form of name to be used, and shows a name authority card with the name properly written for a catalog entry. Whether or not the librarian makes name authority cards, each name must be looked up and the form to be used in the catalog decided upon. For example, in the *Booklist,* volume 48, the heading for *Windows for the Crown Prince* is Vining, Elizabeth (Gray) 1902–   , the form used on Card 12.

The general rule for cataloging is to "Enter a work under the name of its author whether personal or corporate." (A.L.A. 1949.1) "In the heading give the author's name in full and in the vernacular form…" unless another form has commonly been used and is better known. "The form adopted for a given person is used without variation whenever it occurs as a heading, whether as author, added entry, or subject. Refer from forms not adopted." (A.L.A. 1949.36) "Enter persons of modern times under the family name followed by the forenames and the dates of birth and death when available." (A.L.A. 1949.37)

> Gide, André Paul Guillaume, 1869–1951.

The dates are given only if they are found in the search for the name. If the library does not find these dates of birth and death useful in its catalog they should be omitted.

The author's surname is followed by a comma, one space, the forenames, comma, one space, dates of birth and death, period. If only initials for forenames appear on the title page and the forenames cannot be found, eight spaces are left after each initial so that the names may be filled in, if found later.

Title. "The title proper is transcribed exactly as to order, wording and spelling, but not necessarily as to punctuation and capitalization. Capitalization…and punctuation in the catalog entry should follow as far as practicable the current usage of the language concerned. Accents are added in conformity with the general usage….Accents, but not umlauts, are to be omitted from capital letters and initials (except the French capital E).

"*Abridgment.* Long titles are abridged if this can be done without loss of essential information. The first words of the title are always included…The first word of the title may be the name of the author. In the possessive form it is generally omitted…Parts of the title more intelligibly presented in a contents paragraph are omitted from the transcription of the title…." (L.C. 1949.3:5)[2]

Phrases in the title giving the name of the illustrator are omitted,

[2]U. S. Library of Congress, Descriptive Cataloging Division, *Rules for Descriptive Cataloging in the Library of Congress* (Washington: 1949). The citation is to Rule 3:5.

unless the illustrator is of sufficient importance to have an added entry in the catalog under his name. Also omit phrases about the kind and number of illustrations, since the collation states whether or not the work contains illustrations. Unusual illustrations may be mentioned in a note.

"*Additions*. Additions may be made to the title in the language of the title if it needs explanation and if brief statements to clarify it can be taken from the work itself....

"*Alternative title*. An alternative title is always transcribed in the catalog entry because the book may be referred to by it and because another edition may be published with the alternative title as the title.

"*Subtitle*. The subtitle is considered a part of the title and transcribed in the entry in the same manner as the title proper, except that a long subtitle which is separable from the title may be omitted....." (L.C. 1949.3:5)

"*Author statement*. The statement of authorship appearing on a work is incorporated in the catalog entry *only* if it is necessary for one of the following purposes:

"a. To show variation in the form of name in the work from that adopted as the author heading, if the two are not obviously two forms of the same name.

"b. To bring out the pseudonym under which an author has written.

"c. To indicate the statement which veils rather than names the author of an anonymous work....

"d. To name the persons who contributed to a work of joint or composite authorship, and to show their part in the work....

"e. To show the relationship to the work of the person named in the heading (if this is other than author, editor, compiler, etc.) that otherwise would not be shown....

"f. To name the person or persons who prepared a work which is entered under a corporate author heading.

. . . .

"h. To make the title intelligible if the author's name is an integral part of the title.

"*Joint authors*. Two or three joint authors, collaborators, or contributors are named in the author statement. If there are more than three, all after the first name are omitted. The omission is indicated...by the phrase 'and others'...

"Additions to the author statement. If a pseudonymous work is entered under the real name of the author, the designation 'pseud.' is added after the pseudonym in the author statement...." (L.C. 1949.3:6A;C;E)

"Capitalization. In the titles of books, pamphlets, periodicals, documents and other publications...the first word is capitalized....

"The first word of every title quoted and every alternative title introduced by 'or' or its equivalent, is capitalized...." (L.C.1949. App. II, A.1;1a)

Punctuation. Use a colon after the first part of the title, if the second part is in apposition with it and each part makes sense by itself. Use a common, however, if it is just a matter of one or two words, e.g., *Lincoln, the Man.* Use a semicolon before explanatory phrases such as "with an introd. by" and before subtitles, which are subdivided by commas. Use a comma before the phrase beginning "by" introducing joint authors, the pseudonym of an author, etc. Some examples of punctuation of titles are:

> Intelligence in the modern world: John Dewey's philosophy.
> The cavalier's cup; another adventure of Sir Henry Merrivale, by Carter Dickson [pseud.].
> The diplomats: 1919–1939; edited by Gordon A. Craig and Felix Gilbert.
> Electricity and magnetism; theory and applications. 3d ed.
> Is another world watching? The riddle of the flying saucers.
> London homes of Dickens; with an introd. by Walter Dexter.
> Signal, noise and resolution in nuclear counter amplifiers.

The abbreviations used in the illustrations of titles given above and on the sample cards in this book are listed in Appendix II. Words in the title up to the first mark of punctuation are not to be abbreviated. Abbreviations used on the title page are to be used on the card whether or not they are included in the list in Appendix II.

Edition. An edition as recorded in cataloging implies some change in the text, either additions, revisions, corrections, or all three. Since there is no difference between the fifth impression and the first or between the fifteenth printing and the first, so far as the content is concerned, the number of printings or impressions is not mentioned. "The edition of a work is always described in its catalog entry..." (L.C. 1949.3:7) It is given immediately following the title. The wording of the edition statement varies, since it is taken from the title page of the book. Occasionally the information is found only on the back of the title page or in the preface, in which cases the edition statement is given in brackets at the end of the title to show that it was not on the title page. For abbreviations to be used in the edition statement see the list in Appendix II. Some examples of edition statements are:

3d ed.
2d ed. unabr. with reference history.
7th ed. rev. to Jan. 1, 1953.
Rev. and enl.
1951 ed.
A special ed. rev. and with new material.
Concordance ed.

Imprint. The place of publication, name of the publisher, and date of copyright or of publication follow the title, and are separated from each other by commas. "The place of publication is followed by its country, state or similar designation if it is necessary to identify the place or to distinguish it from another place of the same name. Abbreviations are used for most such designations...." (L.C. 1949.3:11A) If the name of the city is well known, e.g., New York, Boston, Chicago, London, the name of the state or country after it is unnecessary. In cases where two or more cities have the same name the best known is given without state, the lesser known with state, e.g., Washington (referring to Washington, D. C.) but Washington, N. C. If two equally well-known cities have the same name, give state in each case, e.g., Portland, Me.; Portland, Ore.

"The publisher statement appearing on a work is abridged as much as possible without loss of...identification of the publisher. Unnecessary parts of the statement are omitted, abbreviations are employed [see Appendix II] and names known to be forenames are represented by initials...." (L.C. 1949.3:12) Necessary data to make the publisher statement intelligible are: "The statement that a work is privately printed; phrases showing that the publisher is also the author of the work, if an author statement is needed." (L.C. 1949.3:12B) Omit: "the phrases 'published by,' 'published for,' and the word, 'publisher';...the initial article, except when necessary for clarity; the phrases 'and company,' 'and sons';...terms meaning 'incorporated' or 'limited' and their abbreviations;...the name of the publishing firm if it is used with the name of a branch or division identified with the publication of a particular

type of book, e.g., McGraw-Hill and its branch, Whittlesey House."
(L.C. 3:12A)

Title page:	Methuen & Co. Ltd. London
	36 Essex Street. Strand W.C.2
Give:	London, Methuen.
Title page:	The Naylor Company
	Publishers to the Southwest
Give:	San Antonio, Texas
	San Antonio, Naylor.
Title page:	Columbia University Press
	Morningside Heights, New York
Give:	New York, Columbia University Press.

The imprint for the proceedings and transactions of societies may
or may not repeat the name of the society; in either case the name of the
society is the author of the entry.

"Omission of publisher. For a work entered under a corporate author
heading with the same body responsible both for authorship and for
publication, the publisher statement is omitted from the imprint...."
(L.C. 1949.3:12C) An exception is made if the publisher statement is
given in the imprint simply as The Association, The Society.

Title page:	National Education Association of the United States
	Washington, D.C.
Give:	Washington
Title page:	Worcester, Massachusetts
	Published by the Society
Give:	Worcester, Mass., The Society

When publishers are well known the place of publication may be
omitted and the publishers' names abbreviated. Appendix II gives a list
of well-known publishers, with abbreviations, to be used without place.
If the publisher of a given book is not included in this list, the place
appearing first on the title page and the name of the publisher listed
first are to be given in the entry with such abbreviations as are authorized in this appendix. When a publisher's name becomes more common
in catalog entries, it may be used in abbreviation and without place if it
is added to the list in the appendix. There are two exceptions which
should be made: (1) if the first place and publisher are foreign ones,
and one in the United States is given, give the latter; and (2) if a place
other than the first is given in larger print, that is the home office of
the publisher and is the one to give in the entry.

The date of publication is the date given at the foot of the title page. This date is usually changed when the book is reprinted. The important point is not when the book was printed, but when it was written and when the latest changes in it were made. The latest copyright date shows this, for books can be recopyrighted only when important changes are made in them; therefore, the latest copyright date is used, e.g., "Copyright, 1914, 1942"—choose the latter. The person or firm copyrighting an average volume is of no importance in the catalog, so variation in this fact is not noted. The letter *c* before a date, c1952, shows that it is the copyright date. If there is no copyright date, give the date of publication; i.e., the date at the foot of the title page; if no publication date, give the date in or at the end of the preface or introduction, preceded by the abbreviation *pref.* or *introd.* or the appropriate word written out; if no date is given anywhere, write *n. d.* Some librarians may prefer to use *no date* instead of the abbreviation *n. d.* Use arabic figures for dates even though the book uses roman numerals.

Place, publisher, and date, if not found on the title page, are enclosed in brackets.

    Bloomington, Indiana University Press, 1953.
    Harper [c1950]
    Morrow, 1953.
    New York, The Modern Library [pref. 1880]
    [New York] Fordham University, n. d.
    New York, Pantheon Books, n. d.
    Van Nostrand [1950]

Collation. This term is used to include the number of pages of a one-volume work, or the number of volumes of a work in more than one volume, and information about the illustrations.

The title page may include a statement as to the number of volumes and the number of and type of the illustrations, or this information, like the paging, may be discovered only through an examination of the book. In giving the number of pages the preliminary paging is to be ignored and the last numbered page in the book is to be recorded, whether it is the last page of the text, the next to the last, or the last page of the index. If a work is in two or more volumes and the library does not have them all, give what it has in pencil so that the changes may be made easily if other volumes are added, e.g., *v. 1, 3.* When a book does not have its pages numbered, write "unpaged."

Frontispieces, plates, portraits, maps, diagrams, charts, plans, facsimiles, tables, etc. are to be included in the general term *illustrations*. Unusual illustrations, such as colored plates which add much to the work, may be mentioned in a note.

> 210 p.   illus.
> 3 v.   illus.

Two typewriter spaces are left between the paging or number of volumes and the statement about the illustrations. This makes each subgroup of the collation stand out clearly.

Series note. Many books belong to a series and it is sometimes important to include this information in the catalog entry. A series is "A number of separate works, usually related to one another in subject or otherwise, issued in succession, normally by the same publisher and in uniform style, with a collective title..."[3] There are three kinds of series: author, subject, and publisher's. *Pilgrimage,* parts I-XII, by Dorothy M. Richardson, which includes *Dawn's Left Hand* and *Clear Horizon,* is an example of an author's series; "American Guide Series" and "Rivers of America" are examples of subject series; Everyman's Library, an example of a publisher's series.

The name of the series is found at the top of the title page, on the cover of the book, or on one of the pages preceding the title page. A series note states the name of the series to which the book belongs. If the name of the series begins with an article, the second word as well as the article begins with a capital letter. The series note is enclosed in parentheses and begins on the fifth space after the collation; if there

18 Main entry with subtitle, series note, and notes

```
973.917
B86    Brogan, Denis William, 1900-
           The era of Franklin D. Roosevelt; a chronicle
       of the New Deal and global war.    New Haven, Yale
       University Press [c1950]
           382 p.  illus.    (The Chronicles of America
       series, v. 52)

           "Bibliographical note": p. 365-372.
```

---

[3]*A.L.A. Glossary of Library Terms* (Chicago: A.L.A., 1943), p.124.

is not space on that line, it begins at the first indention on the following line. If the series is not of sufficient importance for an added entry, it is unnecessary to make a series note. Sample Card 18 shows a series note.

Notes. Notes may be added to catalog entries when needed to explain the title or to correct any misapprehension to which it might lead; to supply essential information; to give important bibliographical details not included in the title, imprint, or collation. They should be brief and clear. The safest rule is not to add a note if there is doubt as to its value. The following order is suggested for notes:

1 Added information about the physical make-up of the book, e.g., that the title page is lacking (something which may occur when an old library is being cataloged); that it contains unusually fine colored plates.
2 Notes on pseudonyms, sequels.
3 Source of the book, e.g., that it has been published previously in some periodical; the fact that it is bound with some other work; that it has been published under some other title.

Contents.

"*Scope.* Either all of the contents or a part of them are specified in the catalog entry if it is necessary to bring out important parts of the work not mentioned in the title, or to give a fuller and more detailed description of the contents than the title supplies.... The complete contents are listed in the entry for collections of works by the same author (especially if they are on different subjects) or for collections of works by different authors, unless the articles are numerous and slight or of the same type.

"Contents are especially necessary for works in several volumes, whether they are single works (with a formal division of matter that can be described) or collections of works by one or more authors.

"Partial contents are noted if one or more selected items in the work need to be specified. Bibliographies are noted unless they are obviously of little value. Bibliographical footnotes are mentioned only if they seem to be particularly important or take the place of a bibliography that would have been noted. Appendices are noted only if they contain matter that is important enough to be specified.... Supplements or other appended matter not printed with the work are always noted.

"*Position.* The contents note...is the last note in the catalog entry.

"*Form.* Give the precise heading of the item as it is found in the work (generally as a...heading...or in the table of contents)...the contents are arranged in one paragraph, beginning with the word 'Contents' or the phrase 'Partial contents.' The items are given in the order in which they appear in the work. Except in works of one volume, the parts of the work are designated, the terms being those used in the work itself, except that arabic numerals are substituted for roman numerals unless both are required for clarity. If the parts are unnumbered, volume or part numbers are supplied....

"For works of one volume, the items in a contents paragraph are separated by a dash; for works of more than one volume, the dash precedes the volume number and items within the volumes are punctuated as separate sentences.

"Introductions described in the title are not mentioned again in the contents paragraph...."

Example taken from Gamaliel Bradford's *American Portraits 1875-1900:*

> Contents.—Mark Twain.—Henry Adams.—Sidney Lanier.—James McNeil Whistler.—James Gillespie Blaine.—Grover Cleveland.—Henry James. —Joseph Jefferson.

Example from De la Mare's *Collected Poems, 1901–1918,* a work in two volumes:

> Contents.—v. 1 Poems, 1906. The listeners, 1914. Motley, 1919.—v. 2 Songs of childhood, 1901. Peacock pie.

"In listing works by different authors, the title precedes the name of the author...Initials are used for one or more forenames. Brackets are not used to show that the word 'by'...has been supplied."
Example from *Critics' Prize Plays,* published in 1945:

> Contents.—Winterset, by M. Anderson.—High Tor, by M. Anderson.—Of mice and men, by J. Steinbeck.—Time of your life, by W. Saroyan.—Watch on the Rhine, by L. Hellman.—The patriots, by S. Kingsley.

Example from E. V. Heyn's *Twelve More Sport Immortals,* published in 1951:

> Contents.—Christy Mathewson, James J. Corbett, Bobby Jones, Grover Cleveland Alexander, John L. Sullivan, Rogers Hornsby, by J. Sher.—Red Grange, Judge Landis, Eddie Shore, by E. Fitzgerald.—Walter Johnson, by S. Povich.—Bill Tilden, Jim Thorpe, by A. Stump.

The example from Heyn shows the importance of using "by" in giving contents for biography in order to make clear who is the subject and who is the author. It also shows how one may list the titles by one author together rather than giving each one separately and repeating the author's name, e.g., Christy Mathewson, by J. Sher.—James J. Corbett, by J. Sher., etc.

"Paging is given in the contents paragraph only for bibliographies, and for a particular item that occupies a disproportionately large portion of the work. If given, it is cited within parentheses.

"Contents of a set in many volumes may be paragraphed, one paragraph to a volume, with 'Contents' centered as heading...." (L.C. 1949.3:22A-C)

Sometimes partial contents are useful, e.g., for F. C. Lincoln's *Migration of Birds:*

> Appendices: I. List of birds mentioned in the text.
> II. Bird banding.

Different editions of the same book. The title page of the third edition of Garrett's *Statistics in Psychology and Education* reads:

STATISTICS IN
PSYCHOLOGY
AND EDUCATION
BY
HENRY E. GARRETT, PH. D.
PROFESSOR OF PSYCHOLOGY, COLUMBIA UNIVERSITY
WITH AN INTRODUCTION BY
R. S. WOODWORTH
PROFESSOR EMERITUS OF PSYCHOLOGY
COLUMBIA UNIVERSITY
THIRD EDITION
LONGMANS, GREEN AND CO.
NEW YORK. LONDON. TORONTO

Examination of this book shows the latest copyright date to be 1947. It has twelve preliminary pages numbered in roman numerals, 487 pages numbered in arabic, and diagrams and tables.

The title page of the fourth edition of Garrett's book on statistics reads just as that for the third edition except that "Fourth Edition" is given instead of "Third Edition" and the date of publication, "1953," is given at the foot of the title page below the place of publication.

This edition also has bibliographical footnotes, diagrams, tables, twelve preliminary pages numbered in roman numerals, but 460 pages numbered in arabic. The latest copyright date on the reverse of the title page is: 1953.

19 **Main entry with edition statement**

```
311
G23    Garrett, Henry Edward, 1894-
            Statistics in psychology and education.   3d ed.
       Longmans ⌐c1947⌐
            487 p.   illus.
```

20 **Main entry with edition statement**

```
311
G23A  Garrett, Henry Edward, 1894-
            Statistics in psychology and education.   4th ed.
       Longmans ⌐c1953⌐
            460 p.   illus.
```

Should these two editions of Garrett's book on statistics be cataloged as two different books or as two copies of the same book? In some small general libraries only the latest edition of a book is wanted and the earlier edition is withdrawn when the later one is secured. In such a library the catalog cards for the earlier edition would be destroyed, and new cards would be made for the new edition. A librarian wishing to keep all editions would make separate cards for the added edition as for any other book. The difference between the cards for these two editions of Garrett would be in the edition statement, the copyright dates in the imprint, the number of pages. Note that the book number would have an added symbol to distinguish it from that for the third edition as otherwise the two books would have the same classification number. The edition statement would in each instance be taken from the title page and would give the exact wording, as explained on page 82.

In books published in England there is frequently found on the back of the title page such a statement as:

First Printed in 1949
Reprinted 1950

or:

First published, 1940
Reprinted 1942

As 1949 or 1940 in the second case more nearly represent the time of the writing of the books the earlier dates would be preferred for the catalog cards rather than the later dates or the ones, if any, on the title pages. When there are several copyright dates, however, the latest one is given on the catalog card, since it signifies a change in the content of the book.

Works in two or more volumes. De la Mare's *Collected Poems, 1901–1918,* whose contents were given earlier in this chapter, is in two volumes. The title page for the first volume reads:

Collected Poems
1901–1918
By
Walter de la Mare
In Two Volumes
Vol. I
New York
Henry Holt and Company
1920

The title page for Volume II is identical with that of Volume I except that it reads: "In Two Volumes, Vol. II." One entry records both volumes. "A...work in several volumes is, as a rule, cataloged from the title page of the first volume. Variations on the title pages of subsequent volumes are shown by incorporating the data with those from the first volume or by adding supplementary notes." (L.C. 1949.3:4B) The collation would be: 2 v.

"If the work is in more than one volume and the publication or copyright dates of the individual volumes vary, the inclusive dates are given in the imprint..." (L.C. 1949.3:13A)

Supplements, indexes. Channing's history, for which a card is given, has a general index which forms a supplementary volume to the work but was not compiled by Channing. "Continuations of, and supplements and indexes to,...publications that are not independent of the work to which they belong are described in the entry for the main work. ...the supplementary volumes may be included as part of the contents statement [of the main work] even though they are not numbered consecutively with the other volumes....If, however, a more complete description of the supplement is required, the following form is used: a dash...to represent the repetition of the author heading, is added to the catalog entry following all of the...notes relating to the main work... It is followed by the title of the supplement or index, the author state-

21 Author entry for work of more than one volume with different copyright dates for different volumes and with contents

```
973
C45    Channing, Edward, 1856-1931.
           A history of the United States.    Macmillan
       [c1905-25]
           6 v.  illus.

           Contents.-v. 1 The planting of a nation in the
       new world, 1000-1660.-v. 2 A century of colonial
       history, 1660-1760.-v. 3 The American Revolution,
       1761-1789.-v. 4 Federalists and Republicans, 1789-
       1815.-v. 5 The period of transition, 1815-1848.-
       v. 6 The war for Southern independence.
                           (Continued on next card)
```

ment (if necessary to show the compiler or other person responsible for the work), the edition statement, imprint, collation, etc., as for an independent work....

"If the title of the supplement or index includes the title of the main work and can be separated from it, the title of the main work is represented by a second dash...following the dash that represents the author." (L.C. 1949.5:1) If author and title of the supplement or index both differ from the main work, the supplement or index is cataloged separately.

When there is not space on the card for all of the information, added

22 Extension card also shows general index added to card for main work

```
973
C45    Channing.              2

973    --- --- Supplementary volume, general index, comp.
C45    by Eva G. Moore.    Macmillan [c1932]
           155 p.
```

cards known as extension cards are made. Whenever an extension card follows, "Continued on next card" is typed (or stamped with a rubber stamp) aligned with the hole in the card, and immediately to the right of it. The call number and the first or filing word of the first card are repeated on all extension cards and the number of the card is written in the center of the card, on the line above the heading. On an author or main card, the filing word at the top of the extension cards would be the author's surname; if the name of an organization, however, the full heading would be repeated as so many organizations begin with the same word, the name of the country, and so forth. On extension cards for added entries repeat the entire added heading, then proceed as usual.

Extension cards may be tied to the first card with heavy white thread. A pencil may be slipped in while the thread is being tied, so that the cards may be turned easily without being cut. Tying makes it easier to handle the cards before they are filed, and if for any reason they have to be removed from the catalog for additional information or a correction they can be kept together.

Works by joint authors. The title page of a work by joint authors reads:

You Can't
Take It With You
A Play
by
Moss Hart
and
George S. Kaufman
Farrar & Rinehart
New York   Toronto

This statement appears on the back of the title page:

Copyright 1937 by Moss Hart and George S. Kaufman

There are 207 pages, no illustrations except the frontispiece, which represents one scene in the play. There are no bibliographies or appendixes. Note that the author whose name comes first on the title page is given in author place on the top line of Card 23 and the names of both are given in the entry.

If the work is by more than one author "Enter under the first author mentioned on the title page..." (A.L.A. 1949.3A) Include all the names in the title, i.e., up to three.

23 **Main entry for a work by two authors**

```
812
H32    Hart, Moss, 1904-
            You can't take it with you, a play by Moss Hart
       and George S. Kaufman.    New York, Farrar & Rine-
       hart ⌐c1937⌐
            207 p.  illus.
```

For a work by four or more authors whose names appear on the title page, the name listed first is used as the author entry and also included in the title followed by the words *and others*. *And others* is given in brackets, since it is not on the title page of the book but is supplied by the librarian. If the authors are well known the names may be given in contents or in a note.

Names of organizations as authors. Chapter V gives the rules covering the forms of names of organizations to be used as headings in the catalog. The author card for a government document would be just like that for a book with a personal author, except that the heading would frequently be the official name of the government body, adapted to agree with the rules in Chapter V.

Note that the name is given on the same line as if it were a personal author. There are periods at the end of the main heading and each subheading, e.g., U. S., and each subheading is preceded by two spaces.

In headings as well as in the body of the card capitalize "names of countries and administrative divisions." (A.L.A. 1949. Appendix III, E5)

U.S.   Maritime Commission.
Virginia.   Conservation Commission.

"Capitalize names of organized bodies (first word and all important words)." (A.L.A. 1949. Appendix III, E4)

Minneapolis.   Public Library.
National Conference on City Planning.

"Capitalize: proper names, derivatives of proper names, common nouns and adjectives forming an essential part of a proper name." (A.L.A. 1949. Appendix III, E.1–3)

Child Study Association of America.
Association of American Geographers.

24 Author entry for a government document

```
385.2
U58   U. S. Congress.  House.  Committee on Foreign Af-
         fairs.
         Special mission to Panama to study the Panama
      Railroad Company; report by Thomas S. Gordon.
      U. S. Govt. Print. Off. 1951.
         22 p.  maps.
```

As in the case of government documents, publications of societies, associations, institutions and miscellaneous bodies are cataloged as are works of personal authors except that the name of the society, association, etc. is used as heading. "Phrases indicating the official status of a government printer..." should be included in the imprint for government documents. (L.C. 1949.3:12B.3)

The same book with two different titles. Mireille Cooper's *The Happy Season,* published by Pellegrini & Cudahy in New York in 1952, was published in London in 1951. The content of the English and the American editions is the same, but the English edition has the title *Swiss Family Burnand.* If the library has a copy of one title, an entry is made under the author for that title and a reference is made from the author and the other title so that the reader will be sure to find the book. A note on each entry informs the reader of the changed title.

If on the other hand the library has a copy of the book under each of its titles, each title will be cataloged separately, with the appropriate note on each entry giving the information as to the other title.

25 Main entry for book with changed title—book in library

```
Cooper, Mireille (Burnand) 1893-
      The happy season.   New York, Pellegrini &
   Cudahy ₁1952₎
      214 p.  illus.

      First published in London in 1951 under ti-
   tle: Swiss family Burnand.
```

26 Main entry for book with changed title—book in library

```
Cooper, Mireille (Burnand) 1893-
     Swiss family Burnand.    London, Eyre & Spottis-
woode, 1951.
     220 p.  illus.

     Published in New York in 1952 under title:  The
happy season.
```

27 Reference for book with changed title—book not in library

```
Cooper, Mireille (Burnand) 1893-
     Swiss family Burnand.
     see her
     The happy season.
```

Another kind of book it may be well to mention here is the book with more than one title page. In some instances there is an added title page for the series to which the book belongs, a special title page for a second volume, or a facsimile of the title page of an earlier edition. Catalog the book from the title page for the volume rather than the series, for the set rather than the volume; catalog from the printed title page if there is also an engraved one. If such information would be useful in the particular library give information in a note about the other title page or title pages.

* * *

Information in catalog entries for fiction. Since the reader who wants fiction uses the catalog only to find whether or not a certain book is in the library or what books the library has by a certain author, cards for fiction may be simpler than for nonfiction. For this reason most public libraries do not classify fiction nor assign a book number, and catalog it more simply than nonfiction when they type the cards. Some school and college libraries, however, prefer to classify their fiction as literature and to catalog it exactly as they do their nonfiction.

Others do not classify fiction, but catalog all books the same way whether fiction or nonfiction.

The simplest form of entry may contain only the author's full name, without dates, and the title. Many librarians prefer, however, to follow the same policy regarding author's dates for fiction as for nonfiction. Some librarians find the copyright date or the date of publication useful as the date answers the reader's query as to which of the titles is the most recent.

If more information regarding the book, e.g., the publisher, is desired on the catalog entries, it is better to catalog fiction and nonfiction alike. But if this information is available in trade catalogs and bibliographical tools which are at hand, time may be saved by making simple catalog entries such as Card 28 and by referring to these printed aids for the occasional calls for such information.

If the printed catalog cards described in Chapter X are used for fiction there are very few books for which the author's name and dates have to be established. If only author and title, or author, title, and dates are given for fiction, however, it may be less expensive, takes less time, and is as satisfactory to type the cards for fiction in the library as it is to order Wilson or Library of Congress printed catalog cards.

On the title card the information given on the author card is simply reversed, the title given on the top line, the author on the line below. As the reader frequently remembers the title rather than the author, title entries for fiction are important.

Another type of fiction is the anonymous book the author of which is unknown. This is the easiest of all to catalog. Obviously there can be no author card, and the only items that could go on the title card are the title and the copyright date. The latter item may be omitted. When the author is known but his name is not given on the title page, the book is cataloged as any other work of fiction, and a note states that the book is published anonymously.

28 Main entry for fiction

Edmonds, Walter Dumaux, 1903–
    The Boyds of Black River.   ₍c1953₎

chapter VII

Added catalog entries

Introduction. An added entry is a "secondary entry, i.e., any other than the main entry. There may be added entries for editor, translator, title, subjects, series, etc....an added entry card is a duplicate of the main entry, with the addition of a special heading." (A.L.A. 1949, p. 229)

Title entries. Title entries are made for all books of fiction and may or may not be made for all books of nonfiction. Consider Channing's *A History of the United States* and Gunther's *Inside Asia*. The former title is neither striking nor distinctive and may be used for many different histories of the United States. Undoubtedly many readers, however, will remember the latter and look for it in the catalog. A given library should have a definite policy and either always make title cards for nonfiction, or have a list of introductory words commonly used in titles for which title cards are not to be made, e.g., "Introduction to," "The principles of," "A story of." Title entries may well be omitted from the catalog also if the first word (or words) is the same as that of the subject heading on the subject card. Since directions for using the catalog commonly state that it contains an author and a title entry for every book in the library and in addition subject entries for nonfiction, many readers expect to find a book under its title, even though it is a common one, and may think the book is not in the library if it is not found under its title.

There are two possible forms for title entries, namely, the short form and the unit card form. The short form title card has classification number, book number, title, and author. Title cards may be just like the main entry, however, with the brief title added above the heading of the unit card. This form is in accordance with the statement made

29 Title entry—short form

```
950
G97        Inside Asia.
         Gunther, John, 1901-
```

30 Title entry—unit card

```
950        Inside Asia.
G97      Gunther, John, 1901-
             Inside Asia.    Harper ⌐c1939⌐
           599 p.  illus.

           Bibliography: p.578-581.
```

31 Title entry for book with changed title—book in library

```
         The happy season.
       Cooper, Mireille (Burnand) 1893-
         The happy season.    New York, Pellegrini &
       Cudahy, 1952.
         214 p.  illus.

         First published in London in 1951 under title:
       Swiss family Burnand.
```

32 Reference card for book with changed title—book not in library

```
         Swiss family Burnand,    see
       Cooper, Mireille (Burnand) 1893-
         The happy season.
```

above that "an added entry is a duplicate of the main entry, with the addition of a special heading." If the unit card is used, the reader need not refer to the author card.

In the preceding chapter the author card for Cooper's *The Happy*

Season is given as an illustration of what is done with books published under different titles. Corresponding cards would be made for the titles.

The latter part of the title of some books is better known than the full title, e.g., *The Tragedy of Macbeth*. In such cases a catch or partial title card is made. This card begins with the first striking word of the title, for example, *Macbeth*. If the card is a unit card, the full title is given after the author entry.

> Macbeth.
> Shakespeare, William, 1564–1616.
> > The tragedy of Macbeth.
>
> Robinson Crusoe.
> Defoe, Daniel, 1661?–1731.
> > The life and strange surprising adventures of Robinson Crusoe.

There are other books for which full *and* partial titles should be brought out in the catalog, e.g., J. George Frederick's *A Primer of "New Deal" Economics*. This work should have title cards as follows:

> A primer of "new deal" economics.
> Frederick, Justus George, 1882–
> > A primer of "new deal" economics.
>
> "New deal" economics.
> Frederick, Justus George, 1882–
> > A primer of "new deal" economics.

Subject entries. There are usually more inquiries for material on a specific subject than there are for books by a particular author or with a special title. The most used cards in the catalog are the subject cards, that is, the cards which indicate on the top line the subject of which the book treats. For this reason a subject entry should be made for every book which deals with a definite subject. Sometimes a book includes several different subjects and requires two, three, or even more subject entries. Subject entries are not necessary for books containing a single poem or a single play, or for a collection of all or part of the works of an individual author. Chapter II, "Choice of Subject Headings," deals with the question of ascertaining what a book is about and what subject headings best express its contents. There is also the possibility of making general subject references for entire groups of books, e.g., books on birds, airplanes, etc., or for all books of a certain form, e.g., books of American poetry. See Sample Cards 1 and 2.

If one turns back to Card 1, one will note that the classification num-

33 Subject entry—heading with subdivision

```
952      JAPAN.  SOCIAL LIFE AND CUSTOMS.
V78  Vining, Elizabeth (Gray) 1902-
         Windows for the Crown Prince.  ₍1st ed₎
      Lippincott ₍c1952₎
         320 p.  illus.
```

ber for this general subject reference is given in the same position as on the main card, described in Chapter VI; the subject heading in the same position as the added title on Card 30. A line is skipped and a paragraph, beginning on the second line below the heading and at the same indention as the heading, tells where books on the given subject may be found. The second and succeeding lines of this paragraph begin at the first indention. Another line is skipped; then the second paragraph about the use of the shelf list card is given with the same indentions as the first paragraph.

On the subject card the subject heading is given on the third line from the top of the card, the line above the author or main heading (two lines above if the length of the heading requires it), beginning at the second indention, so that the author heading may be more prominent. If the subject heading occupies more than one line, succeeding lines begin at the third indention. Subdivisions of a main heading may be separated from it by a period and two spaces, or other punctuation marks agreed upon locally, as a long dash (e.g., u.s.—history). This heading is usually given in red ink or in full capitals in black ink to make it stand out conspicuously. In all other respects the subject card is a copy of the author card.

Added entry for joint author, compiler, editor, etc. Added entry cards may be made for the second of two joint authors, for a compiler, editor, illustrator, translator, or for the person who writes the introduction to the book of another, provided these added entries are likely to be useful. If there are more than two joint authors or joint editors, added entries are made only for the first one. An added entry under Kaufman would be useful for Hart and Kaufman's *You Can't Take It with You*. This play is frequently referred to as Hart and Kaufman's play, and some readers will look under Hart, some under Kaufman. The abridgment given on page 47 will need an added entry under Lanier, since it is spoken of as Lanier's *Boy's King Arthur*. Also, though the main entry for the example which follows, *The Book of King Arthur and His Noble Knights* is under Macleod, an entry is needed under Malory for the reader who is interested in everything Malory has written.

If a writer, Pope or Longfellow for instance, translates another's work, an added entry would enable the student to consider not only Pope's or Longfellow's original writings but his translations as well. The student of *The Iliad* may be interested in the Pope translation and think of it as Pope's *Iliad*, though knowing it is Homer's *Iliad*. Occasionally an added entry is necessary for a compiler or an editor, for the same reason. If the library is likely to have a call for illustrations by a well-known artist, e.g., Walter Crane, an added entry under his name would make it possible to find examples of his illustrations. If the library has a copy of the H. W. Wilson Company's *Children's Catalog*, it may be used to locate books with illustrations by a particular artist and no added entry need be made under illustrator.

To make added entries of the kind mentioned, the full name in its best-known form (see Chapter III, "Choice of Personal Names") with dates, if the library uses them, is written on the line above the author. Begin at the second indention, so that the heading of the main entry may remain in a prominent position. If this added heading occupies more than one line, succeeding lines begin at the third indention. The abbreviation, *comp., ed., illus.,* or *tr.* (or the full word if preferred) is given one space after the comma at the end of the heading (Card 35). In the case of an added entry for a joint author or for the individual

34 Added entry for a joint author

```
812        Kaufman, George S          1889-
H32        Hart, Moss, 1904-
              You can't take it with you, a play by Moss Hart
           and George S. Kaufman.    New York, Farrar & Rine-
           hart ₍c1937₎
              207 p.  illus.
```

35 **Added entry for a translator**

```
220        Moffatt, James, 1870-1944, tr.
B58    Bible.
           A new translation of the Bible, containing the
       Old and New Testaments ⌐by⌐ James Moffatt.  ⌐Con-
       cordance ed.⌐    Harper ⌐c1950⌐
           2 v. in 1.  illus.
```

36 **Added entry for the author and title of a work dramatized by another writer**

```
           Benson, Sally, 1900-
812            Junior miss.
C54    Chodorov, Jerome.
           Junior miss, a new comedy by Jerome Chodorov
       and Joseph Fields, based on the book by Sally Ben-
       son.    Random ⌐1942⌐
           209 p.
```

who writes the preface or introduction for another's work, no designation follows the name (Card 34).

Another type of added entry is one for the author and title of a work
which has been dramatized by another writer (Card 36). The name of
the author and the title of the original work are added above the unit
card at the second and third indentions respectively.

Added entries, except title and subject cards, are made sparingly
in the small library where the collection is accessible.

Analytical entries. Some books are made up of two or more separate
works of an author, or of different authors; or they may treat of several
distinct subjects or phases of a subject. For example, the two-volume
edition of De la Mare's *Collected Poems,* the title page for which is
reproduced in the preceding chapter, contains his well-known poems
for children, published under the title *Peacock Pie.* In this collection the
library has the work, *Peacock Pie,* whether or not it has the separately
bound edition. How can this be shown in the catalog? By making
author and title analytical entries for it. Law's *Science in Literature*
contains an essay by Madame Curie on her discovery of radium. This

material on radium is as important as any that will be found in many libraries. It can be brought out by means of a subject analytical entry, i.e., a subject entry for a part of a book. Small collections and special libraries need to have their material analyzed freely, since the analytical entry may represent the only work by the author, the only copy of the essay, play, etc., or the only material on the subject. Frequently the analytical entry is used to call attention to an extra copy of popular material already available in another form.

In this connection it should be stated that advantage should be taken of work already done. The H. W. Wilson Company's *Children's Catalog,* eighth edition, includes 6491 analytical entries for 419 of the 3400 books it lists. Their *Standard Catalog for High School Libraries,* sixth edition, analyzes 621 of the 3610 books it lists. Dull, Metcalfe, and Brooks' *Modern Physics* has thirty subject analytics listed in this catalog; they include such specific subjects as Lenses, Television, and Thermometers and Thermometry. Printed indexes less likely to be found in the small library are Firkins' *Index to Short Stories,* Logasa and Ver Nooy's *Index to One-Act Plays* and other similar indexes.

For an author analytical entry the name of the author of the play, essay, or other separate work is given on the unit card on the second line above the author of the book, the title on the line below the author of the part, followed by: "p. 00–00:". For a title analytical entry this is reversed and the title is given on the top line, the author of the analytical entry on the next line followed by the same phrase and punctuation, namely: "p. 00–00:".

Note on Card 37 that the regular unit card is used as it is for all added entries, with the appropriate heading added. The author of the analytical entry is given on the second line of the card, the title on the third line, followed by: a comma, the paging, and a colon (in case of a work of two or more volumes, the volume number precedes the paging, e.g., v. 2, p. 56–112:). The indentions deserve special attention. In order that the author of the main book may stand out as well as the author and title of the particular part, the author in the added heading (i.e., the analytical author) is given at the second or title indention and the title of the part analyzed at the third indention. If the name of the author of the analytical entry takes two lines, it begins on the first line and continues on the second line, third indention; and if the title of the analytical entry runs over, it comes back to the second indention.

37 Author analytical entry

```
              Sheridan, Richard Brinsley Butler, 1751-1816.
 808.82          The school for scandal, p. 182-265:
 C67      Cohen, Helen Louise, 1882-        ed.
              Milestones of the drama.    Harcourt ⌐c1940⌐
              580 p.

              Includes bibliographies.
              Contents.-Sophocles.  Oedipus, King of Thebes.-
         Everyman.-Marlowe, Christopher.  Doctor Faustus.-
         Sheridan, R. B.  The school for scandal.-Ibsen, Hen-
         rik.  A doll's house.-Rostand, Edmond.  Cyrano de
         Bergerac.-O'Neill, Eugene.  The Emperor Jones.-
         Further explorations.
```

If the author of the analytical entry and the author of the book are the same, an author analytical entry is unnecessary, as the person searching for the play or short story will look under the author's name, then in the contents listed on the card, for collections of plays, short stories, etc.

The two title analytical cards (numbers 38 and 39), like the author analytical card (number 37), are unit cards with the title and author of the respective analytics added as headings, followed by the paging. On Card 38, the author of the analytical entry and the author of the book are the same. It would be absurd to give the same author twice in succession, hence the title of the analytical entry is simply added in the regular place for an added title heading, and is followed by the paging

38 Title analytical entry—book and analytical entry by the same author

```
 821         Peacock pie, v.2, p. 95-218:
 D33      De la Mare, Walter John, 1873-
              Collected poems, 1901-1918.    Holt ⌐c1920⌐
              2 v.

              Contents.-v. 1 Poems, 1906.  The listeners,
         1914.  Motley, 1919.-v. 2 Songs of childhood, 1901.
         Peacock pie.
```

39 Title analytical entry—book and analytical entry by different authors

```
                  The school for scandal.
                  Sheridan, Richard Brinsley Butler, 1751-1816,
    808.82            p. 182-265:
    C67    Cohen, Helen Louise, 1882-        ed.
                  Milestones of the drama.      Harcourt  ⌐c1940⌐
                  580 p.

                  Includes bibliographies.
                  Contents.-Sophocles.  Oedipus, King of Thebes.-
           Everyman.-Marlowe, Christopher.  Doctor Faustus.-
           Sheridan, R. B.  The school for scandal.-Ibsen, Hen-
           rik.  A doll's house.-Rostand, Edmond.  Cyrano de
           Bergerac.-O'Neill, Eugene.  The Emperor Jones.-
           Further explorations.
```

as for all other analytical entries. In the first example, Card 39, since
the authors are different, the same items are given as for the title
analytical entry, but in reverse order. If the title runs over, the second
line begins at the same indention, i.e., the third indention; and if the
author's name runs over, it continues on the next line beginning at the
third indention.

For a subject analytical entry the subject heading is given as on any
subject card. The heading is followed by the phrase regarding the paging. If the author of the chapter or section whose subject is being
brought out in the catalog in this way is different from the author of the
book, his name comes on the line below the subject, and the phrase
regarding the paging follows that. If the work is in more than one

40 Subject analytical entry including title of the part analyzed

```
                  BOONE, DANIEL, 1735-1820.
    973        Roosevelt, Theodore, 1858-1919, p. 18-28:
    L82    Lodge, Henry Cabot, 1850-1924.
                  Hero tales from American history, by Henry Cabot
           Lodge and Theodore Roosevelt.    New York, Century
           Co. ⌐c1922⌐
                  335 p.  illus.

           Daniel Boone and the founding of Kentucky.
```

volume and the analytical entry is for an entire volume, the volume number is substituted for the paging (e.g., v. 2:).

On subject analytical entry cards it is observed that the title of the part analyzed is omitted because the name of the author and the subject heading are more important than the title and there is not space for all three at the top of the unit card. Dropping the author, title, etc., of the unit card another line would make all other items too low on the card. To omit these items in subject analytical entries only would mean remembering the difference each time or giving special instructions to the typist. If the title is very important, an exception may be made by omitting the notes and contents of the unit card from this copy of the card and substituting a note giving the title of the analyzed part.

Series entries. A series entry is defined as "an entry, usually brief, of the several works in the library which belong to a series under the name of that series as a heading." (A.L.A. 1949, p.233) "Enter a series under its title...Make added entry or reference under name of editor." (A.L.A. 1949.5F)

The title of the series is given (see Card 41) on the fourth line from the top at the first indention; if it runs over, the succeeding lines begin at the second indention. Following a comma, the words *ed. by* and the name of the editor of the series as found in the book are given. There is a period at the end. If there is no editor, or it seems unnecessary to give the editor's name, the phrase is omitted. The classification number is given on the next line, and below that, on the same line with the book number, are given: the author's name inverted, beginning at the second

41 Added entry under series—short form

```
        Rivers of America.
975.1
C21         Canby, Henry Seidel.     The Brandywine.
              ₍c1941₎
978.9
C77         Corle, Edwin.     The Gila.     ₍c1951₎

977.3
G77         Gray, James.     The Illinois.     ₍c1940₎
```

indention, with his dates omitted to conserve space; after four typewriter spaces, the title of the work, omitting explanatory and alternative
titles; then after four typewriter spaces, the date. The second line of
the entry for each individual work begins at the second indention.
Other volumes in the series are added to the card in the same form. A
line skipped, as shown on Card 41, makes it easier to read the entry for
any one volume. For a numbered series in which the volumes are preferably read in a certain order (see Card 42), the volume numbers are
given at the first indention, and the surname of the author of the individual book at the third indention.

Another way to make a series entry is to write the name of the
series above the heading of the unit card. Thus a series entry is made
for each book in the set, and these cards file together in the catalog
alphabetically by author.

**42 Added entry under series, giving volume number and editor of series—short
form**

```
        The Chronicles of America series, ed. by Allen
           Johnson and Allan Nevins.
970
H94    v. 1  Huntington, Ellsworth.    The red man's conti-
              nent.    ₍c1919₎
973.16
R53    v. 2  Richman, Irving Berdine.    The Spanish con-
              querors.    ₍c1919₎
```

43 Added entry under series—unit card

```
973.917   The Chronicles of America series, v. 52.
B86    Brogan, Denis William, 1900-
           The era of Franklin D. Roosevelt; a chronicle
       of the New Deal and global war.    New Haven, Yale
       University Press ₍c1950₎
           382 p. illus.    (The Chronicles of America
       series, v. 52)

           "Bibliographical note": p.365-372.
```

For the unit card form for a numbered series, if it is desirable to have the cards file in order by number rather than alphabetically by the author, the volume number is added to the heading; for instance, Card 43 has as heading: "The Chronicles of America series, v. 52."

Special entry under series is necessary for important subject series, i.e., for series in which all the books deal with the same subject, e.g., "Rural Science Series," "The Chronicles of America Series." School libraries especially will find these entries useful. Even the smallest public library which owns "The Chronicles of America Series" would probably find a series entry useful.

Another kind of series for which an added entry under the series title is useful is an author's series, e.g., "The Leatherstocking Tales," by James Fenimore Cooper (see Card 45). Added entries under series

44 Added entry under series—biography

```
        Golden hind series.
92
H39        Hawkins, by Philip Gosse.      ⌐c1930¬

92
H88        Hudson, by Llewelyn Powys.     ⌐c1928¬

92
R16        Raleigh, by Milton Waldman.     ⌐c1928¬
```

45 Added entry under series—author the same

```
    The Leatherstocking tales, by James Fenimore Cooper.

        The deerslayer.

        Last of the Mohicans.

        The pathfinder.

        Pioneers.
```

46 Reference from the name of the editor of the series

```
          Nevins, Allan, 1890-     ed.
             See
        The Chronicles of America series.
```

titles are also useful for standard works in an attractive format, for example, "Scribner Illustrated Classics," "The Windermere Series."

Card 46 shows the form to be used for a reference card from the editor of a series to the entry under the title of the series.

Extension cards for added entries. Extension cards for added entries follow the same rule for the added heading, if it is a person's name, as for main entries; otherwise, the entire added heading and the heading on the unit card are given as usual. Extension cards are omitted for added title entries and for analytical entries, unless the part given in the added heading is mentioned on an extension card, in which case that extension card is made. The phrase "Continued on the next card" is omitted in these cases.

Name reference cards. On page 50 it is stated that the librarian must choose one form of an author's name and always enter his works under that form, and that a reference must be made from any other forms with which the public may be familiar. This applies to all name entries in the catalog: author, subject, editor, compiler, etc. These reference cards (number 47-49) are very brief. They should be made for all names which might be searched for in the catalog under any other form than the one chosen for entry. The form of name not used for entry is given on the fourth line from the top, at the second indention, the word *See,* at the third indention on the succeeding line. The form of

47 Name reference card—pseudonym

```
          Gorham, Michael, pseud.
             See
        Folsom, Mary Elting, 1914-
```

48 Name reference card—heading for anonymous classic

```
        Roland
          See
  Chanson de Roland
```

49 Name reference card—name of an organization

```
      American Library Association.   Section for Libra-
         ry Work with Children.   Book Evaluation Commit-
         tee
           See
      American Library Association.   Editorial Committee.
      Subcommittee on Inexpensive Books for Boys and
      Girls.
```

name that has been adopted for entry is given on the next line at the first indention. If the name referred from runs over, the next line begins at the third indention; and if the name referred to runs over, the next line begins at the second indention.

Subject reference cards. Cards 3 and 4 in Chapter II are illustrations of *see* and *see also* reference cards. Note that both the term not used and the term used as a subject heading are given in full capitals, as are the subject headings on Card 33. If red ink is used for the headings on the subject cards, it should also be used for the subject references. The indentions and spacing are the same as for name references.

Tracing. Tracing is the memorandum on the main entry card of all other cards made for a book. It is necessary in order that all the cards may be found and taken out of the catalog if it is decided to make a correction on or addition to them, or if the book is withdrawn from the library. The headings for the other cards decided upon as necessary for the book are traced on the main entry card as soon as it is made. These added entries may be typed by the librarian or preferably by a typist who has been taught how to make them.

Rules for tracing. The record of the added entries, in a single paragraph, is typed on the front of the main entry card, just above the hole. The first line begins at the second indention. On printed cards the tracing is put on each card, as all cards are made from the same copy, but in typed cards it should be omitted on the added entry cards. If necessary, part of the tracing can be put on the back of the card, in which case type the word "Over" on the front of the card, just below the hole.

"The subject headings are listed first, numbered consecutively with arabic numerals, followed by the other secondary entries, numbered with roman numerals except for the series entry which is unnumbered and enclosed in parentheses....added entries for persons or corporate bodies...are listed in the order in which they appear in the catalog entry....Added entries for title entry, the partial title if such entry is to be made, and for the series follow in this order. Each is traced to show the form in which it is to be found in the catalog. Unless the title is to be found as it appears in the catalog entry, the word 'Title' in the tracing is followed by the selected form of the title." (L.C. 1949.3:25) This applies to both the title of the main book, if it is a partial title, and to title analytical entries. The word "Series" in parentheses is used to trace a series entry.

If author and title analytical entries are made for all the plays, essays, or stories listed in contents on the main entry card, instead of tracing each one, a statement to that effect may appear below the other tracing, e.g., "Author and title analytical entries made for each play," or "See contents for tracing."

The reference card for the author or the editor of a series is traced on the back of the series card by giving his name in full. For example, the tracing for a reference card for "Cooper, James Fenimore, 1789–1851" (see Card 46 for form of this card) is written on the back of the card.

Name and subject reference cards do not need to be traced on any *catalog* card, as they are applicable to all books by or about an individual or on a subject and do not pertain to one particular book. The subject reference cards are traced by checking the printed list of subject headings, or on the subject authority card in the card subject authority list described in Chapter II. Name reference cards are traced on the name authority card, if such cards are made for all names with cross references; if not, they may be traced on the author card for the first book cataloged with which that person is associated, just as they would be on the name authority card. Later if that book is withdrawn from the library and consequently its cards from the catalog, that tracing is transferred to another author card.

Examples of tracing.

Gunther's *Inside Asia.*

> 1. Asia. Biography. 2. Asia. Politics. 3. Chiang, Kai-shek, 1886–   4. China. 5. Gandhi, Mohandas Karamchand, 1869–1948. 6. Statesmen. I. Title.

Numbers 1, 2 and 4, in the above example of tracing, are subject entries for the entire book; numbers 3 and 5 are subject analytical entries. Note that the word "Title" is used to trace the title, which may readily be determined by looking at the card.

Burt's *Powder River.*

> 1. Cattle. 2. Dakota Indians. 3. Powder River. 4. Wyoming. History. (Series).

No title card would be made for Burt's *Powder River,* as it would be the same as the subject entry.

Hart and Kaufman's *You Can't Take It with You.*

> I. Kaufman, George S., 1889–   II. Title.

Chodorov and Field's *Junior Miss.*

> I. Fields, Joseph. II. Benson, Sally, 1900–   III. Title.

An added entry is made under Sally Benson as she is the author of the story on which the play is based, but only one title entry is necessary as it is the same for both the story and the play.

Cohen's *Milestones of the Drama.*

> 1. Drama. Collections. I. Sheridan, Richard Brinsley Butler, 1751-1816. School. II. Title. III. Title: The school for scandal.

The added entry for Sheridan is an author analytical entry; number III is the record of a title analytical entry. Author analytical entries are traced by the heading for the author, followed, if not apparent from the card, by the first word, not an article, of the title of the analytical entry.

The shelf list. The shelf list is "a brief...record of the books in the library...arranged in the order of the books on the shelves." (Cutter) Hence its name. It is a very important record.

Uses of a shelf list. The shelf list is used—

To take the inventory to see if any books are missing.

To show how many copies of a given book the library owns.

To show what kind of books are in a given class as an aid in classifying.

To show the librarian who is making out book orders how many books the library already has in any given class.

To serve in a limited way as a classed catalog.[1]

To give source, date, and cost if no accession record is kept.

To serve as a basis for a bibliography or reading list on a specific subject.

To serve as a record for insurance.

Rules for shelf-listing. The shelf-list card is a unit card; i.e., it is a duplicate of the main card, except that the notes, contents, and tracing are omitted. This saves space for the *shelf list information*. If an accession book is used, the accession number, described in Chapter XII, is added to this card. If an accession book is not used the source, date of acquisition, and cost of the book are added to the shelf-list card. If no accession book is kept, but an accession number is used, this number is added to the shelf-list card, as shown on Card 51, followed by the name of the source, the date received, and cost. Some libraries consider the accession book unnecessary duplication of other records, but like the convenience of having one number which stands for the book.

If an accession number is used, it begins on the second space from the left edge of the card on the second line below the last line of the description—imprint, collation, or series note, as the case may be. If there are two or more copies or volumes of a work, the accession numbers are listed on the shelf-list cards in numerical order. The volume numbers or the copy numbers are written at the first indention opposite their respective accession numbers. Thus all copies and volumes of one work go on the same shelf-list card, and there are as many shelf-list cards as there are titles in the library, i.e., different works in the library. Copy numbers may be omitted if the librarian wishes, as long as accession numbers are used.

If accession numbers are not used, the source, date, and cost of the book are given instead. Abbreviations which will be clear to the librarian, e.g., B. & T. for Baker and Taylor, may be given for the source; if the book is a gift, the name of the donor is given, e.g., Mrs. J. H. Jones.

---

[1] A classed catalog has its entries arranged by classification numbers rather than alphabetically as in a dictionary catalog, and there is an alphabetical subject index. This classed arrangement brings together all the entries on a given subject.

50 Shelf-list entry showing accession numbers for a two-volume work of which the library has two copies

```
821
D33    De la Mare, Walter John, 1873-
           Collected poems, 1901-1918.    Holt ⌐c1920⌐
           2 v.

3016   v. 1
3017   v. 2
3511   v. 1
3512   v. 2
```

51 Shelf-list entry showing source, date, and cost for a two-volume work of which the library has two copies

```
821
D33    De la Mare, Walter John, 1873-
           Collected poems, 1901-1918.    Holt ⌐c1920⌐
           2 v.

1201   B. & T. 2-16-52 $2.00 v. 1
1202      "            $2.00 v. 2
1622   Jones, Mrs. J. H. 6-7-53 gift v. 1
1623      "                     gift v. 2
```

The number of the month, day, and last two figures of the year are given, separated by hyphens, e.g., 2-16-52. The date follows the source, with one space between; then the cost, or, if it is a gift, the word *gift*.

Note that one ditto mark is sufficient for both source and date, but that the cost, or word *gift*, is repeated for each volume or copy.

Shelf-list cards for nonfiction are arranged exactly as the books are arranged on the shelves, first numerically by classification number and second alphabetically by author, except individual biography, which is arranged alphabetically by the subject of the biography. Since the figures in all book numbers are regarded as decimals, B219 would pre-
$$\frac{973}{B21} \quad \frac{973}{B219} \quad \frac{973}{B31}$$
cede B31, e.g.: B21 B219 B31 for Bancroft's *History of the United States*

of America and Bassett's *A Short History of the United States,* respectively. If book numbers are not used, the name of the subject of a biography may be added on the top line of the card just as it is on the subject card, as an aid in filing the cards by the subject of the biography.

In a public library the adult and the juvenile shelf-list cards are filed separately. The juvenile shelf-list cards as well as the juvenile catalog cards are marked with a location symbol in connection with the classi-

$$+ \quad J$$

fication number, e.g., 973 or 973. Also the shelf-list cards for the refer-

$$R \quad *$$

ence collection are marked with a location symbol (e.g., 394 or 394) to distinguish them and are filed separately. The books, of course, have these location symbols added to the classification number.

When to shelf-list. If the library is not yet cataloged, the fiction shelf list may serve also as an author list and the nonfiction shelf list may serve as a subject catalog (since it brings together all of the botanies, all of the United States histories, etc.) until such time as the library can be cataloged. Before beginning the cataloging of an old library, be sure that there is a correct shelf list to use as a basis for the work. In a new library, if it is not possible to catalog the new books as rapidly as they are being bought, it is well to accession (if an accession record is to be made), classify, and shelf-list them at once. Later, using the shelf list as a check, catalog the different classes. In a well-organized and well-established library it is best to make the shelf list and catalog cards for each book when it is added to the library.

If printed catalog cards are used whenever they can be secured, they are used for the shelf list also. The H. W. Wilson Company prints a special shelf-list card.

chapter VIII

Cataloging sets, serials, and independent publications bound together

S ets. The cataloging of sets differs as do the sets themselves. If there is a common title for the entire set, if one volume gives the contents for two or more volumes and the last volume contains the index to the set, then, needless to say, the set must be given one classification number and be cataloged as one work. If the common title is distinctive the set will be known by that title, and this fact is another argument for keeping the volumes together. If the volumes are bound alike and have a common title, but each volume is complete in itself, has a distinctive title, an index, etc., there is no reason for keeping them together. Besides, the average reader will not select a volume from a set as readily as he will pick up an individual book. For example, a set of the Waverley Novels, the different volumes all bound alike—on the back of each volume: "The Waverley Novels, Vol. XXI" (or XII, etc.)—does not attract readers as does a binding reading "Rob Roy," even though "Vol. XI," or even "Waverley Novels, Vol. XI," appears below "Rob Roy." If this volume XI is shelved with other editions of *Rob Roy,* it is likely to be chosen for reading more often than if it is one of twenty-five books in the same binding shelved together.

To consider examples of different kinds of sets:

The Works of
John Milton
Volume I

Part I

New York
Columbia University Press
1931

All of the volumes of this set of Milton's works have identical title pages, except for the volume number and date. Volume I has two parts, bound separately but with the table of contents for both in Part I. The two parts are paged consecutively. The same is true of Volumes II and III. But Volumes IV to XVIII are each bound separately. Each one has the copyright statement on the back of the title page, running from 1931 to 1938 in the different volumes.

This set of Milton has a two-volume index with the same binding and style of title page as the set, but it is not included in the volume numbering of the set. The title page is given below:

An Index
To the
Columbia Edition of the
Works of John Milton

By Frank Allen Patterson
Assisted By
French Rowe Fogle

Volume I. A–K

New York
Columbia University Press
1940

The title page of the second volume of the index is the same as that for Volume I, except that it has: "Volume II. L-Z." These index volumes will be cataloged in the same way as the index for Channing's *History of the United States,* described on page 91. Obviously this set of

52 Main entry for a set

```
828
M66    Milton, John, 1608-1674.
           Works.    New York, Columbia University Press
       ₍c1931-38₎
            18 v. in 21.    illus.

       ---- An index to the Columbia edition of the Works
       of John Milton, by Frank Allen Patterson, assisted
       by French Rowe Fogle.    New York, Columbia Univer-
       sity Press ₍c1940₎
            2 v.
```

Milton's works will have to be cataloged as a set because of the way in which the works are divided among the different volumes and because of the index. If a set is incomplete, the dates, the number of volumes, and the number of parts would be written in pencil, so that they may be easily changed when another volume is added.

Note that as there are twenty-one physical volumes in this set of Milton's works (Card 52) but only eighteen from the point of view of the division of the works, it is stated as "18 v. in 21."

A type of title page which is found rather frequently in such works of fiction as the Waverley Novels, is the following:

The
Waverley Novels

By
Sir Walter Scott, Bart.

Vol. XXXV
Redgauntlet.— I.

Edinburgh
Adam and Charles Black
1879

Other volumes of this work have the same information on their title pages; the individual volume title and the volume numbers are different. On this particular title page the title of the series is more prominent than that of the work. Yet *Redgauntlet* is one of Scott's well-known novels and will be asked for by title. If fiction is cataloged in the library as nonfiction is, "The Waverley Novels" would be given as a series note. But if fiction is cataloged very simply with only author, title, and date, as recommended in Chapter VI, the card for the above book would not show that it is one of the Waverley Novels. Regardless of how little detail is given on the catalog cards an added entry under the name of the series, "The Waverley Novels," will be found useful.

The *A.L.A. Catalog,* 1926, gives the following note regarding Cooper's *The Deerslayer:* "The first of five novels devoted to the career of the great Leather Stocking, pioneer, hunter, and Indian fighter." The first sentence of the note for *The Last of the Mohicans* is: "The second of the Leatherstocking tales"; for *The Pathfinder:* "The third of the Leatherstocking tales"; for *Pioneers:* "The fourth of the Leatherstocking tales"; and for *The Prairie:* "The fifth of the Leatherstocking tales." The editor's note of Everyman's Library edition of *The Last of the Mohicans* states: "...one of the five 'Leatherstocking tales'..." The introduction to the Illustrated Sterling Edition of *The Prairie,* published by Dana Estes and Company, has: "This book closes the career of Leatherstocking." The Houghton Mifflin edition of *The Pathfinder,* copyright 1898, states in the author's preface: "Following the order of events this book should be the third in the series of 'The Leather-Stocking Tales.'" On the other hand, *The Last of the Mohicans,* in the Riverside Literature Series, also published by Houghton Mifflin, makes no mention of the Leatherstocking Tales.

As has been pointed out, the average reader is not attracted by books which belong to sets, consisting of many volumes bound alike. Yet the reader is apt to be much interested in reading all the volumes in a series in which the same characters appear. The Leatherstocking Tales is a series of this type and should have a series entry. Having read and enjoyed the first work the reader is likely to continue until he has read them all.

Sequels. Closely akin to such series as "The Leatherstocking Tales" are sequels, for instance, Nordhoff and Hall's *Men Against the Sea,* the second volume of a trilogy, the first volume of which is *Mutiny on the Bounty.* Such books are cataloged as are any other works with notes stating the sequence (Card 53). Such notes are very desirable, since readers are usually anxious to read sequels. *Men Against the Sea* would have as a note: "A sequel to Mutiny on the Bounty. Followed by Pitcairn's Island." *Pitcairn's Island* would have as a note: "A sequel to Mutiny on the Bounty, Men against the Sea."

53 Main entry for book with a sequel

```
    Nordhoff, Charles Bernard, 1887-1947.
        Mutiny on the Bounty, by Charles Nordhoff and
    James Norman Hall.    Little [c1932]
        396 p.

        The first volume of a trilogy.  Followed by
    Men against the sea, Pitcairn's Island.
```

Serials. Of quite a different type are serials, the volumes of which are issued at regular intervals, e.g., periodicals, yearbooks, annual and biennial reports, directories. *The World Almanac* is a serial. The title page of the 1953 edition is as follows:

New York World Telegram
THE WORLD ALMANAC
AND
BOOK OF FACTS
FOR
1953
EDITED BY
HARRY HANSEN

Sixty-eighth Year of Publication
PUBLISHED ANNUALLY BY
NEW YORK WORLD TELEGRAM
and
The Sun
A SCRIPPS HOWARD NEWSPAPER
125 Barclay Street, New York 15, N.Y.
Copyright 1953 by New York World Telegram Corporation
Title (T. M.) Registered in United States Patent Office

The title page for the 1952 edition is the same, except that it has: "1952," "Sixty-seventh Year of Publication," and "Copyright 1952."

The reader consults the catalog to see if *The World Almanac* is in the library, and if it is, what volumes the library has. All numbers of *The World Almanac* are, therefore, cataloged on one set of cards and only items of importance common to all numbers are given. Since there is no author and the editor will necessarily change from time to time, the main entry is made under the title, which begins on the top line, so as not to waste that space. In order that it may be readily distinguished from the usual title entry, the information on the card through the series note is written with hanging indention instead of paragraph indention.

Subtitles of serials frequently vary; therefore only the short title common to all issues is given. The editors are omitted, since they change more or less frequently and their names are not needed on the cards.

No date is given in the imprint, which otherwise follows the usual rules. The collation is usually omitted since it may vary for the different volumes. The frequency of publication, if not included in the title, e.g., *Annual,* is given as the first note. As the second note, and in the usual place for notes, is the statement of the holdings of the library—the words *Library has* followed by the volumes and dates covered, arranged in columns. As the information is given in columnar form, unlike other notes, nothing is written directly after *library has.* To make the *library has* statement easier to read a line is skipped wherever there is a gap in the set, e.g., on Card 54 before the first issue held by the library, 1940, and again between 1940 and 1945–46, 1945–46 and 1948, 1948 and 1950, 1950 and 1952–53.

Added entries may be made as usual by duplicating the main card and adding the appropriate heading. Or the unit card may be made, but in the note position, instead of the *library has* statement, the following may be given: "For volumes in the library see the title of this work."

To take another example of a serial:

WHO'S WHO
IN AMERICA

TITLE REGISTERED IN THE UNITED STATES PATENT OFFICE

A BIOGRAPHICAL DICTIONARY OF
NOTABLE LIVING MEN AND WOMEN

REVISED AND REISSUED BIENNIALLY
MONTHLY SUPPLEMENT
(Since 1939)

VOL. 27
1952-1953
TWO YEARS

FOUNDED 1897 AND PUBLISHED SINCE 1899 BY
THE A. N. MARQUIS COMPANY

Marquis Publications Building
CHICAGO–11 U S A

The back of this title page lists the copyright dates of all issues of this work, ending "Copyright, 1952."

The title pages of volumes 25, 26, and 27 differ only in the volume number and the dates, except volume 25, which has FIFTIETH ANNIVER-

54 Main entry for an almanac

```
R
310
W92    The World almanac.     New York, World-Telegram.

          Annual.
          Library has

       1940          1950
       1945-46    1952-53
       1948

                      O
```

55 Main entry for a biennial publication

```
R
920
W62    Who's who in America.     Chicago, A. N. Marquis Co.

          Biennial.
          Library has

       v. 25-27  1948/49-1952/53
```

SARY EDITION just below the date, 1948–1949. It is unnecessary to include this information about the anniversary edition on the catalog entries (see Card 55). The volume numbers are especially helpful in cases like this where each volume covers more than one calendar year. Note that the location symbol *R,* meaning the books are shelved in the reference collection, is placed on the line above the classification number on Cards 54 and 55.

Besides serials which are entered under their titles, there are those which are published yearly, biennially, etc., by a government department or an association, for example:

56 Main entry for a serial with an author

```
R
317.3
U58    U. S.  Bureau of the Census.
              Statistical abstract of the United States.
       U. S.  Govt. Print. Off.


              Annual.
              Library has

       1941

       1948-49

                              ⃝ (Continued on next card)
```

Seventieth Edition

Statistical Abstract

Of the United States

1949

Prepared under the Direction
of Morris B. Ullman in the Office of the
Assistant Director for Statistical Standards

U. S. DEPARTMENT OF COMMERCE

Charles Sawyer, Secretary

BUREAU OF THE CENSUS, Philip M. Hauser, Acting Director

For sale by the Superintendent of Documents, U. S. Government Printing Office
Washington 25, D. C. Price $3.00 (Buckram)

The numbers for 1948, 1949, 1950, 1951 have almost the same information on their title pages; the differences are in the number of the edition, the dates, and the cost.

There is really nothing new about cataloging a work of this kind. It has the same sort of author heading as any other government document and this heading should be established in the usual way. Aside from the fact that it has an author, it is cataloged as is *The World Almanac* or *Who's Who in America* (see Card 56).

Periodicals. Sets of bound periodicals may be cataloged just as almanacs and other serials are cataloged. The title pages have most features in common with the serials discussed on the preceding pages.

The librarian of a small public, school, or even special library with sets of bound periodicals may catalog them in this way, or may not catalog them at all. As they are conspicuous by their make-up, they are easily located on the shelves in a one-room library; and they are used through the general or special periodical indexes rather than through the catalog.

Note that the *library has* statement for *Current History and Forum* (Card 57) gives the months as well as the years covered by the volumes. This form is used when the volumes do not coincide with the calendar years. Since *Current History and Forum* ceased publication with volume 53, number 1, June, 1941, this volume number and final date are typed, thus closing the entry. When *Current History and Forum* united with *Events* in September, 1941, to form *Current History,* a new volume numbering began. The library having this new periodical would add the latest volume, "v. 4, Mar.-Aug. 1943," in pencil to facilitate changing the statement when the next volume is received. The notes on Cards 58 and 60 explain the formation of the periodicals. Because the new periodical *Current History* (Card 59) has a different name and a new volume numbering begins, it is cataloged as a separate periodical.

General encyclopedias are examples of sets that may or may not

57 **Main entry for a periodical**

```
909.82
C97    Current history and Forum.    New York, C-H Pub.
          Corp.

          Monthly.
          Library has

     v. 51-53, no.1    Sept. 1939- June 1941



                          ○   (Continued on next card)
```

58 Main entry for a periodical—extension card

```
909.82                          2
C97    Current.
           Current history combined with The Forum and The
       Century magazine, May 23, 1940, under the title:
       Current history and Forum; Current history and Forum
       was superseded by Current history, September, 1941.
```

59 Main entry for a periodical

```
909.82
C976  Current history.     Philadelphia, Events Pub. Co.

          Monthly.
          Library has
       v. 1-     Sept. 1941-

       v. 20-     Jan. 1951-
```

60 Main entry for a periodical—extension card

```
909.82                          2
C976  Current.

           Formed by the union of Current history and
       Forum with Events.
```

be cataloged. Unless the library has a number of encyclopedias the
reader does not go to the catalog to locate them, but goes directly to
the shelves. Like bound periodicals they may be easily located in a
small library. Shelf-list cards, however, should be made for all bound

periodicals, encyclopedias, and other works, whether cataloged or not, in order that the library may have a record of such works and of what volumes of each it has.

Rules for cataloging serials and periodicals.

Classification number. Classification number is given as usual. If book numbers are used in the library they are assigned for serials as for any other book. If the serial is entered under its title, the book number is derived from the first word of the title not an article. The book number for *The World Almanac* would be W92, for *Who's Who in America,* W62.

Author. Reports of institutions, governments, bureaus, associations, and the like, are entered under the institution, bureau, or association as author (see Chapter V), with the title in its usual place. If there is a change in the author, the work may be recataloged under the new author with a reference from the former author and title; or if many volumes have been cataloged previously, the work may be left under the former author with a reference from the new author and title.

Title as main entry. "Enter a periodical under its latest title using hanging indention. Capitalize the initial article, if there is one, and the word following it. Make a reference or an added entry for any earlier title or titles under which the periodical may have been issued....A publication which does not continue the volume numbering of an earlier publication is usually considered a new periodical, and should have separate entry.

"A periodical issued by a society, institution, or government body is ordinarily to be entered under its title. .with added entry for the issuing body." (A.L.A. 1949.5C1)

"Enter almanacs, general yearbooks and similar serial publications under title." (A.L.A. 1949.5D) Follow the same cataloging procedure as for periodicals.

"Enter encyclopedias and dictionaries under title unless decidedly better known by the name of their editors. In either case make added entry under the form not chosen for main entry, and for the publisher if the work is likely to be referred to by his name." (A.L.A. 1949.5B)

On all cards the title begins on the fourth line at the first indention, succeeding lines at the second indention. In cataloging in a library that has been established for some time several issues of the serial will probably be available so that several title pages may be compared and phrases not common to all omitted. Use the brief title if cataloging the first issue of a yearbook, etc., since the subtitle may vary or be omitted from later numbers. If a radical change is made in the title, keep all numbers on one card and state in a note, "Beginning with_____ issue, title is _____." Make a reference card from the form of title not used. An illustration of such a change in title is the *Magazine of Art,* the title of which from September to December, 1936, was *Art Including "Creative Art";* and from its first publication in January, 1916, to August, 1936, was *The American Magazine of Art.*

If the title of the new periodical begins with the same words as one of the original magazines, a reference from the similar title is not necessary.

Title. Give as usual if the work has an author, except that if the title begins with the number of the report, e.g., *Second Annual Report,* omit the number, as it is given as the volume number in the *library has* statement.

Imprint. Give as usual, but omit date.

Collation. Omit.

Library has. The statement of the numbers or volumes or years of a serial that a library owns begins with the phrase *library has* on the second line below the imprint or, if frequency is given in a note, on the line below the frequency note beginning at the second indention. On the line below, beginning at the first indention, are given the volumes or the years, or both, of the issues in the library in straight columns. They are put on the same line with a dash between the numbers if the volumes are consecutive, giving the latest one in pencil so that it may be changed when the next number comes. A line is skipped to indicate each gap, not each volume lacking, and statements that need to be changed are written in pencil. Such statements as "Forty-third issue," "Third edition," and "Second annual report," may be written "v. 43, v. 3, v. 2." Sample cards 54–57 and 59 illustrate the form of the *library has* statement.

Notes. Unless it is included in the title, give the frequency as the first note. Notes other than that of frequency are given on a separate extension card, since *library has* statements may take up more space if there are many gaps in the set. Later, if the first card should be filled up, a second and, if need be, a third card could be inserted between the first card and the card giving the notes.

Shelf-listing serials. To make the shelf-list card for a serial the same rules are followed as for other shelf-list cards. The *library has* statement is omitted. If accession numbers are used they are given in parallel columns opposite their respective volume numbers or years (see Cards 61 and 62).

61 Shelf-list entry for a serial

```
R
310
W92    The World almanac.      New York, World-Telegram.

1102   1940
3106   1945
3612   1946
4523   1948
5502   1950
6512   1952
7000   1953


                            O
```

62 Shelf-list entry for a serial (alternative method)

```
R
310    The World almanac.      New York, World-Telegram.
W92

Pub.   2-9-40  $1.00   1940
  "    2-15-45 $1.00   1945
  "    2-8-46  $1.00   1946
  "    3-1-48  $1.00   1948
  "    2-16-50 $1.00   1950
  "    2-13-52 $1.25   1952
  "    2-8-53  $1.25   1953

                            O
```

Bound withs. Two or more works of the same author or works of different authors are sometimes bound or published together in one volume. If the book has a title page for each work as well as table of contents, a preface, and separate paging, each work may be called informally a *bound with*. The book is cataloged as a separate book, but on the cards for each work there is a note of the other work or works with which it is bound. The true test of such a volume is that it could be cut into two or more works, each of which if bound separately would be a complete volume, not showing in any way that it had ever been bound with another.

A similar sort of work may have one title page which gives all or at least some of the different titles; or it may have a common title for the volume and the individual titles may be given only on half title pages preceding the different sections of the book. The half title is a brief title on a page preceding a title page, or a separate work where there are several in one volume. It does not include the imprint. The title pages for two such volumes follow:

How to Live

By

Arnold Bennett

A Special Edition for the Bookman Subscribers Only, Containing
"How To Live on Twenty-Four Hours a Day," "The Human
Machine," "Mental Efficiency," "Self and
Self Management."

A BOOK OF
GREAT AUTOBIOGRAPHY

Christopher Morley
Joseph Conrad
Selma Lagerlöf
Helen Keller
William McFee
W. N. P. Barbellion
Walt Whitman
Etsu Inagaki Sugimoto

The first of these examples, the volume of Bennett's works, includes four of his essays, published separately, brought together in one volume under a common title. The *one* title page lists all the essays and each of them has a half title, a table of contents, and is paged separately. But all of the copyright dates, in this case a different copyright date for

63 Main entry for several works with common title—not a bound with

```
 920
 B72    A Book of great autobiography: Christopher Morley,
           Joseph Conrad, Selma Lagerlöf, Helen Keller,
           William McFee, W. N. P. Barbellion, Walt Whit-
           man, Etsu Inaguki Sugimoto.   Garden City,
           N. Y. Doubleday, Doran ⌐c1934⌐
           1 v. (various pagings)
```

each work, are given on the back of the title page. The second example, *A Book of Great Biography,* also has only one title page on which is given the common title for the volume and the list of authors whose works are included in the volume. Each work is separately paged and preceded by a "Publisher's Note." Some works of these types have continuous paging throughout the volume.

While examining these title pages and half titles, the librarian must keep in mind such questions as these: What is there in these volumes that readers would want? Under what would they look in the catalog? A reader may be looking for *The Human Machine, A Daughter of the Samurai,* Helen Keller's *The Story of My Life,* something by Walt Whitman. Title analytics would be needed for each of the essays in the volume by Bennett; and both author and title analytics for each of the works in *A Book of Great Autobiography.* The main entry for the latter work would be under the title (see Card 63).

Similar, yet different, is this bound with:

The Riverside Literature Series

Birds and Bees

Essays

By

John Burroughs

With An Introduction

By

Mary E. Burt

And A Biographical Sketch

Houghton Mifflin Company

Boston: 4 Park Street; New York: 85 Fifth Avenue

Chicago: 378-388 Wabash Avenue

The Riverside Press   Cambridge

On the back of this title page are listed the contents and the copyright dates. This is followed by a biographical sketch, introduction, and the essays, then this title page:

The Riverside Literature Series

A-Hunting of the Deer
And Other Essays

By
Charles Dudley Warner

Houghton Mifflin Company
Boston: 4 Park Street; New York: 85 Fifth Avenue
Chicago: 378-388 Wabash Avenue
The Riverside Press   Cambridge

The imprint on this title page is the same as that on the Burroughs title page. The copyright dates on the backs of the title pages, of course, differ. The back of the title page for Burroughs reads:

Copyright, 1879, 1881 and 1886
By John Burroughs

Copyright, 1887
By Houghton Mifflin & Co.

All rights reserved

The back of the title page for Warner's work reads:

Copyright, 1878
By Charles Dudley Warner

Copyright, 1906
By Susan Lee Warner
All rights reserved

The title page for the third work in this volume with Burroughs' and Warner's works, namely Thoreau's *The Succession of Forest Trees, Wild Apples, and Sounds,* is complete also and has the copyright dates on the back of the title page. The paging for this book is: Burroughs' essays, 88; Warner's essays, 85; and Thoreau's essays, 103.

The works by Burroughs and Warner would be cataloged as shown on Cards 64 and 65. The work by Thoreau would be cataloged in the same way. Neither a series note nor a series entry is necessary, as "The Riverside Literature Series" is a publisher's series, including a great many books by different authors on a variety of subjects. Notice that the cards are identical as far as form is concerned, and that the titles

64 Main entry for the first work in a bound with

```
814
B97    Burroughs, John, 1837-1921.
           Birds and bees; essays, with an introd. by
       Mary E. Burt and a biographical sketch.     Houghton
       ⌐c1887┐
           88 p.

           Bound with: Warner's A-hunting of the deer and
       other essays and Thoreau's The succession of forest
       trees, Wild apples, and Sounds.
```

65 Main entry for a work other than the first in a bound with

```
814
B97    Warner, Charles Dudley, 1829-1900.
           A-hunting of the deer and other essays.
       Houghton ⌐c1906┐
           85 p.

           Bound with: Burroughs' Birds and bees and Tho-
       reau's The succession of forest trees, Wild apples,
       and Sounds.
```

listed in the note vary for each one. If a book number is used it is the same for all of the works since there is only one physical volume on the shelf. The book number is taken from the name of the author of the first volume.

The added cards are traced on each main entry card as usual, and in addition the main cards for Warner and Thoreau (the other works in this volume) are traced on the Burroughs card—simply by giving the author headings in full. There is only one card for the shelf list as there is only one book on the shelf and one call number. The shelf-list card is made for the first work in the volume, in this case Burroughs' *Birds and Bees*.

chapter IX

Audio-visual materials

Introduction. Audio-visual materials, i.e., films, filmstrips, records, slides, stereographs, maps, charts, and pictures, are found in most libraries today. Pictures are generally put in a vertical file, either by themselves or with pamphlets and clippings, and do not need to be classified or cataloged. Stereographs are in special boxes and do not necessarily need to be cataloged. They may, however, be treated much the same as slides and cataloged as sets. As films are rented or borrowed rather than bought by the smaller libraries, they are not included in this chapter. Filmstrips, maps, musical and nonmusical records, and slides are found in the smaller as well as in the larger libraries and for the fullest use they need some kind of classification and cataloging.

Rufsvold's *Audio-Visual School Library Service*[1] is an excellent general book on the selection, care, processing, and use of this type of material. The Library of Congress has issued rules for cataloging motion pictures and filmstrips[2] and for phonorecords.[3] This latter term, "phonorecords," is used to cover phonograph records on discs or cylinders, wire and tape recordings, etc. *Rules for Descriptive Cataloging in the Library of Congress* (1949) includes rules for cataloging maps. Library of Congress printed catalog cards are available for filmstrips, maps, and records.

The H. W. Wilson Company publishes the *Filmstrip Guide,* which cumulates as does the *Readers' Guide to Periodical Literature* and other

---

[1] M. I. Rufsvold, *Audio-Visual School Library Service* (Chicago: A.L.A., 1949).
[2] U. S. Library of Congress, Descriptive Cataloging Division, *Rules for Descriptive Cataloging in the Library of Congress: Motion Pictures and Filmstrips* (Washington: 1953).
[3] U. S. Library of Congress, Descriptive Cataloging Division, *Rules for Descriptive Cataloging in the Library of Congress: Phonorecords* (Washington: 1952).

134

Wilson indexes. The *Filmstrip Guide* consists of two parts: Part I, Alphabetic Title and Subject Index, and Part II, Classified Subject List. The entries for filmstrips in this *Guide* include title of the film-strip, source from which it is obtained, its date of release, etc. If the library, or a library in the vicinity, has this *Guide* it would be helpful to look up the entries for the filmstrips to be cataloged and get the essential information, as the strip itself may not give all of it. Library Music Services[4] sells printed catalog cards with each musical record.

James I. Wyer stated an important principle in organizing materials in a library, "have all materials on the same subject in the fewest places."[5] The nature of the material and how it will be used should be considered in deciding upon its arrangement, whether to classify, and how to catalog.

Classification. Books are classified that those dealing with the same or related subjects may be found close together. They can be examined at the shelves. On the other hand, records must be put on a record player, filmstrips and slides on a projector, and maps spread out on a table. Furthermore, the librarian usually gets the audio-visual material for the patron, as filmstrips are in a special cabinet and are easily mixed up, and records may be broken. For these reasons it does not seem worth while to arrange nonbook materials by a subject classification system.

A few librarians prefer to classify their record albums and let the patron choose his records as he does his books. As he knows that printed material on United States history is together on the shelves under 973, he can also learn to go to that number on the shelves where the album records are kept and find together those on United States history.

But for the majority of libraries an identification number is the most satisfactory way of arranging nonbook materials. The records, filmstrips, etc. can be arranged in order as they are received by the library; no space is wasted, and no shifting is necessary later to fit a new acquisition into its proper place in a classified collection.

The identification number consists of a letter or letters indicating the type of material, e.g., FS for filmstrip, and a number given to the item when it is received by the library. The identification or call number for the first record added to the library would be R1; and for the first record album, RA1; for the first filmstrip, FS1; and for the first map, M1. This number is put on the record, album, filmstrip, map, or set of slides, and it is also placed on the shelf list and catalog cards in the same position as the classification number on the cards for a book.

Cataloging. If the material requires equipment, e.g., a record player or a projector for its use, or if it is difficult to handle, like a map, simple cataloging is important as a catalog is more easily consulted than the materials themselves. In cataloging the four types of materials discussed in this chapter, consider their similarity to books rather than their differences. Books are entered under author or title; so are these materials. Book entries include publisher and date; records have the trade name of the firm and the disc number. What is it the user needs to know about the filmstrip, map, record, or slide that differs from what he needs to know about a book? Is the filmstrip in black and white or in color, how many frames[6] has it? On what scale was the map drawn; what are its measurements? How many records and how many sides of the record are used for a piece of music; what are the revolutions per minute? The person who wishes to use slides wants to know their size, whether or not a study guide is included, etc.

The items in the description of a book, filmstrip, map, record, or slide are given in groups in a predetermined order, with the same indentions and spacing. It is more convenient, especially in a small library, to have the catalog entries for all types of materials in one file. But, that the user of the catalog may know whether he is getting a book, record, or filmstrip, the cards should show clearly the type of material described. Some libraries use colored cards, a different color for each type of material. The Library of Congress, however, prints its entries for audio-visual materials on white cards, so that the library planning to use printed cards whenever they are available will use white for the typed cards. An appropriate symbol, such as those suggested in the section on classification, will identify the material. The Library of Congress printed catalog cards for records and filmstrips have the word *Filmstrip* or *Phonorecord* in italics, enclosed in parentheses, immediately after the title and the library using these cards would do well to do the same, even though its call number has descriptive letters, such as FS and R. It is also desirable to show the approximate age level.

---

[6] A frame is "the area of film that constitutes one exposure." (*A.L.A. Glossary*)

This information may be given in the upper right-hand corner of each card, e.g., p for primary, a for adult. A list of abbreviations commonly used in cataloging audio-visual materials is given at the end of this chapter.

The next chapter tells how to order and use Library of Congress printed catalog cards, which are recommended for records, filmstrips, and maps whenever they are available. Unit cards should be typed following the specific directions given under each type of material in this chapter; and the general rules about items to include, spacing, indentions, and general style of the cards, given in the preceding chapters, should be used for the few maps, records, and filmstrips for which printed cards are not available. The rules given here are based on the A.L.A. rules and the Library of Congress rules referred to in footnotes on page 134.

Records, musical and nonmusical. Assign a number to each record as it is added to the library. This number preceded by the letter R, if it is a single record, is the call number for that record, e.g., R29 would be the call number for the twenty-ninth record added to the collection. RA would indicate a record album, RA16, the sixteenth album added. One set of Library of Congress rules is used for phonodiscs, phono-cylinders, phonotape and phonowire recordings, phonofilms for sound films, and phonorolls for either player piano or player organ, and the term phonorecords is used to include them all. Nonmusical records are treated much as their corresponding literary counterparts. Separate works on opposite sides of a record are cataloged individually with appropriate notes on each as for books bound together (see Chapter VIII, pages 130-33 and Cards 64-65).

The items to be included in the catalog entry for a phonorecord are: name of the author, usually the composer for musical records, author or narrator for nonmusical records; conventional title; title; trade name of the publisher, serial number (i.e., album and record numbers) for identification, and the date of release when available; physical description of the record; series to which it belongs; notes, including contents notes; and the tracing for added entries. This information is found on the label of the record and on the covers of the record album.

The heading for the main entry and the one appearing on all the unit cards is similar to what would be used for visual materials. The rules and examples in Chapters III–V apply to records as they do to printed materials; and the form on the card would be the same.

Conventional titles are formulated for musical works on phono-records, unless the work is entered under its title or the arranger. The conventional title is given on the line below the composer and is in brackets. It is given in order that all the editions and arrangements of a composition may be brought together in the catalog. It includes: the title of the first edition of the work, or is based on that title; the instrument or instruments on which it is played; the number of the composition if that is necessary to identify it; the opus number; and the key.

Examples of conventional titles for phonorecords are:

Conventional title: [Sonata, piano, no. 21, op. 23, C major]
Title on record label: Sonata no. 21 in C major, op. 23 ("Waldstein")

Conventional title: [La traviata. Selections]
Title on record label: Duets from La traviata

Conventional title: [Operas. Selections]
Title on record label: Great Baritone Arias

Note that the items in the conventional title are given in a definite order, regardless of how they are given in the title of a particular record.

The title of the work is taken from the label of the record, the cover of the album, and is given as the title of a book is given. The imprint for the record consists of the trade name of the publisher, album or record number, and the date of release, when it can be ascertained from the work being cataloged. The record number is given on the label, the matrix number is cut into the disc and is not included in the catalog description.

Columbia M-MM-622; Columbia 70365-D; RCA Victor P 154
RCA Victor DM1118; RCA Victor LCT 1023; Decca 202; LLP198/199

The collation for phonorecords includes the number of volumes, i.e., albums, if more than one; the number of sides, including parts of a side; the diameter in inches to the nearest inch; and the speed, i.e., the number of revolutions per minute.

2 albums, (7s.) 12 in. 78 rpm.
2 s. 12 in. 33⅓ rpm.

For tape recordings the number of reels is given, followed within parentheses by the diameter of the reel and the width of the tape unless it is one-fourth of an inch.

1 reel (5 in.) 3¾ in. per sec.
2 reels (5-10 in.) 15 in. per sec.
2 reels (14 in. 1½ in. tape) 15 in. per sec.

A series note is made under the same circumstances and in the same form as for printed material, e.g., (Concert Hall Society, Annual series 6, release F-2). "Columbia Masterworks," however, is like a publisher's series and need not be given.

Notes giving additional information cover the following items and are given in the following order:

1 Names of performers and of performing groups, followed by the medium of performance.

Clifford Curzon, piano; Joseph Roisin, violin.

2 Language of the performance if the title does not show it.

Lily Pons, soprano, with orchestra; sung in French.

3 Length of time required to play the record, if stated on the record.
4 Information about the method of cutting the record which affects the equipment necessary to reproduce it.

Instantaneous recording, vertically cut; reproduced from inner to outer grooves. (Most modern records are laterally cut and run from outer to inner grooves.)

Microgroove. (This note distinguishes discs commonly designated as "long-playing," "LP," etc., recorded at a speed of 33⅓ rpm, from discs recorded at the same speed which have "standard" grooves.)

5 The sequence in which the records should be played, i.e., automatic or manual sequence.

Contents are given for single records or albums if they include several songs, speeches, or a number of short instrumental pieces. The same form is used as for printed collections of short separate works. Sometimes the notes about the performers and the contents can be combined.

On Card 66 note that the word *Phonodisc* is in italics, enclosed in brackets, and comes directly after the title.

When two musical works are on the same disc, each one is cataloged separately, and as the last note on each entry there is a note about

66 L. C. printed catalog card for recording

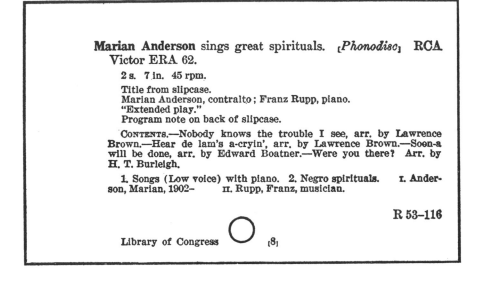

Marian Anderson sings great spirituals. ₍*Phonodisc*₎ RCA
Victor ERA 62.

2 s. 7 in. 45 rpm.

Title from slipcase.
Marian Anderson, contralto ; Franz Rupp, piano.
"Extended play."
Program note on back of slipcase.

CONTENTS.—Nobody knows the trouble I see, arr. by Lawrence
Brown.—Hear de lam's a-cryin', arr. by Lawrence Brown.—Soon-a
will be done, arr. by Edward Boatner.—Were you there? Arr. by
H. T. Burleigh.

1. Songs (Low voice) with piano. 2. Negro spirituals.   ɪ. Anderson, Marian, 1902–   ɪɪ. Rupp, Franz, musician.

R 53–116

Library of Congress   ₍8₎

the other work, introduced by the word "With," and including the
author and title of the other.

> With: Beethoven, Ludwig van. Symphony, no. 1 in C, op. 21. (Note on
> the entries for Brahms' Variations on a Theme by Haydn, op. 56a. A
> similar note would be put on the entries for Beethoven's Symphony
> no. 1.)
> With the composer's Tales from the Vienna woods. (Note on the entry for
> Strauss' Blue Danube.)

Added entries are made for subjects, performer, conductor, narrator,
title if distinctive, and series if an important series. The form is the
same as for books, simply add the appropriate heading to the unit card.
Subject headings are taken from *Sears' List of Subject Headings.* For
instance the heading "Symphony" in *Sears' List* would be used for
books or other printed material *about* symphonies and for the recordings *of* symphonies; the differences in the call number would show
whether a given entry is for a book or a record.

Added entries for records are traced on the front of the main entry
as are added entries for books, using the same form and style of
numbering.

The shelf-list card would follow the unit card through the collation
and series note, if any; with the source, date, and cost of each copy of

a record added on the second line below the collation or series note as on the shelf-list card for a book.

Filmstrips. As each filmstrip is added to the library assign a number. This number preceded by the letters FS forms the call number, e.g., FS6 would be the call number for the sixth filmstrip added to the library. This number should be written on the container for the film-strip and on the catalog and shelf-list cards.

If two or more distinct filmstrips are presented on one strip, a separate entry is made for each title, with an appropriate note, as is done when two or more books are bound together, a method described in Chapter VIII, pages 130-33. On the other hand two or more film-strips presented on a single strip should be cataloged as a single work if they can be considered as forming a whole.

The information needed to describe a filmstrip for the catalog is found on the filmstrip itself, in the accompanying booklet, or in such aids as *Filmstrip Guide.*

The items to be included on the catalog entry are: the title; name of the producer and date; physical description of the filmstrip; series to which it belongs; a summary of its contents; credits, i.e., persons or organizations not mentioned in the description to whom credit should be given; and the tracing of the added entries (see Card 67).

67 L. C. printed catalog card for filmstrip

Bill Clark (*Filmstrip*) Popular Science Pub. Co., 1952. Developed in cooperation with Albert Whitman and Co.

42 fr., color, 35 mm. (Pioneer heroes)

With teaching guide.
A pictorial condensation of the book of the same title by Sanford Tousey.
Summary: Drawings are used to describe the exploration of the Louisiana Territory in 1804 by William Clark and Meriwether Lewis. For intermediate grades.

1. Clark, William, 1770–1838. 2. Lewis and Clark Expedition. I. Tousey, Sanford. Bill Clark. II. Popular Science Publishing Company, inc., New York. (Series)

923.973   Fi 52–1343

Library of Congress   ₍9₎

Filmstrips are entered under the title as the main entry, not under the author. Write the title, given on the filmstrip or in the descriptive material, with hanging indention. Card 63 shows a book entered under title with hanging indention.

The name of the manufacturer of the film corresponds to the publisher of a book and follows the title in "imprint place." The Library of Congress rules for cataloging filmstrips define the producer as "the individual, company, institution, or organization responsible for the film's coming into existence..." In making a filmstrip the photographing, editing, sound recording, and distributing may be done by the same individual or organization, or each process may be done by a different one. If there is more than one they would be given in the following order on the card: name of the individual or organization interested in getting the filmstrip to the public; name of the producer; name of the maker; and name of the individual or organization who releases it. Some examples taken from Library of Congress printed catalog cards are given below:

> Dept. of National Health and Welfare, Ottawa. Made and released by National Film Board of Canada, 1953; made 1950.
> McGraw-Hill Book Co., 1952.
> McGraw-Hill Book Co., 1952. Produced by Teletran.
> Popular Science Pub. Co., 1952.
> Popular Science Pub. Co., 1952. Developed in cooperation with Albert Whitman.
> William P. Gottlieb Co. Released by Encyclopaedia Britannica Films, 1952.
> Margaret Bradfield Associates, 1953. Made by Jam Handy Organization.

As the above examples show it is sometimes necessary to give two or more individuals or organizations to show who is responsible for the filmstrip and the date may be that of the production or release of the filmstrip. Follow the same rules for giving place as are followed for books. If the publisher is in the list in Appendix II to be used abbreviated and without place, use that abbreviation and omit the place; otherwise give the place, then a comma, before each individual or organization in the imprint, and use the abbreviations listed in Appendix II in the name of the organization.

The date is as important as for printed material. The first choice would be the copyright date; second, the date of release; third, approximate date of release, if it can be ascertained; fourth, the date the filmstrip was made. If the dates differ include all.

c1950   1953   1951?   made 1949
Made by Hal Rieff Studios, 1943.
Made and released by National Film Board of Canada, 1953; made 1950.

Following the imprint information in the usual place for the collation give the physical properties of the filmstrip in the following order:
total number of frames, including the opening and closing ones;
whether in color or in black and white; and the width in millimeters.

48 fr. color, 35 mm.
47 fr. b&w, 35 mm.

If there is an accompanying record, its physical description comes immediately after the description of the physical properties of the filmstrip, and on the same line, if there is space.

81 fr. color, 35 mm. and disc: 2 s. 16 in. 78 rpm, 19 min.
48 double fr. color, 35 mm. and tape: 1 reel (10 in.) 7 in. per sec. 10 min.

This information about the filmstrip would be followed by the name of
the series, if any, in parentheses.

Notes, given in their usual place, include such information about
accompanying material as teachers' manuals.

A summary which describes the content of the filmstrip so as to
reduce to a minimum the occasion for handling it comes next. It is
preceded by the word "Summary" followed by a colon.

Credits are noted for certain individuals or organizations who have
assisted in the production of the filmstrip, if their names are on the
filmstrip or accompanying booklet and if they are important.

Credits: Written by Margaret Bradfield; illustrator, Carlos Lopez.

Filmstrips issued in a series may be cataloged as a collection under
the latest title of the series. Inclusive dates are given as is done for volumes copyrighted or published at different times. Card 21 shows
inclusive dates for a book in several volumes. The number of filmstrips is given as the first item in the collation, followed by the usual
items that are common to all of the strips, with variations noted.

4 filmstrips (28 fr. each), b&w (pt. 1 in color), 35 mm. and 4 discs (1s.
each), 12 in. 78 rpm.
4 filmstrips, color, 35 mm. Part 1, 41 fr.; pt. 2, 44 fr.; pt. 3, 49 fr.; pt. 4,
45 fr.

The contents note for a series is given in the same form as for a book. If the number of frames differs for each filmstrip, they are given following the title of each strip:

> Contents.—1 Two to make friends. 29 fr.—2 Bob's little shadow. 27 fr.—
> 3 Quarrel, quarrel. 28 fr.—...

The contents may make a summary unnecessary. Credits, if any, follow the contents.

Added entries, similar to those for books, are made for joint producers, sponsors, the releasing agent in the United States if it is a foreign filmstrip, alternative or partial titles when distinctive, titles of separate parts if important and not used as a separate entry, series if important, and subjects. There is no entry for the person who writes the script or illustrates the work, though he may be mentioned under credits. The form of these added entries is the same as that of added entries for books: the heading is added above the title on the unit card and the entries are traced on the front of the main entry.

Maps. Use the letter M and the number of the map to form the call number, as is done for filmstrips and records, e.g., M14 would be the fourteenth map added to the map collection. The items to include in an entry for a map are very similar to those in a book entry. They are: author; title; place of publication, publisher, and date; collation, which includes the number of maps and their size; notes; and the tracing of the added entries. Information for cataloging a map is usually found on the map itself, sometimes within a fancy border or in the margins.

Maps are entered under the person or corporate body given in the title as responsible for the map: the cartographer; engraver; publisher; or copyright claimant in this order. If there is no individual or organization which can be considered responsible for the map, enter under the title, using hanging indention as is customary when the main entry is under the title. Following the author, in its usual place, give the title. The title is taken from any part of the front of the map.

The place of publication, name of the publisher, and date of the map are given in imprint place; if not found on the front of the map, they are put in brackets, if they can be ascertained. The copyright date is the date of first choice. If the map is entered under the publisher as author the publisher statement is omitted in the imprint.

The collation is given in the usual place. If there is only one map, put "map" or "col. map," if more than one give the number, e.g., "4 maps." If one map is printed on several sheets, it is described as a single map, e.g., "map on 6 sheets." The height and width of the map are given in inches, to the nearest half inch. The height is always given first. The measurements are taken from the outer border lines of the map. If a map is folded, especially if folded within a cover, or has a panel that should come on the outside, give the measurements for it folded as well as spread out.

> map 28 x 27 in. fold. to 10 x 5 in.

The first and most important note gives the scale of the map. This shows the relation that exists between a unit of distance on the map and that same distance on the earth's surface. It is usually given on the map expressed as a fraction or a ratio and is called the natural scale, e.g., $\frac{1}{125,000}$ or 1:125,000; or it may be a linear scale, e.g., 1 mile to the inch. This latter is determined by measuring with a foot ruler the distance marked as one mile on the linear scale drawn on the map. If the scale is not given, a note would read: Scale not given.

Another item which is important for maps is the projection from which the map was drawn. This is taken directly from the map, e.g., "polyconic projection." If not stated somewhere on the map, it is omitted. Notes also give information as to what types of data the map shows, e.g., air routes, population distribution, railroads, etc. Information of a type not usually found on that kind of map is especially important for notes; for instance if a highway map shows points of historic interest, bring it out in a note, as all highway maps do not have such information; but, since all highway maps do show the type of surface of the highways, this fact would not be noted on the card.

Notes also cover such items as: name of surveyor, engraver, cartographer, dates; for instance: "With international boundaries as of September 1, 1939, the day Germany invaded Poland."

Inset maps, if important, are given in a partial contents note.

> Insets: Alaska.—Hawaiian Islands.

If very important the inset map is cataloged separately as an analytic.

Card 68 is for a road map. Notice that it is entered under the association responsible for it; that the title, place, and copyright date are given in their usual positions. The publisher's name is omitted as it is the same as the author. The copyright date is on the face of the

68 L. C. printed catalog card for map

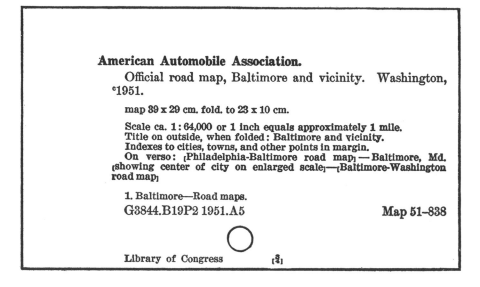

> **American Automobile Association.**
>   Official road map, Baltimore and vicinity. Washington,
> ᶜ1951.
>
>   map 39 x 29 cm. fold. to 23 x 10 cm.
>
>   Scale ca. 1:64,000 or 1 inch equals approximately 1 mile.
>   Title on outside, when folded: Baltimore and vicinity.
>   Indexes to cities, towns, and other points in margin.
>   On verso: ₍Philadelphia-Baltimore road map₎ — Baltimore, Md.
> ₍showing center of city on enlarged scale₎—₍Baltimore-Washington
> road map₎
>
>   1. Baltimore—Road maps.
>   G3844.B19P2 1951.A5   Map 51–838
>
>   ◯
>
>   Library of Congress   ₍²₎

map, so brackets are not used. The Library of Congress measures maps in centimeters instead of inches and gives the approximate scale when the exact scale is not stated on the map or cannot be ascertained. The title, which appears on the outside when the map is folded, is given in a note. There is also a note about the indexes which are printed on the map, and the maps which are on the back of the main map.

A typewritten card for this road map of Baltimore would have author, title, place, and copyright date as on this Library of Congress printed card. The collation would be the same except that the measurements would be in inches, e.g., map 19½ x 14½ in. fold to 11½ x 5 in. As the scale is not given the note would be: Scale not given. The second and third notes would be omitted, but the fourth note about the map on the back would be useful even in the small library's catalog. Remember that it is easier to consult a catalog card than to get a map out and unfold it.

Slides. Assign a number to each unit or series of slides as they are added to the library, adding this number to the abbreviation SL to form the call number, as is done for records, filmstrips, and maps. Miss Rufsvold points out that the individual slides, like the individual records in an album, may have their number in the series added, e.g., SL92(8) for the eighth slide in the series numbered 92. The title is

69 Main entry for a set of slides

pe

SL52   Farm animals.   Chicago, Society for Visual Educa-
           tion, n. d.
           10 2x2 slides.   col.

           Contents.-Bf193 Cattle, Guernseys in farmyard.-
       Ah360 Beef cattle in pasture.-Da29 Pig.-Aal15
       Sheep in pasture.-Bf160 White billy goat.-Bf67
       Horses, team of.-Ar190 Colorado turkey farm.-Bf138
       Farm unit, chickens scratching for their food.-
       Bf198 Duck, white Muscovy.-Bf146 Three geese at
       edge of pond in typical poses.

used for the main entry of a slide as it is for filmstrips. The unit card
would include: title, using hanging indention; place, name of producer, and date; number of slides, if a set; size of the slides; and
whether black and white or in color; in the usual place for title, imprint, and collation. For sets list the number and subject of each individual slide in a contents note.

Added entries are made for subjects only and they are traced just
as they are for books. The shelf-list card is the same as the unit card,
with the omission of notes and contents and the addition of the source,
date received, and cost of the slides.

At the present time no printed catalog cards are available for slides.

Sample Card 69 shows the items described as the ones needed for
slides. Note that the style of card is the same as that for books.

Simplified care of audio-visual materials. The small library may
not have time to do even the simple cataloging of audio-visual materials
described in this chapter. Maps can be folded, given the mark of ownership of the library, have the area written in the upper right-hand corner,
and be filed in the vertical file with other material on the subject.

Records can be kept in albums or in envelopes, in cabinets, or on
shelves with upright partitions close together and sheets of corrugated
pasteboard to hold the records erect and prevent warping.

Records, filmstrips, and slides, however, must have some kind of card index or catalog. If a good plan is worked out, the necessary rules obtained, printed catalog cards used whenever obtainable, and the work kept up to date, it does not take long to catalog such audio-visual materials and it does save time in locating the right one and also saves wear and tear on the materials.

Abbreviations. The abbreviations used in cataloging records, filmstrips, maps, and slides are given below, rather than in Appendix II, since they are needed only for this chapter. They are taken from the work by Rufsvold, the Library of Congress rules for filmstrips and records, and the H. W. Wilson Company's *Filmstrip Guide.*

Type of material:

FS	Filmstrip
M	Map
R	Record, single
RA	Record, album
SL	Slide

Age level:

a	adult
c	college
e	elementary
jh	junior high school
p	primary
ps	preschool[7]
sh	senior high school
t	teacher

Abbreviations used in the description of the material:

b&w	black and white
fr.	frame, frames
ft.	foot, feet
guide	teacher's manual
in.	inch, inches
min.	minute, minutes
mm.	millimeter, millimeters
rpm	revolutions per minute
s.	side, sides
sec.	second, seconds

[7]This abbreviation is not found in any of the sources listed above, but as no abbreviation was found for this term, *ps* was adopted, as it is similar to those used for related terms.

chapter X

Printed catalog cards

The Library of Congress prints the cards which are used in its catalogs and the H. W. Wilson Company prints cards for the material listed in its Standard Catalog series. They are for sale to libraries. Since the cards are somewhat different and the procedure in ordering them differs, they will be treated separately.

Library of Congress printed cards. Differences will be found, not only in Library of Congress printed cards, Wilson printed cards, and the sample typewritten cards in previous chapters, but between Library of Congress cards printed at different times, as shown by the first two figures in the card number (e.g., 52-60002 means that the card was issued in 1952). These latter differences are the result of changes in the cataloging practices of the Library of Congress and should be ignored. Since the older cards and the most recently printed cards both describe the material accurately, variations in the details of certain items do not matter.

Card 70 for Haykin's *Subject Headings* is, incidentally, a card for an unbound book, as the Library of Congress prints cards for books, unbound books, pamphlets, recordings, maps, and filmstrips. The author heading is given in the form adopted by the Library of Congress. The subtitle is included as it is short and shows the point of view from which the subject is treated. These printed cards always give the place of publication, the publisher's name, abbreviated somewhat as it would have been on typewritten cards, and the date of the work. The sample Library of Congress cards in this chapter and in Appendix I show the variety of ways in which the date may be given: imprint

70 L. C. printed catalog card

Haykin, David Judson, 1896–
    Subject headings; a practical guide. Washington, U. S.
Govt. Print. Off., 1951.

    v, 140 p. 26 cm.

    At head of title: The Library of Congress.

1. Subject headings.   I. U. S. Library of Congress. II. Title.

Z695.H36   ◯   025.33   52—60002

Library of Congress   [52r50x15]

---

date (from the title page); copyright date; date found elsewhere in
the book than the title page or in a reliable bibliography; the nearest
approximate date; e.g., 1951, [c1953], [1895], [18–?], [195–?], [1952?].
The brackets, as usual, indicate that the enclosed material is not on the
title page.

Note that different sizes and styles of type are used to emphasize
or make less conspicuous the different items. The collation gives the
last numbered page of each section of the work, information about the
illustrations, and includes the size, i.e., the height of the book in centimeters, e.g., 26cm. 25 cm.

Card 71 includes the authors in the title, as the book was written
jointly by two authors, and also mentions the illustrator.

Card 72 for Gamow gives both the imprint date and the copyright
date, even though they are almost the same, as is the Library of Congress' policy. Note that Gamow's full name is given in the lower right-
hand corner of the card.

Card 73 for Hoover's *Water Supply and Treatment* shows edition
statement and series note in the same form as given on the typewritten
cards in earlier chapters. The brackets around the name of the author
of the series indicate that it was not on the title page of the book, as
was the title, *Bulletin*.

71 L. C. printed catalog card—joint authors

> **Agle, Nan Hayden.**
>   Three boys and a tugboat ₁by₁ Nan Hayden Agle and Ellen
> Wilson; illustrated by Marian Honigman. New York, Scrib-
> ner ₁1953₁
>   121 p.   illus.   20 cm.
>
>
>   ɪ. Wilson, Ellen Janet (Cameron) joint author. ɪɪ. Title.
>
>   PZ7.A2678Tj   ◯   53–7785 ‡
>   Library of Congress   ₁5₁

72 L. C. printed catalog card—imprint and copyright date both given

> **Gamow, George,** 1904–
>   The birth and death of the sun; stellar evolution and
> sub-atomic energy. Illustrated by the author. New York,
> Viking Press, 1949 ₁ᶜ1945₁
>   xvi, 245 p.   illus.   22 cm.
>
>
>   1. Sun.   2. Stars.   3. Atoms.   ɪ. Title.
>   *Full name:* George Antony Gamow.
>   QB44.G26   1949   ◯   523   50–2196
>   Library of Congress   ₁15₁

   Notes and contents, shown on Cards 74 for Priestley and 75 for the
Massachusetts Institute of Technology are given in the same form as
on the sample cards in previous chapters.
   At the bottom of the cards is the tracing for the added entries made
for the Library of Congress catalog. Below the tracing and to the left

73 L. C. printed catalog card—edition and series notes

Hoover, Charles Potter.
    Water supply and treatment. ₍7th ed.₎ Washington,
National Lime Association ₍1951₎

    xi, 211 p. illus. (part col.) map. 24 cm. (₍National Lime As-
sociation₎ Bulletin 211)

    1. Water-supply. 2. Water—Purification. 3. Water—Softening.
4. Water—Analysis.   (Series)

    TD345.H57 1951   628.16   51-25395
    ——————— Copy 2.   TP875.N36 no. 211 1951
    Library of Congress   ₍1₎

---

74 L. C. printed catalog card—contents given

Priestley, John Boynton, 1894–
    Seven plays.   New York, Harper, 1950.

    xi, 477 p.   23 cm.

    CONTENTS. — Dangerous corner. — Eden end. — Time and the Con-
ways.—I have been here before.—Johnson over Jordan.—Music at
night.—The linden tree.

    PR6031.R6A19   1950   822.91   51-118

    Library of Congress   ₍10₎

---

of the hole are given the Library of Congress classification and book
numbers, e.g., Z695.H36 and on the same line to the right of the hole
is given the suggested Dewey Decimal Classification number, e.g.,
025.33. Some cards have two decimal classification numbers. Anderson
and Weidner's *American Government* has: *320.973 and 342.733. The

75 L. C. printed catalog card—name of an organization as heading—
bibliography mentioned in note

Massachusetts Institute of Technology. *Albert Farwell*
Bemis Foundation.
    The prefabrication of houses; a study by the Albert Far-
well Bemis Foundation of the prefabrication industry in the
United States, by Burnham Kelly ₍director. Cambridge₎
Published jointly by the Technology Press of the Massa-
chusetts Institute of Technology and Wiley, New York ₍1951₎

    xxii, 466 p. illus., map. 24 cm.

    Bibliography: p. 446–452.

    1. Buildings, Prefabricated.   i. Kelly, Burnham.

    TH1098.M3   691   51–10730

    Library of Congress   ◯   ₍15₎

---

starred number is from the 15th edition of Dewey, the other from
the 14th edition.
    The Library of Congress card number, e.g., 53-7785, which is to be
used in ordering Library of Congress cards, is given in the right-hand
corner of the card. Such symbols as ₍5₎, ₍516₎1 to the right of the hole
and below the Dewey Decimal Classification number indicate facts as
to the edition of the card and are unimportant to the cataloger.
    Some cards, as those for Hoover's *Water Supply,* indicate that the
Library of Congress has a second copy by giving two long dashes
followed by "Copy 2" (——— ——— Copy 2) below the Library of Congress classification number.
    Ordering Library of Congress cards. If Library of Congress cards
are to be used, write to the Librarian of Congress, Washington 25, D.C.
and ask for a copy of the Library's instructions for ordering printed
catalog cards, a temporary subscriber's card, and the printed forms to
be used for each order. The directions for making out the orders are
detailed and clear.
    The price of Library of Congress cards varies slightly from time to
time, as each year the price is compared with the cost of production
and any necessary adjustment made. The price also varies with the

method of ordering. Current prices vary from 6c to 10c, depending upon the method of ordering, for the first card for a work and 3c for additional copies of the same card ordered at the same time.

When one considers the cost of blank cards and the time required to search the name and do the cataloging printed cards are not expensive.

Wilson printed cards. The printed catalog cards of the H. W. Wilson Company reproduce the entries for books in their printed book catalogs, including the very helpful annotations. Unlike the Library of Congress cards, all the cards of a set are not exactly alike, but have title, etc., added at the top. The sets for each book are available in two forms. One form has subject heading and classification number at the top of the card; the other has subject heading and classification number at the bottom of the card where it may be used as a suggestion but is not in the way if the particular library has used or prefers to use another form of subject heading or a different classification number. The illustrations in this chapter show the two forms. It will also be noted that the shelf-list card omits the annotation and tracing in order to leave space for the special shelf list information.

Cards 76 and 77 will be found upon examination to differ from the typewritten cards given in this book and from Library of Congress

76 **Wilson printed catalog card**

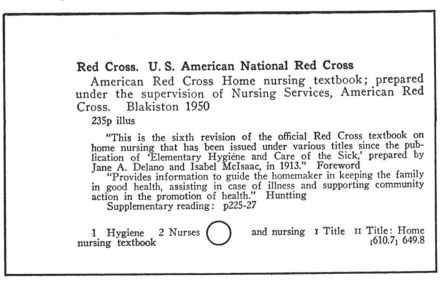

Red Cross. U. S. American National Red Cross
    American Red Cross Home nursing textbook; prepared under the supervision of Nursing Services, American Red Cross. Blakiston 1950
    235p illus

    "This is the sixth revision of the official Red Cross textbook on home nursing that has been issued under various titles since the publication of 'Elementary Hygiéne and Care of the Sick,' prepared by Jane A. Delano and Isabel McIsaac, in 1913." Foreword
    "Provides information to guide the homemaker in keeping the family in good health, assisting in case of illness and supporting community action in the promotion of health." Huntting
    Supplementary reading: p225-27

    1. Hygiene   2 Nurses   and nursing ɪ Title ɪɪ Title: Home nursing textbook   ᵢ610.7ᵢ 649.8

77 Wilson printed shelf-list card

Red Cross. U.S. American National Red Cross
    American Red Cross Home nursing textbook; prepared under the supervision of Nursing Services, American Red Cross.   Blakiston 1950
    235p illus

ₗ610.7₎ 649.8

3-13-53   ◯   (W)   The H. W. Wilson Company

---

catalog cards. The most conspicuous difference is in the annotation and scanty punctuation of the Wilson card. Punctuation is omitted from the printed book catalogs published by Wilson to save expense and space; the cards are printed from the same copy. Each issue of the book catalog includes at the end a "Directory of Publishers"; hence entries for individual books give only the abbreviation for the book publisher which is found in this directory.

Cards 76 and 78 are for the same book, even the same edition. Though there is a difference in the style of printing the author headings are the same. The Wilson cards have the phrase: *American Red Cross* preceding *Home Nursing Textbook,* otherwise the titles are identical. The Library of Congress gives the information about the revision in an edition note, the Wilson card gives it in the annotation. The Library of Congress card includes the place in the imprint, the last numbered page of the preliminary paging, and the size in collation; the Wilson card does not. Both cards give the earlier title in a note and also the fact that there is a bibliography and the paging for it. The suggested subject headings are the same and both indicate an added entry under title. The Wilson set has a second title card, as "American Red Cross" precedes the title "Home nursing textbook"; note how the second title is traced.

78 L. C. printed catalog card

Red Cross. *U. S. American National Red Cross.*
   Home nursing textbook, prepared under the supervision
of Nursing Services, American Red Cross. ₍6th revision₎
Philadelphia, Blakiston, 1950.

   ix, 235 p. illus. 23 cm.

   First published in 1913 under title: American Red Cross textbook
on elementary hygiene and home care of the sick.
   Bibliography: p. 225–227.

   1. Hygiene. 2. Nurses and nursing.   ɪ. Title.

   RT61.R38   1950   649   50—4804

   Library of Congress   ₍51x20₎

---

79 Wilson printed catalog card as author analytical entry

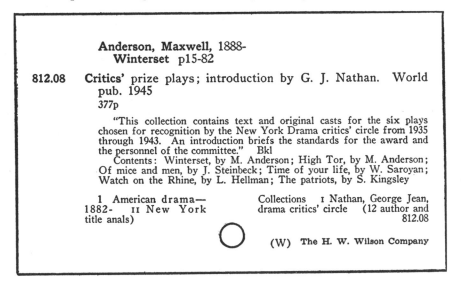

              Anderson, Maxwell, 1888-
                 Winterset p15-82

 812.08   **Critics'** prize plays; introduction by G. J. Nathan. World
              pub. 1945
              377p
                   "This collection contains text and original casts for the six plays
              chosen for recognition by the New York Drama critics' circle from 1935
              through 1943. An introduction briefs the standards for the award and
              the personnel of the committee." Bkl
                   Contents: Winterset, by M. Anderson; High Tor, by M. Anderson;
              Of mice and men, by J. Steinbeck; Time of your life, by W. Saroyan;
              Watch on the Rhine, by L. Hellman; The patriots, by S. Kingsley

              1 American drama—   Collections   ɪ Nathan, George Jean,
              1882-   ɪɪ New York   drama critics' circle (12 author and
              title anals)   812.08

                                          (W) The H. W. Wilson Company

---

The cards for *Critics' Prize Plays* have the classification number at
the left of the first word of the title, since this work has its main entry
under the title; usually the call number is at the left of the author
heading. Note in the tracing: "(12 author and title anals)." The printed
cards for the author and title analytical entries (Cards 79 and 80) have

80 Wilson printed catalog card as title analytical entry

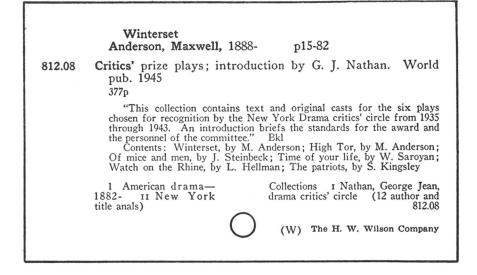

both author and title added at the top of the card; the paging follows the title on the author analytical entry and the author's name on the title analytical entry. The punctuation of the contents note on these cards differs from that used on the typewritten cards in this book and on the Library of Congress cards. However, that is only a minor difference.

Ordering Wilson cards. If one wishes to use the Wilson printed cards, he should write to The H. W. Wilson Company, 950-72 University Ave., New York 52, N. Y. for a copy of their *Complete Checklist of Sets of Catalog Cards* and its supplements. The pamphlet and the monthly supplements give simple, clear directions for ordering the cards and include a printed order form. The company sells sheets of coupons to be used in purchasing the cards, which are sold in sets only; the current price is 8c for each set with one additional 8c coupon to be sent with each order. If the book requires more than the average number of analytical entries, the additional cards are sold separately in sets at the price indicated in the checklist.

Advantages of using printed catalog cards. The copy for printed catalog cards is prepared by expert catalogers, with all that this fact implies in regard to author headings, items included on the cards, suggestions as to subject headings, classification numbers, and added entries to be made. The Library of Congress cards give considerable bibliographical information about the book which may be of great value. The Wilson cards give annotations which are very useful. Printed cards are uniform as to blackness and are very legible. Their use saves time in preparing the entry, in typing cards, and in revising typewritten cards. One printed card may be compared with the book to see if it matches the particular edition which the library has, and only the call number and the typewritten headings added to the cards need to be checked for accuracy. Printed cards are especially useful for books which require several subject cards or numerous analytical entries. The Library of Congress cards do not specify which added cards are analytical entries; but the necessary extra cards may be ordered and by having call number, headings, and paging added are quickly made into analytical entries.

Typewritten reference cards and short form series cards have to be made by each library for its own catalog. If the unit card is used for series entries, printed cards may be used. The simple form of cataloging for fiction recommended in this manual makes the process of cataloging by the library as quick as or quicker than ordering Library of Congress printed cards and adapting them for the catalog. It is recommended, therefore, that typewritten cards be used for fiction even though Library of Congress cards are ordered for all nonfiction. On the other hand, if the Wilson cards are to be used for nonfiction, it is recommended that they be ordered for fiction as well, since they include annotations and are easy to order.

The question of whether to use Library of Congress cards depends largely upon the kind of library. The school or children's library having chiefly books which are listed in the Wilson Standard Catalogs and for which printed Wilson cards are available would do well to use Wilson cards, ordering Library of Congress cards only for older books and others for which Wilson cards are not available. The library for adults and the more scholarly library would do well to use Library of Congress cards with their added bibliographical information. The mixture of Library of Congress cards, Wilson printed cards, and typewritten cards in the same catalog does not reduce the usefulness of the catalog.

Adapting printed cards for use in the catalog. The librarian compares the cards with the book which they are to represent in the catalog to see that they agree, and with the catalog or authority file to see whether or not the form of heading agrees with what has already been used. If, for example, the printed card has the author's real name on the first line and it seems better to use the pseudonym, write it on the line above the real name—beginning at the first indention—followed by a comma, one space and *pseud. of.*

If the library has entered a few books under another form of the name, e.g., Mulock, Dinah Maria, instead of Craik, Dinah Maria (Mulock), it would be better to change those and adopt the form used on the printed cards. If on the other hand there are many cards in the catalog by the author, the headings on the printed cards may be changed. A line can be drawn through the author heading and the preferred form written above, beginning at the first indention, as usual.

It is unnecessary to cross out any item given on the printed card, provided it applies to the book in question. Changes may be made by crossing out or erasing items and typing or writing in the corrections. As few corrections as possible should be made on the printed cards so as not to spoil the appearance of the cards.

If the publisher given in the imprint on the card is not the publisher of the edition to be cataloged, the statement on the card should be changed. If the date given is not the copyright date, *c* should be added and the date changed if necessary. In the case of incomplete sets date and volume should be changed with pencil, so that the card may show what the library has and yet be easily changed when the other volumes are added.

After the librarian makes the corrections or additions which may be necessary in order that the printed card may represent the book correctly, the next step is to add the call number. For most books published since 1930 the Decimal Classification number appears to the right of the hole in the card and may be used if it is not too long and is in agreement with the policy of the library. For instance, if the number suggested for a biography is 923 it would not be used, since the plan recommended for the small school or public library in Chapter I is to use 920 for all collective biography and 92 or B for all individual biography.

The next step is to examine the tracing. Does the library need all of the added entries listed? Are the subject headings those listed in the printed list of subject headings adopted by the library? Does the amount of material on the subject make necessary the subdivisions of the subject given? If the library has only a few books on a country and is unlikely ever to have many, the name of the country alone may be sufficient for all the books about it, e.g., FORMOSA; or the general subdivisions HISTORY and DESCRIPTION AND TRAVEL may be sufficient, rather than the more specific subdivisions such as, CZECHOSLOVAK REPUBLIC. HISTORY. 1938–1945. or IRELAND. DESCRIPTION AND TRAVEL. 19th CENTURY.

The Library of Congress card suggests added entries to be made, subject headings, etc., which fit the book. The librarian should decide which of these added entries will be of use in his catalog, select the term for the subject heading which agrees with the heading given in the list adopted for the given library, and not divide a heading when the amount of material on a subject does not warrant it.

If all of the added entries given in the tracing on the printed card are not used, underscore the number of each item of tracing for which a card is filed in the catalog. If the subject heading given on the card is not the same as that listed in the printed subject headings list, use the heading from the printed list and type it on the front of the card. If there is insufficient space at the end of the tracing, type it on the back, and type the word "over" below the hole on the front of the card.

On the Library of Congress cards which are to be used as added entries the call number is added, the necessary alterations are made, and in addition the appropriate headings are added; no change is made in the tracing, as only the main entry is consulted for tracing. To make a Library of Congress card into an author analytical entry, estimate in advance the number of lines which the added heading will require. If contents or any other extra information has made extension cards necessary, use a full set of cards, i.e., first, second, third, etc., for the main and all other entries except title cards and analytical entries. For title cards, use the first card only, drawing a line through the words, "Continued on next card." For analytical entries, use the card which contains that part of the contents for which the analytic is made, crossing out "Continued on next card."

The Wilson printed cards will rarely need any alteration, as they are more often made for the edition of the book which the library has. The Dewey Decimal Classification number is suggested for the same type of library as that for which the cards are ordered; however, two or, occasionally, three numbers are given and a choice has to be made. The cards for Keith's *White Man Returns* have [919.11] 991.1 and *Profile of Youth* by members of the staff of the *Ladies' Home Journal* has [136.7] 136.73 or 301.15. Choose the number which will put the book with similar books in the library.

Likewise the added entries for joint authors, editors, and subject headings on the Wilson cards are selected for greatest usefulness to the type of library which customarily orders their cards. The suggested subject headings on these cards are chosen from the Sears list. Hence it will not often happen that the indicated entries need not be made or that the subject heading will need to be shortened. However, it is best in many libraries to order the cards that do not have subject headings printed at the top of the subject cards nor the classification number in its place in the upper left-hand portion of the card, as the subject headings and classification number may not agree with those used by the library and may have to be modified.

chapter XI

Arrangement
of cards in a catalog

Introduction. Next in importance to making the cards for the catalog is their arrangement in the trays of the catalog case. Unless all cards with the same heading are found together and all cards are arranged according to some definite plan, a card catalog is of very little use. One of the most important mechanical points is to watch that the trays do not become overcrowded. A good rule is never to fill a catalog tray more than two-thirds full; space is needed to shift cards so that the one being examined may be handled easily.

Another important matter is to label the trays so that the reader can easily locate the tray which contains the author, title, or subject for which he is searching. Adequate guide cards, preferably cut in thirds, should indicate the approximate location of the desired card.

A very good method of arranging guide cards in the catalog is to have the authors' surnames on the left, main subject headings in the center, and subdivisions of the subject on the right. This plan enables the caption on the guide card to be short and near enough to the top of the card so that it may be read. So far as possible there should be a guide card for every inch of tightly held cards. A very minor point is to have a blank card in the front of each tray so that the first card will not become soiled.

One of the signs telling how to use the catalog, which may be purchased from a library supply house, may be placed in a poster holder on top of the catalog if it is a low cabinet, or hung beside it. Be sure that the printed directions fit the catalog.

Catalog guide cards

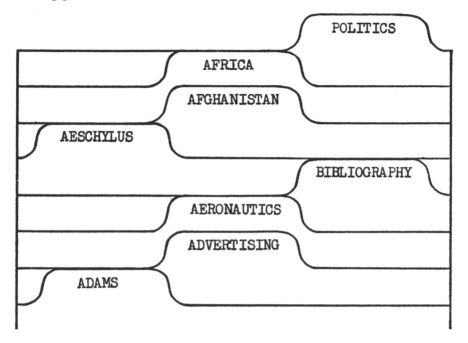

Some large libraries file cards in the catalog once a week; small libraries may file oftener or less often than this. It is not worth while to file a few cards if there will be more tomorrow; if it might be a week or more before there are others, those ready may be filed so that the readers may have the use of these new cards.

Before filing cards, they should be sorted into catalog and shelf-list cards, and counted for the library reports.

After this preliminary sorting the cards are arranged for the catalog alphabetically, according to the rules used in this catalog. The next step is to interfile the cards with those already in the catalog trays, leaving the new cards above the rod. Later go over these new cards, making sure that they are in their right alphabetical place. Next pull out the rod and allow the cards to drop into place, locking them in with the rod.

Filing should not be continued for a long period. Since filing cards requires close attention, the eye becomes tired and mistakes are likely to occur. If the same person both files and revises, several hours should elapse between the filing and the revising.

There is no dictionary catalog with all cards filed absolutely alphabetically, word by word or letter by letter; in all catalogs there will be at least a few logical exceptions. Before beginning to file in an unfamiliar catalog, observe what alphabeting code was used. Whatever code has been used, continue to follow it unless it is unsatisfactory, and be sure that the change will be an improvement before deciding to refile an entire catalog.

RULES FOR ARRANGING CARDS IN A CATALOG

Below are given rules which should prove adequate for filing cards in the dictionary catalog of a small library. These rules are listed by number and topic in Appendix V of the *A.L.A. Rules for Filing Catalog Cards.*[1] If more information on filing catalog cards is desired, it will be found in the main body of this filing code.

There are two fundamental methods of filing alphabetically; namely, word by word and letter by letter.

Word by word filing:	*Letter by letter filing:*
Book	Book
Book collecting	Bookbinding
Book of English essays	Book collecting
Book of famous ships	Bookish
Book scorpion	Book of English essays
Bookbinding	Book of famous ships
Bookish	Books
Books	Books and reading
Books and reading	Book scorpion
Books that count	Booksellers and bookselling
Booksellers and bookselling	Books that count

In word by word filing, each word is a unit, and thus *Books that count* precedes *Booksellers and bookselling*, since *Books* precedes *Booksellers;* while in letter by letter filing no attention is paid to words but each letter is considered. Thus *Books that count* follows *Booksellers* because *b o o k s t* follows *b o o k s e.* To take another example: *Book scorpion* precedes *Bookbinding* in word by word filing as *Book* precedes *Bookb,* but in letter by letter filing *Bookbinding* precedes *Book scorpion* because *b o o k b* precedes *b o o k s.*

---

[1]*A.L.A. Rules for Filing Catalog Cards;* prepared by a special committee, Sophie K. Hiss, Chairman (Chicago: A.L.A., 1942), cited in this chapter as *A.L.A.,* with the number of the rule.

Basic rule (A.L.A.1) "(1) Arrange all entries according to the order of the English alphabet....(2) Arrange word by word, alphabeting letter by letter to the end of each word."

> New Hampshire.
> New viewpoints in American history.
> New York.
> Newer knowledge of nutrition.
> Newton, Alfred Edward.

Abbreviations (A.L.A. 5) "(1) Arrange abbreviations as if spelled in full; *e.g.,* Dr., Mr., Mrs., as Doctor, Mister, Mistress...This includes initials and other abbreviations used for geographical names...An explanatory reference should be made from the abbreviation to the full form whenever necessary."

> American Library Association.
> A.L.A. catalog 1942–1949.
> American Library Institute.

> Dr. Jekyll and Mr. Hyde.
> Doctor Luke.
> Dr. Norton's wife.
> Doctors on horseback.
> Documents of American history.

> Miss Lulu Bett.
> Mr. Emmanuel.
> Mr. Pim passes by.
> Mistress Margaret.
> Mrs. Miniver.
> Mrs. Warren's profession.
> Mitchell, Margaret.

> St. Denis, Ruth.
> Saint-Exupéry, Antoine de.
> Saint-Gaudens, Augustus.
> St. Helena.
> Saint Joan.
> Saint John de Crevecoeur.
> St. Lawrence River.
> St. Louis.
> Ste. Anne des Monts.
> Sainte-Beuve, Charles Augustin.
> Saintsbury, George Edward Bateman.

Ampersand (A.L.A. 3c) "Alphabet the character '&' as 'and,' 'et,' 'und,' etc., according to the language used."

> Aucassin and Nicolete,...
> Aucassin & Nicolette: an old French love story...
> Aucassin et Nicolette,...
> Aucassin und Nicolette;...

Analytics.

Author (A.L.A. 25a (4)) "Alphabet an author analytic by the title of the analytic, not by the title of the book. If there are two analytics of the same title subarrange by the main entry of the book."

> Huxley, Thomas Henry, 1825–1895.
> Collected essays...
> Huxley, Thomas Henry, 1825–1895.
> On a piece of chalk, p.157–187:
> Law, Frederick Houk, 1871–
> Science in literature...
> Huxley, Thomas Henry, 1825–1895.
> Science and education...

Title (A.L.A. 25a (4)) "If the title of an analytic and of a separate work are the same, file the separate work first, disregarding a subtitle or a second title, if any."

> Peabody, Josephine Preston, 1874–1922.
> The piper...
> Peacock pie,
> De la Mare, Walter John, 1873–
> Peacock pie...
> Peacock pie, v.2, p.95–218:
> De la Mare, Walter John, 1873–
> Collected poems...
> Peacocks and pagodas.
> Edmonds, Paul.

Subject (A.L.A. 33) "Arrange...a subject analytic[2] by an author other than the author of the book...by the author of the analytic."

> MASARYK, TOMÁŠ GARRIGUE, PRES. CZECHOSLOVAK REPUBLIC, 1850–1937.
> Masaryk, Jan Garrigue, 1886–1948, p.337–355:
> Ludwig, Emil, 1881–1948, ed.
> The torch of freedom, edited by Emil Ludwig and Henry B. Kranz.

---

[2]Subject headings are given in full capitals.

MASARYK, TOMÁŠ GARRIGUE, PRES. CZECHOSLOVAK REPUBLIC, 1850–1937.
Selver, Paul, 1888–
    Masaryk, a biography...

MASARYK, TOMÁŠ GARRIGUE, PRES. CZECHOSLOVAK REPUBLIC, 1850–1937.
Seton-Watson, Robert William, 1879–
    Masaryk in England.

As shown in the example, the volume or paging or both sometimes given in the top line of an analytic heading are disregarded entirely in alphabeting. Cards with the heading MASARYK, TOMÁŠ GARRIGUE, PRES. CZECHOSLOVAK REPUBLIC, 1850–1937 are arranged by authors, and the phrase, "p.337–355" following the subject heading for Ludwig has no effect upon its alphabetical place. The method of filing analytics in the catalog of a given library depends upon the way the analytics are made, but the reader's point of view should always be kept in mind: Is he searching for material on a given subject? for a work by a given author? for a work with a given title? Thus author analytics should be subarranged by title with the books by that author, as shown under Huxley.

Articles (A.L.A. 7) "In alphabeting titles, disregard an initial article..."

Laski, Harold Joseph.
The last of the Vikings.
The last of Uptake.
LATIN AMERICA.

Powder River.
Power, Richard Anderson.
POWER (MECHANICS).
The power of a lie.
The power of color.
Powers, Francis Fountain.

Author arrangement (A.L.A. 25a1-2;b(1)) "Under an author's name, personal or corporate, arrange the entries in two files:..."

1 "Arrange in one file all the entries...for a person as author, joint author, compiler, editor, illustrator, translator and general added entry. Subarrange alphabetically by the title of the book;...disregard the main author heading on the secondary entry cards and subarrange by title. To make this clear, underline the word in the title by which the entry is subarranged..."

2 "Arrange in a second file the entries for works about the author,

alphabeting by the main entry of the book; or, if an analytic, by the author of the analytic....

"*Exception:* The subject entry for a criticism of an individual title files immediately after the author entries for the title."

> Hall, James Norman, 1887–1951.
> Nordhoff, Charles Bernard, 1887–1947.
>> Botany bay, by Charles Nordhoff
> and James Norman Hall.
>
> Hall, James Norman, 1887–1951.
>> Doctor Dogbody's leg...
>
> Hall, James Norman, 1887–1951.
> Nordhoff, Charles Bernard, 1887–1947.
>> The hurricane, by Charles Nordhoff
> and James Norman Hall.
>
> Hall, James Norman, 1887–1951.
>> The tale of a shipwreck...
>
> Lang, Andrew, 1844–1912.
>> Ballads of books.
>
> Lang, Andrew, 1844–1912.
>> A batch of golfing papers.
>
> Lang, Andrew, 1844–1912, comp.
>> Blue poetry book.
>
> Lang, Andrew, 1844–1912.
>> Complete works.
>> Lang, Andrew, 1844–1912.
>>> Homer and anthropology, p.44–65.
>
> Marett, Robert Ranulph, 1866–1943.
>> Anthropology and the classics.
>
> Lang, Andrew, 1844–1912.
>> Homer and the epic.
>> Lang, Andrew, 1844–1912, tr.
> Homer.
>> Iliad; tr. by Andrew Lang.
>> Lang, Andrew, 1844–1912, tr.
> Homer.
>> Odyssey; tr. by Andrew Lang.
>> LANG, ANDREW, 1844–1912.
> Gosse, Sir Edmund William, 1849–1928.
>> Andrew Lang.
>> LANG, ANDREW, 1844–1912.
> James, Henry, 1843–1916.
>> Lang: a biography.

Thus the reader looking for Lang's original works or his compila-tions, such as the *Blue Poetry Book* and the *Red Fairy Book,* finds entries for them all together, arranged alphabetically by title, *Complete Works* following *Blue Poetry Book.* If he is interested in seeing whether or not the library has Lang's translation of *The Iliad* or *The Odyssey,* he finds the entry for it in its alphabetical place among the same group of cards, arranged by the title of the work, and, if there are entries for several works by the same author, alphabetically by title; thus Lang's translation of Homer's *The Iliad* follows Lang's *Complete Works.* After that are the biographies of Lang, arranged alphabetically by authors, James following Gosse. The advantage in this arrangement is that all of an author's works, whether written jointly with someone else or alone, whether originals or translations, are together in one file and all the works about him are together in another.

The reader finds author and title analytics filed in with entries for works published separately. Lang's *Homer and Anthropology* would come between his *Complete Works* and his *Homer and the Epic.* Sub-ject analytics would come with other works about him, in alphabetical place according to their authors.

Bible. Arrange Bible entries as follows.

I.   Whole Bible

1. As author
2. As subject

II.   New Testament
Whole:

1. As author
2. As subject

Individual books, alphabetically:

1. As author
2. As subject

III.   Old Testament
Whole:

1. As author
2. As subject

Individual books, alphabetically:

1. As author
2. As subject

IV.   Bible as first word of a title

Bible.

BIBLE.   COMMENTARIES.

BIBLE.   STUDY AND TEACHING.

Bible. New Testament.

BIBLE.   NEW TESTAMENT.   HISTORY.

Bible. New Testament. Acts.

BIBLE.   NEW TESTAMENT.   ACTS.

Bible. New Testament. Matthew.

Bible. Old Testament. Daniel.

Bible. Old Testament. Genesis.

Bible and the rights of labor.

Bible talks for heart and mind.

Compiler. *See* Author arrangement.

Compound names (A.L.A. 20b) "Arrange personal surnames compounded of two or more words after the simple surname, interfiled in alphabetical order with titles and other headings beginning with the same word."

> Smith, Woodrow.
> Smith College.
> Smith Hughes, Jack.
> Smith-Masters, Margaret Melville.

Congresses. *See* Numerical and chronological arrangement.

Editor. *See* Author arrangement.

Elisions (A.L.A. 6) "Arrange elisions as they are printed and not as if spelled in full. Treat as one word the contraction of two words resulting from an elision."

> Who owns America?
> Who reads what?
> Who'd shoot a genius?
> Who's who in American art?
> Whose constitution.

Figures. *See* Numerals.

Firm names (A.L.A. 22) "Arrange a firm name without forename, a compound firm name, or a phrase firm name, alphabetically with the titles and other headings following the same name as surname."

> Rand, Edward Kennard.
> Rand, Winifred.
> Rand, McNally and Company.

Randall, John Herman.
Randall-MacIver, David.

Wilson, Forrest.
Wilson, James Calmar.
Wilson, Margery.
Wilson, William Jerome.
Wilson and allied families.
Wilson & Greene Lumber Co. Inc.
Wilson (The H. W.) Company.
WILSON'S CREEK, BATTLE OF, 1861.
Wilstach, Frank Jenners.

Forename entries. "Arrange a forename entry after the surname entries of the same name, interfiling with titles and other headings beginning with the same word. Include compound forename entries. Alphabet with regard to all words, articles and prepositions included." (A.L.A. 18) "Disregard a numeral following a forename except when necessary to distinguish between forenames with the same designation." (A.L.A. 16b)

Charlemagne.
Charles, Robert Henry.
Charles d'Orleans.
Charles, duke of Burgundy.
Charles Edward, the Young Pretender.
Charles I, Emperor of Austria.
Charles V, Emperor of the Holy Roman Empire.
Charles VIII, King of France.
Charles I, King of Great Britain.
Charles II, King of Great Britain.
Charles XII, King of Sweden.
Charles the Bold.
Charles the Second.   (title of a book)
Charleston, S.C.
Charleston, historic and romantic.
Charleston, historic city of gardens.

Hyphened words (A.L.A. 11a;c) "Arrange hyphened words as separate words."

Happy home.
Happy-thought hall.
Happy thoughts.

"Arrange as one word, words with a hyphened prefix, such as, anti-, co-, inter-, mid-, non-, pan-, post-, pre-, pro-, re-, trans-, tri-, etc."

> Anti-defamation league.
> Bicentennial.
> Co-operative movement in India.
> Inter-parliamentary union from 1889–1939.
> Non-self governing territories.
> Pre-Raphaelite.
> Pro-British.

Illustrator. *See* Author arrangement.

Initial articles. *See* Articles.

Initials (A.L.A. 4) "*a*) Arrange an initial before a word beginning with the same initial letter.

"*b*) Arrange initials standing for names of organizations, broadcasting stations, airships, etc., whether punctuated or not, as initials and not as abbreviations, i.e., not as if spelled in full. For initials standing for geographical names, *see* Abbreviations.

. . . .

"*d*) Arrange initials standing for authors' names, whether inverted or not, alphabetically with initials standing for organizations or beginning a title, disregarding the inversion and punctuation."

> T., A. O., *pseud.*
> T. A. P. P. I.
> T. A. T.
> T., L. G.
> T., R. M.
> T V and electronics as a career.
> Tabb, John Bannister.
> Table decorations for all occasions.

Joint author. *See* Author arrangement.

Names with a prefix (A.L.A. 13) "*a*) Arrange a name with a prefix as one word. This includes names in which an article or a preposition is written as part of the name and is not transposed....

"*b*) Names beginning with the prefix M' and Mc are filed as if spelled Mac, because they are so pronounced. An explanatory reference should be made from the abbreviated form to the full form:

> M' (or Mc)
> Names beginning with M' or Mc are filed as if spelled Mac."

Debussy
De la Mare.
DELAWARE.
De Scheinitz.
DESERTS.
De Wilde.
Dickens.
DRIVERS, AUTOMOBILE.
DRUGS.
Du Bois.
Ducal palaces.
Du Chaillu.
Dugan.
Dunsany.
Du Puy.
Durant.
The lady and the panda.
La Farge.
La Gorce.
Laing.
McAlpine, Roy Kenneth.
Macartney, Carlile Aylmer.
Macaulay, Thomas Babington.
MacBride, Ernest William.
McBride, Robert Medill.
McCartney, Singerly.
MacDonald, James Ramsey.
Macdonald, Zilla K.
Machiavelli, Niccolo
Machine shop training course.
McIlwain, Charles Howard.
MacInnes, Duncan Arthur.
Macintire, Horace James.
McIntire, Samuel.
VALENTINE'S DAY.
Van Arsdale.
Van Buren.
Vanity fair.
Van Loon.
VARNISH AND VARNISHING.

Names compounded of two words (A.L.A. 12) "Arrange names consisting of two or more words, with or without a hyphen, as separate **words.**

"This includes names beginning with New, Old, East, North, Saint, San, Santa, etc."

> New citizens of India.
> NEW ENGLAND.
> New Jersey State Bar Association.
> New man in Soviet psychology.
> New York times.
> Newberry Library, Chicago.
> Newport, Cecil Archer.
> Newspaper reporting.

Numerical and chronological arrangement (A.L.A. 38) "A numerical or a chronological arrangement, rather than an alphabetical, should be made when number or date distinguishes between entries, or headings, otherwise identical."

> The Chronicles of America series, v. 51.
> The Chronicles of America series, v. 52.

> Congress of the Universities of the Empire, 5th, Cambridge, Eng., 1936.
> Congress of the Universities of the Empire, 6th, Oxford, 1948.

> U. S.   ARMY.   FIRST ARMY.
> U. S.   ARMY.   FIFTH ARMY.

Numerals (A.L.A. 9) "Arrange numerals in the titles of books as if spelled out in the language of the rest of the title. Spell numerals and dates as they are spoken, but omit the 'and' in spoken numerals except at a decimal point between two digits and in mixed numbers."

> EGYPT.
> 1848: chapters of German history.
> Ekblaw, Sidney E.
> ELECTRIC BATTERIES.

> Nilson, Arthur Reinhold.
> 1940: our finest hour.
> 1939: how the war began.
> 99 stanzas European.
> Norcross, Carl.

> On borrowed time.
> ONE-ACT PLAYS.
> 100,000,000 allies—if we choose.
> One hundred non-royalty one-act plays

One man caravan.
1001 mechanical facts made easy.
1000 questions and answers on T. B.
O'Neill, Eugene Gladstone.
OPERA.

Order of entries (A.L.A. 24b) "When the same word, or combination of words, is used as the heading of different kinds of entry, arrange the entries alphabetically by the word following the entry word. Disregard kind of entry and form of heading, *except* as follows: Arrange personal surnames before the other entries beginning with the same word... Subject entries under a personal or corporate name are to be filed immediately after the author entries for the same name... file the title entries after the subject entries."

Buffalo, William.
BUFFALO, AMERICAN.
Buffalo Bill's wild West show.
Buffalo, N. Y.

Manchester, Alfred.
Manchester, Arthur Livingston.
Manchester, Daniel W.
Manchester, Daniel Wilbert.
Manchester, Robert.
Manchester Cathedral.
Manchester city news.
Manchester, Eng.   Board of Education.

Authors' forenames need to be considered in filing only when there is more than one person with the same surname, in which case the personal headings are subarranged by the forenames; e.g., Manchester, *Daniel* follows Manchester, *Alfred* because *D* follows *A* in the alphabet.

Place arrangement (A.L.A. 32) "File entries beginning with the same geographical name in one alphabet, arranging by the word following the name, disregarding... punctuation....

"Subject entries are filed immediately after the author entries of the same heading.

"Two or more places of the same name are alphabeted by the distinguishing designation following the name."

New York (City)   Health Dept.
NEW YORK (CITY)   HEALTH DEPT.
New York (City)   Police Dept.
NEW YORK (CITY)   POOR.
New York (Colony)
NEW YORK (COLONY)
New York (Colony)   Council.
New York (County)   Court House Board.
New York (State)
NEW YORK (STATE)   GEOLOGY.
NEW YORK (STATE)   HISTORY.
New York Edison Company.
New York tribune.

U. S.   Dept. of <u>Agriculture.</u>
U. S.   Office of <u>Education.</u>
U. S.   Forest Service.
U. S.   HISTORY.
U. S.   President.
U. S.   PRESIDENT.
U. S.   Statutes.
U. S.   War Dept.
U. S.   WAR DEPT.
United States catalog.
UNITED STATES GRAIN CORPORATION.
United States Steel Corporation.

Washington and Jefferson College.
Washington College.
Washington Co., Ohio.
Washington Co., Pa.
Washington Co., Va.
WASHINGTON CO., VA.
Washington County reports, 1934.
Washington digest annotated, 1854 to date.
Washington, D.C.
Washington, D.C. Playground Association.
Washington Housing Association, Incorporated.
Washington in Lincoln's time.
Washington national monument.
Washington (State)   University.

Possessive case. *See* Punctuation marks.
Prefixes. *See* Names with a prefix.
Publisher. *See* Firm names.

Punctuation marks (A.L.A. 8) "In alphabeting titles, disregard punctuation marks and the apostrophe...."

Boys' book of photography.
Boys' life of Will Rogers.
Boy's Odyssey.
Boys of 1812.
Boys will be boys.

References (A.L.A. 36) "File *See also* references after entries of the same headings but before further subdivision of the same."

CHILDREN.
CHILDREN.   See also
CHILDREN.   CARE AND HYGIENE.
CHILDREN.   CARE AND HYGIENE.   See also

Subject arrangement (A.L.A. 35) "Arrange a subject, its subheads, etc., in the following order:

"1. Subject without subdivision.

"2. Form, subject and geographical subdivisions, inverted subject headings, and subjects followed by a parenthetical term interfiled in one alphabet, disregarding punctuation.

"3. Period divisions, arranged chronologically.

"4. Phrase subject headings, interfiled with titles and other headings beginning with the same word."

AGRICULTURAL RESEARCH.

AGRICULTURE.   CHINA.

AGRICULTURE, COOPERATIVE.

AGRICULTURE.   ECONOMIC ASPECTS.

AGRICULTURE.   HANDBOOKS, MANUALS, ETC.

AGRICULTURE.   INDIA.

AGRICULTURE.   PERIODICALS.

AGRICULTURE.   STATISTICS.

AGRICULTURE.   STUDY AND TEACHING.

Agriculture and economic progress.

AGRICULTURE AND STATE.

Biographical dictionary of the Anglo-Egyptian Sudan.

BIOGRAPHY.

BIOGRAPHY.   DICTIONARIES.

BIOGRAPHY (AS A LITERARY FORM)

Biography of an idea.

U. S. HISTORY.

U. S. HISTORY. BIBLIOGRAPHY.

U. S. HISTORY. SOURCES.

U. S. HISTORY. REVOLUTION.

U. S. HISTORY. 1783–1865.[3]

U. S. HISTORY. 1783–1809.

U. S. HISTORY. WAR OF 1812.

U. S. HISTORY. CIVIL WAR.

U. S. IMMIGRATION AND EMIGRATION.

Title arrangement (Pittsburgh, modified)[4] Title entries are arranged alphabetically, considering each word in turn; the initial article is disregarded, but all other articles and prepositions are to be regarded.

> In an unknown land.
> In and out of the old missions of California.
> In and under Mexico.
> In little America.
> In the Amazon jungle.
> In the days of giants.
> In the days of the guilds.
> In the footsteps of the Lincolns.
> In this our life.
> In tidewater Virginia.

> Why Europe fights.
> Why I believe in religion.
> Why the chimes rang.
> Why the weather.

If two or more titles under an author's name are the same, distinguish by edition or date, publisher, place of publication, illustrator, translator, editor, etc.

Translator. *See* Author arrangement.

Umlaut (A.L.A. 2) "Disregard the umlaut. Arrange ä, ö as a, o…In the case of headings with an umlaut in the first syllable, cross references should be made from, and to, the form spelled with an e."

United States. *See* Place arrangement; Subject arrangement.

Words spelled in two ways (A.L.A. 10a) "When title headings begin with a word that may be spelled in two ways (e.g., Labor and Labour)

---

[3]Inclusive periods file before subordinate periods.
[4]Pittsburgh, Carnegie Library, *Rules for Filing Cards* (5th ed.; Pittsburgh: Carnegie Library, 1932), p.31.

choose one spelling according to an accepted authority and file all titles under this form. Refer from the other spellings."

LABOR CONTRACT.
Labor in America.
LABOR LAWS AND LEGISLATION.
Labour production of the cotton textile industry.
Labor supply.

chapter XII

Related topics and miscellaneous information

Introduction. For the librarian of the small library there are a few closely related matters about which some information may be helpful. With a staff of one or possibly two, ordering, accessioning, classifying, cataloging, and preparing books for circulation are so closely associated that they are thought of almost as one process. This chapter contains some practical hints regarding these processes.

Acquisition of the books. The books are usually selected and ordered by the librarian, although a committee of the board of a public library may make suggestions and in rare cases place the orders. In most schools the librarian prepares the order but it is sent out by the principal, superintendent, or school purchasing office. When the books and the bill are received, the bill is checked with the books to be sure that the titles and editions received are those which were ordered. Some librarians write the name of the dealer from whom the book is purchased, the date it is received, and the cost in the inner margin of the book on the right-hand page following the title page, writing it parallel to the sewing of the book. This information is useful when one is examining a book with reference to having it rebound, or to seeing how long it has been in the library when one is checking its use with the time it has been available for circulation.

Weeding the book collection. Before beginning to classify and catalog an old library, weed the collection, removing books that are out of date, worn out, unsuitable for that particular library, have very poor print, or have been superseded by a better book. In doing this it is well for the inexperienced librarian to seek the guidance of a trained and experienced librarian, or to check with the best printed book selection aids in the field represented in that library. Books that need mending or rebinding should be put in good physical condition before being cataloged.

Mechanical processes. After checking the bill for a new book, one should cut the pages and open the book correctly, i.e., take a few pages at the front and at the back alternately and press them down gently against the covers, until the middle of the book is reached. This makes it easier to open and read the book and minimizes the danger of breaking its back.

The next step is to put in the mark of ownership, which usually means stamping certain pages of the book with an embossing, perforating, or rubber stamp that gives the name of the library. Stamp the page following the title page and a certain arbitrary right-hand page, e.g., page 89. If book plates are used, they are pasted on the inside of the front cover and no stamp is necessary.

Accessioning. When these mechanical processes are completed, the next task is to accession the book. Some librarians consider this process essential for the library records and some do not. The records of the library usually include information as to the total number of bound volumes in the library, and they may include the number of volumes in the different classes; e.g., a library of 5000 volumes may have one hundred to two hundred books on history. Besides the total number of bound volumes in the library, record of the number of volumes which were added the last year, the last month, etc., may be desired. The accession number is a serial number given to each bound volume as it is added to the library. It is useful in identifying books from the book card when charging or discharging books—e.g., number 1312 means a certain book—and if there is more than one volume in a set, it represents a specific volume.

One of the best accession records for the small library, especially if there are frequent changes in personnel, is the book accession record. Such books may be purchased from any of the library supply houses. The lines in an accession record are numbered consecutively, beginning with one. The entry descriptive of each volume or copy of a book is written on a separate line, and the number of that line becomes the accession number of that volume or copy. This accession number should be written in each volume or copy of the book on the first right-hand page after the title page, in the center of the lower margin about one inch from the bottom, or as nearly in this place as possible considering the printing on the page. The accession number should also be written on one other page, e.g., the page which is stamped. By means of the accession number one can turn at once to the description of the book in the accession book. Since entries in the accession book are dated, it serves as a chronological list of all the books the library has ever owned. It shows how many and what books have been added to the library during any specified length of time, from whom they were purchased, and what they cost.

To accession is to write in the accession book under the proper column heading: (1) the date of the bill of the book, or if there is no bill, the date on which the book is being accessioned; (2) the author heading as found on the title page; (3) the brief title of the book; (4) the publisher in abbreviated form as on a catalog card; (5) the date from the title page or, if none, the copyright date; (6) the volume number; (7) the name of the dealer through whom the book was purchased; and (8) the cost of the book to the library. Some accession books give more items than these, but these are the essential ones. Follow rules for cataloging in giving the title, capitalizing, etc. If the book is a gift, give the donor's name instead of the dealer's, and use the word *gift* instead of cost. Use ditto marks—one ditto mark to a column—where items for successive books are the same. Give the date of accessioning (month, day, and year) on the top line of each page of the accession book. If a page is not filled during one day, give the new date on the line for the first entry made later. Since the source, date, and cost are the only information which the accession book gives that the shelf list ordinarily does not, these items may be added to the shelf-list cards instead of keeping an accession book.

Cataloging routine. The first step in the cataloging process is to order the cards if the printed cards of the Library of Congress or of the H. W. Wilson Company are used. If printed cards are not used, the first step is to classify and assign subject headings, processes described in Chapters I and II. In either case, as soon as the classification number is determined, it should be written in pencil on the page following the title page, about one inch from the top of the page and one inch from the hinge of the book. If the number is placed too close to the top or the hinge, it may be cut off when the book is rebound.

The next step is to decide on the form of the heading for the main entry and for other added entries besides subject entries. Check with the name authority file or the catalog to insure consistency in headings and search the aids if the name is new to the catalog and there is no printed card for the book. If book numbers, which are discussed in Chapter I, are used, they are assigned as soon as the heading for the main entry is determined. The book number is written below the classification number on the page following the title page. If there are printed cards, they are checked with the book to be sure they match; and if there are no printed cards, the items to be included on the cards are decided upon.

The third step is to type the main card, including the tracing for the added cards, or to add the headings and call number and make any changes which may be necessary on the printed cards. If there are no printed cards, the added entry cards and the shelf-list card are typed and revised. The book card and the book pocket are typed at the same time that the catalog and shelf-list cards are typed. The book card should have the call number typed in the upper left-hand corner, the accession number (if one is used) in the upper right-hand corner; the surname of the author or full heading, if a corporate author, on the line below the call number, and the title below that. Indent the first letter of the title to the third space to the right, to make both author and title more prominent.

When an added copy is acquired by the library, it is only necessary to remove the shelf-list card from the tray and add the accession number (or the source, date, and cost of the new copy) and refile the card, since no change is made on the catalog cards. On the other hand, when another volume is added to the library, notation of the new volume must be added to the catalog cards as well as to the shelf-list card. When a new edition is added, it is necessary to catalog it as a new book, except that the same classification number and, as a rule, the same subject headings will be used for the new edition as for the old one.

After each new book order is cataloged, or once a week in a library buying books continuously, the catalog and shelf-list cards should be sorted, counted, and recorded for the annual report. They are then filed above the rod in the catalog and shelf list respectively, the filing is revised, the rod pulled out, and the cards are dropped and locked in the trays.

Marking the spines of books. Books of nonfiction should have their call numbers written on the backs for greater convenience in locating a given book or in returning it to the shelf. The call number should be placed at the same distance from the bottom of all books for the sake of ease in locating books and the appearance of the shelves. A stiff card with this distance marked on it should be used as a guide. One and a half inches from the bottom of the book usually avoids any printing and is a convenient height. The process of marking may be outlined as follows:

1 Mark the place to be occupied by the call number, noting the exact place where each line begins if the call number consists of two lines.
2 Remove the sizing by painting over the spot with acetone or shellac.
3 Write the call number in white ink or with an electric stylus and transfer paper at the place marked. For light colored books use black ink or dark transfer paper.
4 Cover the lettering with a thin coat of white shellac.

Make the figures of the call number vertical, without any flourishes, and round, not angular, so that they may be easily read and so that there may be less variation when the lettering is done by different workers.

Check list of preparation processes.

Librarian:	1 Check books with the bill.
Clerical assistant:	2 Write in each book the name of the dealer, date received in the library, and cost. (This step may be omitted.)
	3 Cut pages.
	4 Open correctly.
	5 Stamp with mark of ownership unless book plate is used.
	6 Accession. (This process may be omitted.)
Librarian:	7 Order printed cards. (Many libraries order the printed cards, especially for new books known to be in print, when they order the book.)
	8 Classify and assign subject headings, making note of them on a slip. (If printed cards are available, compare suggested classification number and headings with the shelf list and library's record of subject headings.)
	9 Decide upon the added entries other than subject entries.
	10 Determine heading for author and such added entries as editor, translator, illustrator. (If printed cards are used, compare forms of names with those in catalog or name authority list.)

	11 Adapt printed cards or type main card and shelf-list card.
	12 Revise these typed cards.
Clerical assistant:	13 Type added cards, book card, and items on book pocket.
Librarian:	14 Revise typed cards and book pocket.
Clerical assistant:	15 Paste in book pocket, date slip, and book plate (if used).
	16 Mark book on spine, put book card in pocket, and put book out for use.
Librarian:	17 Sort cards and count for annual report.
Clerical assistant:	18 File cards in shelf list and catalog trays above rod.
Librarian:	19 Revise filing and lock cards in trays.

Withdrawals. When a book is added to the library it is noted in various records; when it is withdrawn from the library, those records must be changed. If, for instance, a book wears out and is to be replaced by a new copy, note is made on the shelf-list card that that particular copy has been withdrawn from the library, and note is made of the addition of the new copy. Since the catalog cards do not show how many copies of a given title are in the library, withdrawing a book does not affect the catalog so long as other copies remain. If, however, there is only one copy of the book and it is not to be replaced, the catalog cards must be taken out of the catalog, and the shelf-list card (after having the *withdrawal note,* the abbreviation *W* and the date, written on it, e.g., "W 5-17-52") must also be removed from the shelf list. Some libraries give the cause, e.g., "W 5-17-52 Worn out." If one wishes to make a study of the number of books being lost by borrowers, being worn out, etc., with reference to a possible change in policy, it is worth while to include in the note the cause of withdrawal.

If it is a volume which is being withdrawn, note should be made, usually in pencil, on the catalog card that such and such a volume is lacking. If it is to be replaced as soon as it can be secured, this penciled note can be easily erased when the new copy of the missing volume is added to the library.

If the library keeps an accession record, the librarian *may* also write the withdrawal note in the accession book in the *remarks column.* And when the accession book is consulted for any purpose, there is a record of whether or not the book is still in the library and if it is not, the date on which it was withdrawn.

Occasionally it will happen that the book being withdrawn is the only one entered under that name, under that subject, etc. If that is the case, not only should the catalog cards and the shelf-list card be removed, but the name or subject cross references to and from these headings and the corresponding cards in the name and subject authority files should be withdrawn. If a book is to be replaced as soon as funds are available, the cards may be withdrawn from the files, properly labeled, and put aside to be used later.

If there are more copies or volumes in the library, after making the proper withdrawal note on the shelf-list card, refile the card in the shelf list.

If the book withdrawn is the only copy or volume, the shelf-list card for that book, with the withdrawal note on it, should be filed alphabetically by author in a special file called a *withdrawal file*. This file will be found a great convenience when some question comes up as to what has become of a book, whether or not the library ever had a copy, etc. The cards do not need to be kept indefinitely, but might well be kept for five years.

A count of books withdrawn is to be made, just as the count of books added is made. The annual report should show the number of books in the library at the beginning of the year for which the report is being made, the number added during that period, the number withdrawn, and the number in the library at the end of the year.

All library marks of ownership should be removed or "Withdrawn by—(name of library)" should be written or stamped in the book before selling it for old paper or giving it away. Some libraries are governed by definite laws affecting disposal of books.

The first time that a book is withdrawn, the policy should be carefully worked out, note made of the procedure to be followed, and a withdrawal file set up.

Where to catalog. The smallest library should have a place in which to catalog, even though it is only a desk or table in a corner. Have shelves nearby on which may be kept the necessary cataloging tools and aids and the books to be cataloged. Label these shelves, so that it will be possible to tell at a glance what stage of preparation the books are in. Leave any unfinished work clearly marked so that it may be resumed with a minimum loss of time. A quarter of an hour or half an hour may be used advantageously to accession a dozen books, to mark ten on the back, to order printed cards, or the like. The longer periods may be used for determining the form of the author's name, classifying and assigning subject headings, or typing the main cards. The added

cards can be typed by any good typist if he is given adequate instruc-
tion and supervision at first.

Cataloging supplies. A few suggestions as to the supplies which will
be found necessary in cataloging a collection as described in this manual
may prove useful.

Accession record book. Any of the simplified accession record books
which are sold by Demco,[1] Gaylord,[2] or Library Bureau[3] will be found
satisfactory. Accession books are listed according to the number of lines
they contain. As each volume in the library requires one line, the
number of lines desired depends upon the number of volumes on hand
and the approximate number that will be added in the next two or
three years. Loose-leaf accession books, which may be used on a typewriter, are also available from the firms mentioned above.

Catalog cards. Cards of the same quality may be used for the shelf
list and for the catalog. Medium-weight cards are best as they are strong
enough to stand the wear, without taking up unnecessary room or adding unnecessary weight to the card cabinets. The medium weight is
similar to that of the printed cards, and for that reason is much more
satisfactory if the library uses printed cards in addition to its own. It
pays to buy the best catalog cards, and it is important to use only one
kind so that all the cards in the catalog will be of the same size
and thickness and, therefore, can be handled more quickly in the trays.
For fiction at least three cards for each book, namely, author, title, and
shelf list, will be necessary. For nonfiction, if many analytical entries
are made, an average of five cards for each book is the minimum number to count on. Catalog cards come in boxes of 500 or 1000 and cost less
if bought in this or larger numbers.

Medium-weight cards, number 263-2, unruled, are the most suitable
cards from Demco. Medium-weight cards, number 311, unruled, from
Gaylord are most suitable. Medium-weight cards, number 33080 cm
unruled from the Library Bureau are most suitable.

Catalog guide cards. Guide cards should be inserted at intervals of
about an inch. Satisfactory plain buff guide cards, punched for a catalog
tray rod, cut in thirds or halves (i.e., the tab is one-third or one-half
the width of the card) may be purchased in packages of one hundred

[1]Demco Library Supplies, Madison, Wis. and New Haven, Conn.
[2]Gaylord Bros., Inc., Syracuse, N. Y. and Stockton, Calif.
[3]Library Bureau, Remington Rand, Inc., New York 10, N. Y.

or one thousand. The Library Bureau has number 4310 cm; Gaylord has Wearever guide cards; Demco has number 601 cut in thirds. All of these are plain, punched for tray rod, and cut in thirds or halves.

Gaylord's titled tab guides, cut in halves, catalog number 305; the Library Bureau's angle tab visible name guides, half cut, catalog number 45529 cm; and Demco's visible angle tab insertable catalog guides, cut in halves, number 644, are good. Demco also has insertable catalog guides, with left, center, and right cut tabs, catalog number 622. These visible angle guide cards are, as is to be expected, more expensive than the others.

Demco, Gaylord, and the Library Bureau all have center cut sets of shelf-list guide cards for libraries using the Dewey Decimal Classification. Demco has number 640 of gray pressboard and 640-C buff celluloided; Gaylord, number 91 of pressboard; and the Library Bureau number 431-10SL buff celluloided.

Miscellaneous supplies. If extension cards for the catalog are to be tied to the first card, use heavy linen thread, which may be purchased at any dry goods store.

The special supplies needed for marking call numbers on the spine of the books are an electric pencil or an electric stylus and transfer paper, which may be obtained from Demco, Gaylord, or the Library Bureau. Transfer paper may be secured in white, gold, and dark blue or black. Use the white or gold on dark colored books, the dark paper on light colored books. Call numbers may also be put on the spine with white ink; black ink is used on the light colored books. Library Bureau has "David's White Letterine"; Demco, "Radiant White Ink"; and Gaylord, "Gaylord's White Ink." All three firms have Higgins Black Engrossing Ink, which is good for marking light colored books. A bottle of acetone is needed to remove the sizing from the back of the book before applying the ink; and a bottle of white shellac to put over the ink when it is dry. Any good pen point, the type depending upon the personal choice of the person doing the lettering, is satisfactory. Usually a bowl pointed pen is preferred.

The American Library Association's *Lettering on Library Books*[4] gives practical instructions about lettering books on the back and includes a sample alphabet and pictures of the process.

---

[4]American Library Association, *Lettering on Library Books* (Chicago: A.L.A., 1919).

A good steel eraser or a razor blade with a bar top with which to erase words, or more especially letters, is a necessity. Gaylord, Library Bureau, and Demco have steel erasers. A good bar pencil and ink eraser is also very useful, as well as a typewriter eraser.

A typewriter is a necessity in any library for the typing of cards for the books and other material for which printed cards are not available, for typing book orders and business letters, and for typing book lists, etc. Get a typewriter having a removable platen with special card attachment and then buy an additional platen for use in typing letters, etc. If subject headings are to be in red, bichrome typewriter ribbons will be necessary. Royal, L. C. Smith-Corona, and the semi-noiseless Remington are very good typewriters for card work as well as other typing.

Card catalog cabinets. Although there are many firms making card catalog cabinets, it pays to get the best, such as those manufactured by Demco, Gaylord, and the Library Bureau, whose catalog cabinets are especially well adapted for library use. These firms have cabinets varying in size from one to sixty trays, and their catalogs give an estimate of the number of cards which the cabinets of different sizes will hold. Knowing the number of books in the library and the approximate number of new books added each year, one can easily decide by counting five cards to a book the size of cabinet needed.

Card catalog cabinets should have standard trays and should be purchased from the same firm so that they will match exactly and so that the trays will be interchangeable when cards are shifted with the expansion of the catalog. Gaylord trays are about fourteen inches long; Demco, fifteen inches; Library Bureau, seventeen inches. Each tray should have a follower-block to hold the cards erect when the tray is only partially filled, and a rod which runs through the holes in the cards and locks them into the tray. It is also very important to have the cards fit the tray exactly so that they will stand straight, drop in easily, and remain in alignment for the rod. The three firms mentioned have trays which meet these requirements. Catalog trays should be only two-thirds full if the cards are to be consulted easily. The shelf-list cards may be filed in one or more trays of a catalog cabinet.

If the library can afford it, the sectional cabinet is best, as added units are less expensive than the same number of trays in a separate cabinet and the sections fit together and form one cabinet. If as many as eight or nine trays are needed or will be needed relatively soon, it will pay to buy the sectional catalog cabinet, which may be bought in units of five, ten, or fifteen trays from Gaylord or Library Bureau. The same base and top will serve for several units.

Sample catalog cards

I Wilson printed catalog cards

1 Main entry

530   **Blackwood, Oswald Hance,** 1888-
High school physics, by Oswald H. Blackwood, Wilmer B.
Herron and William C. Kelly.   Ginn 1951
670p illus

"The content is organized in accord with the main branches of the
subject,—mechanics, heat, electricity, sound, light, and electronics,—
and the closely integrated chapters under each main branch develop the
important aspects of that division. At the end of each division and of
each chapter there are carefully constructed reviews, problems, and
tests." Preface

1 Physics   I-II Jt.   auths.   III Title   530

2-29-52   ◯   (W)   The H. W. Wilson Company

2 Subject card with heading printed on

> **PHYSICS**
>
> 530   Blackwood, Oswald Hance, 1888-
>   High school physics, by Oswald H. Blackwood, Wilmer B.
>   Herron and William C. Kelly.   Ginn 1951
>   670p illus
>
>   "The content is organized in accord with the main branches of the
>   subject,—mechanics, heat, electricity, sound, light, and electronics,—
>   and the closely integrated chapters under each main branch develop the
>   important aspects of that division. At the end of each division and of
>   each chapter there are carefully constructed reviews, problems, and
>   tests." Preface
>
>   1 Physics   I-II Jt.   auths.   III Title   530
>
>   2-29-52   ◯   (W) The H. W. Wilson Company

3 Added entry for joint author

> **Herron, Wilmer B**   jt. auth.
>
> 530   Blackwood, Oswald Hance, 1888-
>   High school physics, by Oswald H. Blackwood, Wilmer B.
>   Herron and William C. Kelly.   Ginn 1951
>   670p illus
>
>   "The content is organized in accord with the main branches of the
>   subject,—mechanics, heat, electricity, sound, light, and electronics,—
>   and the closely integrated chapters under each main branch develop the
>   important aspects of that division. At the end of each division and of
>   each chapter there are carefully constructed reviews, problems, and
>   tests." Preface
>
>   1 Physics   I-II Jt.   auths.   III Title   530
>
>   2-29-52   ◯   (W) The H. W. Wilson Company

4 Added entry for title

    High school physics

530 **Blackwood, Oswald Hance, 1888-**
   High school physics, by Oswald H. Blackwood, Wilmer B.
  Herron and William C. Kelly. Ginn 1951
   670p illus

    "The content is organized in accord with the main branches of the
  subject,—mechanics, heat, electricity, sound, light, and electronics,—
  and the closely integrated chapters under each main branch develop the
  important aspects of that division. At the end of each division and of
  each chapter there are carefully constructed reviews, problems, and
  tests." Preface

  1 Physics I-II Jt.   auths. III Title   530

  2-29-52   ○ (W) The H. W. Wilson Company

5 Shelf-list card

530 **Blackwood, Oswald Hance, 1888-**
   High school physics, by Oswald H. Blackwood, Wilmer B.
  Herron and William C. Kelly. Ginn 1951
   670p illus

                   530

  2-29-52   ○ (W) The H. W. Wilson Company

II Library of Congress printed catalog cards

6 Main entry

Cady, Ernest.
We adopted three.   New York, Sloane ₍1952₎
250 p.   22 cm.

1. Adoption.   ɪ. Title.

HV875.C25   362.73   52–10307 †

Library of Congress   ₍25₎

7 Main entry

530
B62   Bischof, George P
Atoms at work; a preview of science.   Drawings by Jere
Donovan.   ₍1st ed.₎   New York, Harcourt, Brace ₍1951₎
130 p.   illus.   21 cm.

1. Physics—~~Juvenile literature~~.   ɪ. Title.

QC25.B5   530   51—10007

Library of Congress   ₍52x15₎

8 Added entry for subject

```
530        PHYSICS.
B62      Bischof, George P
                Atoms at work; a preview of science.  Drawings by Jere
         Donovan.  ₁1st ed.₁  New York, Harcourt, Brace ₁1951₁
                130 p.  illus.  21 cm.




                1. Physics—Juvenile literature.    ɪ. Title.

                QC25.B5              530              51—10007

                Library of Congress        ₁52x15₁
```

9 Added entry for title

```
530        Atoms at work.
B62      Bischof, George P
                Atoms at work; a preview of science.  Drawings by Jere
         Donovan.  ₁1st ed.₁  New York, Harcourt, Brace ₁1951₁
                130 p.  illus.  21 cm.




                1. Physics—Juvenile literature.    ɪ. Title.

                QC25.B5              530              51—10007

                Library of Congress        ₁52x15₁
```

10 Shelf-list card

530
B62   Bischof, George P
            Atoms at work; a preview of science. Drawings by Jere
        Donovan. ₁1st ed.₁ New York, Harcourt, Brace ₁1951₁
            130 p. illus. 21 cm.

B. & T. 10-5-53 $3.50

            1. Physics—Juvenile literature.   I. Title.

            QC25.B5   530   51—10007

            Library of Congress   ₁52x15₁

III Main entries

11 Compound surname with hyphen

            Fraser-Tytler, *Sir* William Kerr, 1886–
                Afghanistan; a study of political developments in Central
            and southern Asia. 2d ed. London, New York, Oxford
            University Press, 1953.
                xiv, 348 p. illus., maps (part fold.) 23 cm.
                Bibliography: p. 333–336.

            1. Afghanistan--Hist. 2. Eastern question (Central Asia)

            DS356.F7 1953   958   53–1888

            Library of Congress   ₁5₁

12 Compound surname without hyphen

García Lorca, Federico, 1899-1936.
    The gypsy ballads; translated by Rolfe Humphries, with
3 historical ballads.   Bloomington, Indiana University
Press, 1953.

    64 p.   24 cm.   (Indiana University poetry series)

    ɪ. Title.

    PQ6613.A763P72   861.6   53-9826

    Library of Congress   ɪ7ɪ

13 Married woman's name—maiden name in parentheses

Gilbert, Katharine (Everett) 1886-1952.
    A history of esthetics, by Katharine Everett Gilbert and
Helmut Kuhn.   Rev. and enl.   Bloomington, Indiana University Press, 1953.

    xxi, 613 p.   22 cm.

    Includes bibliographies.

    1. Aesthetics—Hist.   ɪ. Kuhn, Helmut, 1899-   joint author.

    BH81.G5   1953   *101   701.17   53-7022

    Library of Congress   ɪ10ɪ

14 Nobleman entered under his title

Chorley, Robert Samuel Theodore Chorley, *baron*, 1895–
　　Leading cases in the law of banking, by Lord Chorley
　and P. E. Smart.   London, Pitman ₁1953₁
　　329 p.   23 cm.

　　1. Banking law—Gt. Brit.—Cases.　　ɪ Smart, P. E., joint author.
ɪɪ. Title.
　　　　　　　　　　○　　332.1　　　　　　53–24018 ‡
　　Library of Congress　　　　₁1₁

---

15 Real name as entry with pseudonym in title

Norway, Nevil Shute, 1899–
　　The far country, by Nevil Shute ₁pseud.₁　New York, Mor-
　row, 1952.
　　　343 p.   21 cm.

　　ɪ. Title.

　　PZ3.N83Far　　　　　　　　　　　52–9696 ‡
　　　　　　　　　　　　○
　　Library of Congress　　　₁10₁

---

16 Surname with prefix

De Voto, Bernard Augustine, 1897–
    The course of empire; with maps by Erwin Raisz. Boston, Houghton Mifflin, 1952.

xvii, 647 p. maps (part col.) 22 cm.

Bibliographical references included in "Notes" (p. 561–631)

1. North America—Disc. & explor. 2. U. S.—Territorial expansion. 3. Indians of North America—Hist.   I. Title.

E179.5.D4   973.1   52—5261

Library of Congress   ₍53m³30₎

---

17 Personal name heading with unused forename

Bate, H   Maclear, 1908–
    Report from Formosa. ₍1st ed.₎ New York, Dutton, 1952.

290 p. illus. 21 cm.

1. Formosa—Pol. & govt.   I. Title.

DS895.F75B3   *951.24 952.9   52–5316 ‡

Library of Congress   ₍20₎

18 Government publication—government agency as author

> **Gt. Brit.** *Ministry of Housing and Local Government.*
>   Memorandum on the control of mineral working. London, H. M. Stationery Off., 1951.
>
>   60 p. 25 cm.
>
>   At head of title: Ministry of Town and Country Planning.
>
>
>
>   1. Mining law—Gt. Brit.
>
>   52–32798 rev ‡
>
>   Library of Congress   ○   [r53b2]

19 Government publication—person as author

> **Harrison, Jack Edward,** 1924–
>   Preliminary report on the Jo Reynolds area, Lawson-Dumont district, Clear Creek County, Colorado, by J. E. Harrison and B. F. Leonard. Washington, 1952.
>
>   9 p. maps (1 fold. col.) diagr., fold. plan. 27 cm. (Geological Survey circular 213)
>
>   Part of illustrative matter in pocket.
>   "Literature cited": p. 8–9.
>
>   1. Petrology—Colorado—Clear Creek Co. 2. Uraninite.   I. Leonard, Benjamin Franklin, 1921–   joint author. II. Title: Jo Reynolds area, Lawson-Dumont district, Clear Creek County, Colorado.   (Series: U. S. Geological Survey. Circular 213)
>
>   QE75.C5   no. 213   553.49   G S 53–71
>   ——— ——— Copy 2.   TN490.U7H3
>   U. S. Geol. Survey. Libr.   ○
>   for Library of Congress   [3]†

20 Firm as author

Andersen (Arthur) and Company.
    Oil and gas Federal income tax manual. 7th ed., rev. to Jan. 1, 1953. Prepared by and for the use of members of the staff of the Natural Resources Division of Arthur Andersen & Co. ₍Chicago₎ 1953.

    251 p. 23 cm.

    1. Petroleum industry and trade—Accounting. 2. Income tax—U. S.—Law. ɪ. Title.

                        665.5   53–24020 ‡

    Library of Congress   ₍1₎

---

21 Association as author

American Dental Association. *Bureau of Economic Research and Statistics.*
    Distribution of dentists in the United States by state, region, district, and county. Chicago ₍1953₎

    62 p. 25 cm.

    1946 ed. by the Economics Committee, American Dental Association.

    1. Dentists—U. S.   ɪ. American Dental Association. Economics Committee. Distribution of dentists in the United States. ɪɪ. Title.

    RK34.U6A52   617.6   53–25622 ‡

    Library of Congress   ₍1₎

22 Name of conference as heading including number of conference, place and date held

---

National Conference on Higher Education. *6th, Chicago, 1951.*

Charting the course for American higher education in a period of partial mobilization; reports of the study groups in the Sixth Annual National Conference on Higher Education, April 2, 3, 4, 1951, Chicago, Illinois. Washington, Dept. of Higher Education, National Education Association of the United States ₁1951₁

79 p.   23 cm.

1. Education, Higher—1945-   2. Education, Higher—Congresses.   i. Title.

LB2301.N425   1951b   378.06373   52–1159

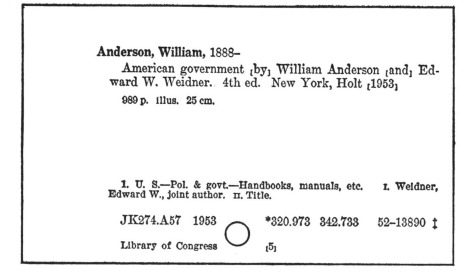

Library of Congress   ₁7₁

---

23 Main entry under first author, both authors in title

Anderson, William, 1888–

American government ₁by₁ William Anderson ₁and₁ Edward W. Weidner. 4th ed. New York, Holt ₁1953₁

989 p. illus. 25 cm.

1. U. S.—Pol. & govt.—Handbooks, manuals, etc.   i. Weidner, Edward W., joint author. ii. Title.

JK274.A57   1953   *320.973 342.733   52–13890 ‡

Library of Congress   ₁5₁

24 Compiler in author position

Creamer, Jack B   *comp.*
    Twenty-two stories about horses and men; with decora-
tions by Ned King. New York, Coward-McCann ₁1953₎
    309 p. illus. 22 cm.

    1. Horses—Legends and stories.   ɪ. Title.

QL795.H7C7   636.1   53–5300 ‡

Library of Congress   ₁20₎

25 Editor in author position

Botkin, Benjamin Albert, 1901–   *ed.*
    A treasury of western folklore. Foreword by Bernard
De Voto. New York, Crown Publishers ₁1951₎
    806 p. illus. 22 cm.

    1. Folk-lore—The West.   ɪ. Title.

GR109.B6   398   51—12013 ‡

Library of Congress   ₁a53v²10₎

26 Main entry for an adaptation

```
398
M16   Macleod, Mary, d. 1914.
          The book of King Arthur and his noble knights:
      stories from Sir Thomas Malory's Morte Darthur.
      New York, F. A. Stokes Co. ₍n. d.₎
          370 p.  illus.
```

27 Main entry for dramatization of another's work

```
812
C54   Chodorov, Jerome.
          Junior miss, a new comedy by Jerome Chodorov
      and Joseph Fields, based on the book by Sally Ben-
      son.    Random ₍1942₎
          209 p.
```

28 Anonymous classic—main entry

Arabian nights.
 The portable Arabian nights; edited and with an introd.,
by Joseph Campbell. ₍John Payne, translator₎ New York,
Viking Press, 1952.

 xlv, 786 p. 17 cm. (The Viking portable library)

 ɪ.ʳCampbell, Joseph, 1904–   ed.

 PJ7715.P3 1952   [398.21] 892.73   52–7413

 Library of Congress   ₍12₎

29 Sacred book—main entry

220
B58   **Bible.**
   A new translation of the Bible, containing the
Old and New Testaments ₍by₎ James Moffatt. ₍Con-
cordance ed.₎   Harper ₍c1950₎
   2 v. in 1. illus.

30 Periodical title in author position—main entry for book

Ladies' home journal.
 Profile of youth, by members of the staff of the Ladies'
home journal; edited by Maureen Daly. ₁1st ed.₎ Philadelphia, Lippincott ₁1951₎
 256 p. 21 cm.

 1. Youth—U. S.   ɪ. Daly, Maureen, 1921-   ed. ɪɪ. Title.

 HQ796.L23   301.1584   51—10016

 Library of Congress   ₁51d²15₎

---

31 Periodical title in author position—main entry for book

Ladies' home journal (Periodical)
 Profile of youth, by members of the staff of the Ladies'
home journal; ed. by Maureen Daly.   Lippincott 1951
 256p

   Twelve profiles of teen-agers, from all backgrounds and parts of the
country. With these are ten general articles on teen-age life covering
such topics as: going steady, necking, driving, sex education, trade
schools, teen-age cruelty, blanket parties, parked cars, social inferiority,
subsidized marriage, teen-age fads and fun

 1 Adolescence   2 Conduct of life   3 Youth   ɪ Daly, Maureen, 1921-
ed.   ɪɪ Title   ₁136.7₎ 136.73 or 301.15

 8-24-51   (W)   The H. W. Wilson Company

---

32 Main entry for paper-bound book

Heard, Gerald, 1889–
    Is another world watching? The riddle of the flying
saucers. A special ed., rev. and with new material. New
York, Bantam Books ₁1953₎

    182 p.   17 cm.   (A Bantam book, 1079)

    First published in London in 1950 under title: The riddle of the
flying saucers.

    1. Flying saucers.   ɪ. Title.
                             Full name: Henry FitzGerald Heard.

    TL789.H4   1953   ◯   *629.13   629.133   53–26428 ‡

    Library of Congress   ₁1₎

33 Composite book—main entry under title

Civil liberties under attack, by Henry Steele Commager ₁and
others. Clair Wilcox, editor₎ Philadelphia, University of
Pennsylvania Press, 1951.

    xl, 155 p.   23 cm.   (Publications of the William J. Cooper Founda-
tion, Swarthmore College)

    Contents.—The pragmatic necessity for freedom, by H. S. Com-
mager.—Progress in civil rights, by R. K. Carr.—Investigations of
radicalism and laws against subversion, by Z. Chafee, Jr.—Security,
secrecy, and the advancement of science, by W. Gellhorn.—Censorship
and the arts, by C. Bok.—Freedom in education, by J. P. Baxter, ɪɪɪ.

    1. Civil rights—U. S.   2. Liberty.   ɪ. Commager, Henry Steele,
1902–   ɪɪ. Wilcox, Clair, 1898–   ed.   (Series: Swarthmore
College, Swarthmore, Pa.   William J. Cooper Foundation lectures)

    JC599.U5C56   ◯   323.4   51–12905 rev

    Library of Congress   ₁r53q³15₎

34 Composite book—main entry under editor—first contributor mentioned in title

Hoffman, George Walter, 1914-   *ed.*
    A geography of Europe. Contributors: Nels A. Bengtson
₍and others₎ New York, Ronald Press Co. ₍1953₎

    ix, 775 p. illus., maps. 24 cm.

    Includes bibliographies.

1. Europe—Descr. & trav.—1945-   ɪ. Title.

D907.H6   ◯   914   53–5719

Library of Congress   ₍20₎

35 Main entry for compilation without an editor

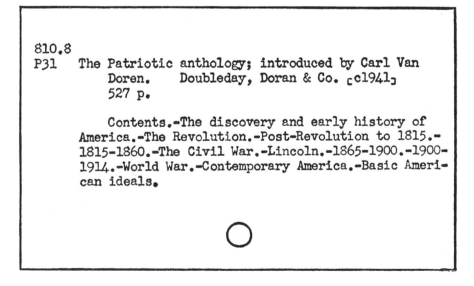

810.8
P31   The Patriotic anthology; introduced by Carl Van
        Doren.   Doubleday, Doran & Co. ₍c1941₎
        527 p.

        Contents.-The discovery and early history of
    America.-The Revolution.-Post-Revolution to 1815.-
    1815-1860.-The Civil War.-Lincoln.-1865-1900.-1900-
    1914.-World War.-Contemporary America.-Basic Ameri-
    can ideals.

36 Encyclopedia—main entry under title

> The **Columbia** encyclopedia, edited by William Bridgwater
> and Elizabeth J. Sherwood. 2d ed. New York, Columbia
> University Press, 1950.
>
> 2203 p. 31 cm.
>
>
>
>   1. Encyclopedias and dictionaries.   I. Bridgwater, William, ed.
> II. Columbia university.
>
>   AC5.C725   1950   031   50—11218
>   Library of Congress   [53x²10]

37 Continuation—main entry under title gives date of first volume, frequency, etc.

> The **Journal** of teacher education.   v. 1–
> Jan./Mar. 1950–
> [Washington]
>
>   v. 25 cm. quarterly.
>
>   Published by the National Commission on Teacher Education and
> Professional Standards.
>
>
>   1. Teachers, Training of—Period.   I National Education Asso-
> ciation of the United States. National Commission on Teacher Edu-
> cation and Professional Standards.
>
>   LB1705.N27   370.73   52–652
>   Library of Congress   [5]

38 Main entry for government publication with supplement added

> **Arkansas.** *State Board of <u>Health</u>. Division of <u>Public</u>*
> *Health Education.*
>   Health film catalog. ₍Little Rock, 1950?₎
>   158 p.   25 cm.
>
>   —— ——Supplement. Little Rock, 1952.
>   54 p.   26 cm.
>   RA420.5.A72   Suppl.
>
>
>   1. Hygiene—Film catalogs.   ɪ. Title.
>
>   RA420.5.A72   613.084   51–62465 rev
>   Library of Congress   ₍r53b1₎

39 Main entry for a dictionary

> **Webster, Noah,** 1758–1843.
>   New international dictionary of the English language.
> 2d ed. unabridged, with reference history ...   William Allan
> Neilson, editor in chief, Thomas A. Knott, general editor
> ₍and₎ Paul W. Carhart, managing editor.   Springfield,
> Mass., G. & C. Merriam Co., 1952.
>   cxxxii, 3214, 146, 105 p. illus. (part col.) ports. (part col.) 31 cm.
>   "A reference history of the United States of America and of
>   Canada, including the States and Provinces" (146 p.) has special t. p.
>
>   1. English language—Dictionaries.   ɪ. Title.
>
>   PE1625.W3   1952   423   52—1747
>   Library of Congress   ₍53f5₎

40 Title of periodical in author position—special issue of a periodical

---

Saturday review.
 America and the mind of Europe; with an introd. by
Lewis Galantière, and contributions by Raymond Aron [and
others] London, H. Hamilton [1951]
 125 p. 19 cm.

 Originally published as a special issue of the Saturday review of
literature.

 1. U. S.—Relations (general) with Europe. 2. Europe—Relations
(general) with the U. S. I. Galantière, Lewis, 1893-   ed. II.
Title.
E183.7.S3 ◯ 327.73094 52–7772 rev
 Library of Congress [r53i²10]

IV Edition statement, imprint, collation, series and other notes

41 Edition statement for first edition—unnecessary for small general library,
 but correct so *not* marked out

De Jong, Meindert, 1910–
 Shadrach. Pictures by Maurice Sendak. [1st ed.] New
York, Harper [1953]
 182 p. illus. 21 cm.

 I. Title.

PZ10.3.D372Sh ◯ 53–5250 ‡
 Library of Congress [7]

42 Name of state omitted in imprint because first word of heading

---

New York. State College of Ceramics, *Alfred. Library.*
  Publication.

  Alfred.
          no. in   v. 29 cm.

      Z881.N675   ◯   58–16064 ‡
      Library of Congress   [3]

**43 Entry for pamphlet without title page—title taken from cover title
and imprint in brackets**

The Library journal.
          Recommended children's books of 1951 as professionally
      evaluated by librarians for librarians in Library journal,
      arranged by grade and subject with author-title index. Com-
      piled under the direction of Louise Davis. [New York, 1952]

          95 p. illus. 23 cm.

          Cover title.

          1. Children's literature—Bibl.   I. Davis, Louise (Farwell) 1892–
      comp.   II. Title.

                                          A 52–8349

      Wisconsin. Univ. Libr.   ◯
      for Library of Congress   [53f5]

---

44 Book privately printed and so stated in imprint

Bible. *O. T.   Psalms.   English.   1952.   Authorized.*
   The book of Psalms, from the Authorized King James
version of the Holy Bible.   New York, Priv. print., press of
A. Colish, 1952.

   xii, 195 p.   15 cm.

   "Four hundred and fifty copies ... number 94."

   BS1422   1952   ◯   53–26242

   Library of Congress   [1]

**45 Imprint date and copyright date both given in imprint—unnecessary
in small general library, but correct so *not* marked out**

Fowler, Helen Marjorie, 1910–
   The intruder.   New York, Morrow, 1953 [c1952]

   248 p.   22 cm.

   First published in Sydney in 1952 under title: The shades will
not vanish.

   i. Title.

   PZ4.F786 In   ◯   52—13828 ‡

   Library of Congress   [53d7]

46 Date of publication uncertain

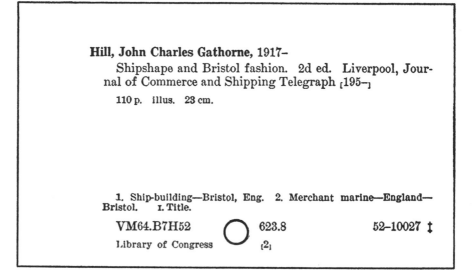

Hill, John Charles Gathorne, 1917–
    Shipshape and Bristol fashion. 2d ed. Liverpool, Jour-
nal of Commerce and Shipping Telegraph ₍195–₎
    110 p. illus. 23 cm.

    1. Ship-building—Bristol, Eng. 2. Merchant marine—England—
Bristol.   I. Title.
    VM64.B7H52   623.8   52–10027 ‡
    Library of Congress   ₍2₎

47 Main entry showing imprint for mimeographed material

Adams, James Frederick, 1927–
    A workbook to occupations. ₍Spokane₎ Mimeographed by
the Mimeograph Office of Whitworth College, °1953.
    1 v. illus. 30 cm.

    To be used with Dictionary of occupational titles, prepared by Divi-
sion of Occupational Analysis, U. S. Employment Service.

    1. Occupations—Terminology. 2. Occupations—Classification.   I.
U. S. Employment Service. Dictionary of occupational titles. II.
Title.
    HB2595.A52   331.7   53–25801 ‡
    Library of Congress   ₍1₎

48 Collation for two volumes bound as one

Di Lemme, Philip, 1900–
    Luminous advertising sketches; a treatise on electric signs, store front designs, abstracts of modern alphabets. ₁New York₁ White House Publications, **1953.**

  2 v. in 1 (chiefly illus.) 24 x 31 cm.

  1. Electric signs. 2. Advertising, Point-of-sale.   I. Title.
  HF5841.D5   53–24906 ‡
                          ◯   *659.134   659.136
  Library of Congress   ₁1₁

---

49 Publisher's series—unnecessary to include in description, but correct
    so *not* marked out

Hausman, Leon Augustus, 1888–
    Field guide for birds, wild flowers and nature study. New York, Grosset & Dunlap ₁ᶜ1948₁

  ix, 107 p. illus. 26 cm. (Grosset's library of practical handbooks)

  1. Natural history—U. S. 2. Natural history—Outdoor books.
  I. Title.

  QH104.H3   574.973   50–6134
                          ◯
  Library of Congress   ₁15₁

---

50 Subject series—give series note and make added entry under series

---

Dickinson, Emily, 1830–1886.
Poems; selected and edited with a commentary by Louis
Untermeyer, and illustrated with drawings by Helen Sewell.
New York, Heritage Press ₁1952₎

xxviii, 284 p. illus. 26 cm. (The American poets)

(Series)

PS1541.A6   1952a   811.49   53–1806

Library of Congress   ₁5₎

---

51 Subject series by author of the book—give series note
and make added entry under series

Ghirardi, Alfred A   1904–
Radio and television, receiver troubleshooting and repair,
by Alfred A. Ghirardi and J. Richard Johnson.   New York,
Rinehart ₁1952₎

xxiv, 822 p. illus. 24 cm. (*His* Modern radio and television
servicing library, 2)

1. Radio—Repairing. 2. Television—Repairing.   i. Title.
(Series)
TK6553.G482   vol. 2   621.3841366   52—5780

Library of Congress   ₁52k10₎

---

52 Series note for series with author and title

Hill, William W
    Land capability for soil and water conservation in Oregon,
prepared by William W. Hill and W. L. Powers. ₁Corvallis,
Or.₁ 1953.

    30 p. illus., fold. map (in pocket) 28 cm. (Oregon. Agricultural
Experiment Station, Corvallis. Station bulletin 530)

    Oregon Agricultural Experiment Station and the Soil Conservation
Service, U. S. Dept. of Agriculture, cooperating.

    1. Soil conservation — Oregon. 2. Water-supply — Oregon.   I.
Powers, Wilbur Louis, 1887–   joint author. ɪɪ. Title.   (Series)

    [S105.E32 no. 530]   A 53–9241

    Oregon. State College.   ◯   Library
    for Library of Congress   ₁2₁

**53 Note for bibliography—first page of bibliography not numbered in book,
hence bracketed**

Hignett, Charles.
    A history of the Athenian Constitution to the end of the
fifth century ʙ. ᴄ. Oxford, Clarendon Press, 1952.

    x, 420 p. 23 cm.

    Bibliography: p. ₁398₁–401.

    1. Athens—Constitutional history

    JC79.A8H5   342.3809   53–1875

    Library of Congress   ◯   ₁2₁

54 Note for bibliography, paging not given

Grant, Madeleine Parker, 1895–
    Microbiology and human progress. New York, Rinehart
₁1953₎
    718 p. illus. 24 cm.
    Includes bibliography.

    1. Micro-organisms.   ɪ. Title.

    QR41.G65   ◯   589.95   52–12517 ‡
    Library of Congress   ₁20₎

55 Appendixes important for small library added on printed card

598.2
L73   **Lincoln, Frederick Charles,** 1892–
    Migration of birds. Illustrated by Bob Hines. Garden
City, N. Y., Doubleday, 1952.
    102 p. illus. 20 cm.
    Bibliography: p. 94–98.
    Appendixes: I. List of birds mentioned in
the text.–II. Bird banding.

    1. Birds—Migration.

    QL698.L479   ◯   598.2   52–5234
    Library of Congress   ₁20₎

56 Contents for work in one volume

Clark, Barrett Harper, 1890–   *ed.*
    Nine modern American plays, edited by Barrett H. Clark
and William H. Davenport. New York, Appleton-Century-
Crofts ₁1951₁
    xiii, 432 p. 25 cm.
    CONTENTS.—The hairy ape, by E. O'Neill.—Street scene, by E. L.
Rice.—Green grow the lilacs, by L. Riggs.—High Tor, by M. Anderson.—Stage door, by E. Ferber and G. S. Kaufman.—You can't take
it with you, by M. Hart and G. S. Kaufman.—Abe Lincoln in Illinois,
by R. E. Sherwood.—The glass menagerie, by T. Williams.—Command
decision, by W. W. Haines.—Supplementary reading (p. 430)—Plays
by dramatists in this volume (p. 431–432)

    1. American drama—20th cent.   I. Davenport, William Henry,
1908–   joint ed.

    PS634.C49   812.5082   51—9988
    Library of Congress   ₁53x10₁

57 Contents for work in two volumes

Cézanne, Paul, 1839–1906.
    Paul Cezanne sketch book, owned by the Art Institute of
Chicago. New York, C. Valentin, 1951.
    2 v. illus. 15 x 23 cm.
    CONTENTS.—1. Introductory text, by C. O. Schniewind. Contents
of the sketchbook.—2. Plates.

    I. Chicago. Art Institute.

    NC248.C37A47   741.91   52–1411
    Library of Congress   ₁7₁

58 Wilson printed catalog card with note about sequel

Keith, Agnes (Newton)
  White man returns; sketches by the author. Little 1951
310p illus

    Sequel to: Three came home
    "The Keiths are back in North Borneo. While her husband's job is
connected with conservation and lumber, the greatest contribution the
Keiths are making—to the island and, through Mrs Keith's writings,
to the world—is to demonstrate the power of the brotherhood of man."
Huntting

1 Borneo—Social conditions ɪ Title   ₜ919.11ₗ 991.1

11-2-51   ◯   (W) The H. W. Wilson Company

**59 Wilson printed catalog card with note about changed title—
tracing for added entries for title and former title**

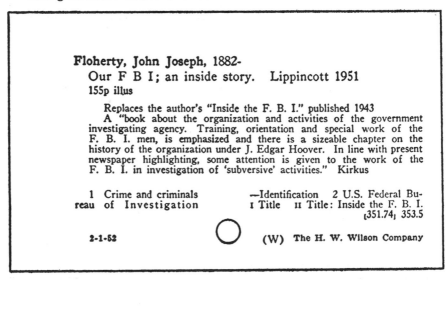

Floherty, John Joseph, 1882-
  Our F B I; an inside story. Lippincott 1951
155p illus

    Replaces the author's "Inside the F. B. I." published 1943
    A "book about the organization and activities of the government
investigating agency. Training, orientation and special work of the
F. B. I. men, is emphasized and there is a sizeable chapter on the
history of the organization under J. Edgar Hoover. In line with present
newspaper highlighting, some attention is given to the work of the
F. B. I. in investigation of 'subversive' activities." Kirkus

1 Crime and criminals   —Identification 2 U.S. Federal Bureau of Investigation   ɪ Title ɪɪ Title: Inside the F. B. I.
                                 ₜ351.74ₗ 353.5

2-1-52   ◯   (W) The H. W. Wilson Company

60 Tracing—title and catch title

> Hogan, Inez, 1895–
>   Read to me about the littlest cowboy; written and illus-
> trated by Inez Hogan. ₁1st ed.₎ New York, Dutton ₁1951₎
>   45 p. illus. 26 cm.
>   Music on lining papers.
>
>
>   ɪ. Title. ɪɪ. Title: The littlest cowboy.
>
> PZ7.H683Re   51–9926 rev
>
> Library of Congress   ₁r53k10₎

61 Tracing—subject and title entries

> Hoffman, George Walter, 1914–   ed.
>   A geography of Europe. Contributors: Nels A. Bengtson
> ₁and others₎ New York, Ronald Press Co. ₁1953₎
>   ix, 775 p. illus., maps. 24 cm.
>   Includes bibliographies.
>
>
>   1. Europe—Descr. & trav.—1945–   ɪ. Title.
>
> D907.H6   914   53–5719
>
> Library of Congress   ₁20₎

62 Tracing—subject, title, and series entries

Summers, Robert Edward, 1918–   *ed.*
      America's weapons of psychological warfare. New York,
Wilson, 1951.
      206 p. 20 cm. (The Reference shelf, v. 23, no. 4)
      Bibliography: p. ₍198₎–206.

      1. Propaganda, American. 2. U. S.—Relations (general) with for-
eign countries. 3. Psychological warfare.   i. Title.   (Series)

      E744.S98   301.1523   51—8838

      Library of Congress   ₍52v²20₎

---

63 Tracing—translator, editor, catch title, series entries

Goethe, Johann Wolfgang von, 1749–1832.
      George Ticknor's The sorrows of young Werter; edited
with introd. and critical analysis by Frank G. Ryder.
Chapel Hill, 1952.
      xxxiii, 108 p. 24 cm. (The University of North Carolina studies
in comparative literature, no. 4)
      Bibliographical references: p. ₍105₎–108.

      i. Ticknor, George, 1791–1871, tr. ii. Ryder, Frank Glessner, 1916–
ed. iii. Title: The sorrows of young Werter.   (Series: North
Carolina. University. Studies in comparative literature, no. 4)

      PT2027.W3 1952   832.62   52–4994

      Library of Congress   ₍7₎

---

64 Subject begins with same word as title, hence no title entry

---

Ley, Willy, 1906–
 Rockets, missiles, and space travel. New York, Viking Press, 1951.

  xii, 436 p. illus., ports. 22 cm.

  Bibliography: p. 413–430.
  First published in 1944 under title: Rockets.

  1. Rockets (Aeronautics)

  TL782.L43   1951   629.13338   51—11482

  Library of Congress   ₍52x10₎

V Dramatization of a work

65 Main entry for work dramatized, note concerning dramatization

---

McLean, Kathryn (Anderson) 1909–
 ... Mama's bank account. New York, Harcourt, Brace and company ₍1943₎

  5 p. l., 3–204 p. 20 cm.

  Author's pseud., Kathryn Forbes, at head of title.
  "First edition."
 Dramatized by John Van Druten and published under title: I remember mama.

  I. Title.

  PZ3.M22367Mam   43—4313

  Library of Congress   ₍52r45n²₎

---

66 Main entry for dramatization of another's work—tracing shows added entry
for original author and title

Van Druten, John, 1901–
I remember mama, a play in two acts, by John Van Druten,
adapted from Kathryn Forbes' book Mama's bank account.
New York, Harcourt, Brace and company ₁1945₁

6 p. l., 3–177 p.   21 cm.

"First edition."

ɪ. McLean, Kathryn (Anderson) 1900–   Mama's bank account.
ɪɪ. Title.
₁*Full name:* John William Van Druten₁

45—35067

Library of Congress   PR6043.A4 I 2
₁480²5₁   822.91

---

67 Main entry for dramatization—same author for both—tracing shows added
entry for joint author of dramatization

Wright, Richard, 1909–
Native son (the biography of a young American) a play
in ten scenes by Paul Green and Richard Wright, from the
novel by Richard Wright. A Mercury production by Orson
Welles, presented by Orson Welles and John Houseman.
New York and London, Harper & brothers ₁ᶜ1941₁

ix p., 1 l., 148 p.   front.   21 cm.

Includes songs with music.
"First edition."

ɪ. *Green, Paul, 1894–   joint author. ɪɪ. Title.
₁*Full name:* Richard Nathaniel Wright₁

41—6481

Library of Congress   PS3545.R815N25
₁50n1₁   812.5

VI Audio-visual materials

68 Main entry for filmstrip with number of frames, color, width in millimeters

---

The Northeast (*Filmstrip*) Young America Films, 1952.
Produced by Key Productions. © Key Productions, inc.;
1Mar52; JP1216.

    48 fr., color, 35 mm. (U. S. regional geography series)

    Summary: Photographs of the Northeast region, which includes
Maine, Vermont, New Hampshire, Massachusetts, Connecticut, and
Rhode Island. Shows that the thin, sterile soil and the short grow-
ing season have necessitated specialized farming, and have led to
heavy industrialization and the development of the lumber and fish-
ing industries.

    1. New England—Descr. & trav. 2. New England—Indus.   I.
Key Productions, inc., New York. . II. Young America Films, inc., New
York.   (Series)

                           917.4   Fi 52–1058

    Library of Congress   [18]

---

69 Main entry for filmstrip with accompanying record

Carol had problems (*Filmstrip*) McGraw-Hill Book Co.,
1952. Produced by Aljac Productions.

    44 fr., b&w, 35 mm. (Work habits series, no. 5)

    With synchronized record.
    Summary: Carol, who makes careless mistakes on her tests, finds
that by checking her work she catches her own mistakes and thus
improves her grades. For middle grades.
    Credits: Technical advisers, Clayton Williamson, Josephine L.
Wright.

    1. Examinations.   I. McGraw-Hill Book Company, inc. II. Aljac
Productions.   (Series)

                           371.27   Fi 52–1300

    Library of Congress   [8]

---

70 Main entry for filmstrip with teacher's manual

Beyond the stars (*Filmstrip*)   Moody Institute of Science of the Moody Bible Institute, 1952.

54 fr., color, 35 mm. (Sermons from science)

Adapted from the motion pictures God of Creation and Hidden treasures.
With teacher's manual and guide book.
Summary: Photographs of the heavens are presented as evidence of the power and glory of God.
Ansco color.

1. God—Omnipotence.   I. Moody Bible Institute of Chicago. II. God of Creation (Motion picture) III. Hidden treasures (Motion picture)*   (Series: Sermons from science (Filmstrip))

231.4   Fi 52–1322

Library of Congress   ₍₉₎

---

71 Main entry for map with measurements, scale, projection

New York (*State*)   *Dept. of Commerce.*
Physical map, New York State and adjacent areas. ₍Albany, 1952₎ °1951.

col. map 80 x 105 cm.

Scale 1: 750,000 ; 1"=12 miles (approximately)
"Lambert conformal conic projection."
"Base map and control by sectional charts; United States Coast & Geodetic Survey."
Relief shown by hypsometric tints.

1. New York (State)—Maps, Physical.

G3801.C1 1951.N4   Map 52–365

Library of Congress   ₍₂₎

---

72 Main entry for map showing measurements when folded

American Automobile Association.
  AAA members' guide to New York City & vicinity; Manhattan, Bronx, Brooklyn, Queens, Staten Island, Nassau, Suffolk, Westchester, Putnam. ₁New York, Automobile Club of New York, 1948₁

  23 p. incl. illus., col. maps. 23 x 41 cm. fold. to 23 x 21 cm.

  "Prepared in cooperation with the Automobile Club of New York."

  1. New York (City)—Road maps. 2. New York (City)—Suburbs—Road maps. 3. Long Island—Road maps.   I. Automobile Club of New York.

  Map 49–173*

  Library of Congress   ₁1₁

---

73 Main entry for phonodisc, conventional title, title, number of sides, diameter, revolutions per minute

---

Gounod, Charles François, 1818–1893.
  ₁Faust. Ballet₁ *Phonodisc.*

  Faust, ballet music.   RCA Victor ERA 64.

  2 s. 7 in. 45 rpm.

  Boston Pops Orchestra ; Arthur Fiedler, conductor.
  "Extended play."
  Program note on back of slipcase.

  1. Ballets. 2. Operas—Excerpts.   I. Boston Pops Orchestra.
  II. Fiedler, Arthur, 1894–   III. Title.

  R 53–149

  Library of Congress   ₁9₁

74 Subject entry for phonodisc—with decimal classification number and Cutter book number

786.4   PIANO MUSIC.
R11   **Rachmaninoff, Sergei, 1873–1943.**
          ₁Prelude, piano, op. 3, no. 2, C♯ minor₁ *Phonodisc.*

          Prelude in C sharp minor, op. 3, no. 2 ₁and₁ Prelude in G minor, op. 23, no. 5.   Capital H–8186.
          1 s.   12 in.   33⅓ rpm.   (Capitol classics)

          Leonard Pennario, piano.
          Microgroove.
          Program note on back ȯf slipcase.
          With: Liszt, Franz. Rhapsodie hongroise, piano, no. 2.

          1. Piano music.   ɪ. Rachmaninoff, Sergei, 1873–1943. Prelude, piano, op. 23, no. 5, G minor. ɪɪ. Pennario, Leonard.

                                                        R 53–142

          Library of Congress   ₁7₁

Abbreviations

These abbreviations are used anywhere in the entry except that words in the title up to the first mark of punctuation are not to be abbreviated. Abbreviations given on the title page are to be used whether included in this list or not. For a list of abbreviations used in the cataloging of audio-visual materials, see page 148.

abridged	abr.
association	assoc.
augmented	augm.
baronet	bart.
book	bk.
born	b.
Brother, Brothers	Bro., Bros.[1]
bulletin	bull.
colored	col.
Company	Co.
compiled, compiler	comp.
Congress	Cong.
copyright	c
Corporation	Corp.
corrected	corr.
County	Co.
Department	Dept.
died	d.
edition, editor, editors	ed., eds.
engraved, engraver	engr.
enlarged	enl.
et cetera	etc.

---

[1]Used only in names of firms and other corporate bodies.

His (or Her) Majesty's Stationery Office . . . . . .H. M. Stationery Off.
illustration, illustrations, illustrator . . . . .illus.
incorporated . . . . .inc.
introduction, introductory . . . . .introd.
Junior . . . . .Jr.
limited . . . . .ltd.
no date of publication .n.d.
number, numbers . . . . .no., nos.
page, pages . . . . .p.
part, parts . . . . .pt., pts.
portrait, portraits . . . . .port., ports.
preface, prefatory . . . . .pref.
President . . . . .Pres.[2]
printing . . . . .print.
privately printed . . . . .priv. print.
pseudonym . . . . .pseud.
publishing, publisher, publishers . . . . .pub.
revised . . . . rev.
Saint . . . . .St.[3]
second . . . . 2d[4]
Senior . . . . .Sr.
series . . . . .ser.
session . . . . .sess.
supplement . . . . .suppl.
table . . . . .tab.
Territory . . . . .Ter.
third . . . . .3d[4]
translator . . . . tr.
United States . . . . U. S.
volume, volumes . . . . v., vol.,[5] vols.[5]

Geographical names. Abbreviations for geographical names in headings are to be decided upon and a list made of those to be used in a given catalog. U. S. for United States is customarily used in all headings, but in titles the usage of the title page is followed. The usual abbreviations for states are used when they follow the name of a city. A library may also compile a list of abbreviations for well-known cities to be used whenever they occur on catalog cards, except as the first word of a heading.

---

[2]Used only in a personal name heading.
[3]Used only when preceding the name, as St. Paul's Cathedral.
[4]All other ordinal numbers are abbreviated as usual, e.g., 1st, 4th.
[5]Used at the beginning of a statement and before a roman numeral.

Publishers. List of publishers, with their abbreviations, to be used without place:

Abingdon-Cokesbury Press	Abingdon-Cokesbury
Allyn & Bacon	Allyn
American Book Co.	Am. Bk.
American Library Association	A.L.A.
Appleton-Century-Crofts, Inc.	Appleton
A. S. Barnes & Co.	Barnes
The Blakiston Co.	Blakiston
Bobbs-Merrill Co., Inc.	Bobbs
R. R. Bowker Company	Bowker
British Book Centre, Inc.	British Bk. Centre
Coward-McCann, Inc.	Coward-McCann
The Thomas Y. Crowell Co.	Crowell
Crown Publishers	Crown
John Day Co., Inc.	Day
Dodd, Mead & Company, Inc.	Dodd
Doubleday & Co., Inc.	Doubleday
E. P. Dutton & Co., Inc.	Dutton
Farrar, Straus & Young, Inc.	Farrar, Straus
Samuel French, Inc.	French
Funk & Wagnalls Company	Funk
Ginn & Co.	Ginn
Grosset & Dunlap, Inc.	Grosset
C. S. Hammond & Co., Inc.	Hammond
Harcourt, Brace & Co., Inc.	Harcourt
Harper & Brothers	Harper
D. C. Heath & Company	Heath
Henry Holt & Co., Inc.	Holt
Houghton Mifflin Company	Houghton
Orange Judd Publishing Company, Inc.	Judd
Alfred A. Knopf, Inc.	Knopf
Lane Publishing Co.	Lane Pub.
J. B. Lippincott Company	Lippincott
Little, Brown & Co.	Little
Liveright Publishing Corporation	Liveright
Longmans, Green & Co., Inc.	Longmans
A. C. McClurg & Co.	McClurg
McGraw-Hill Book Co., Inc.	McGraw
The Macmillan Co.	Macmillan
G. & C. Merriam Co.	Merriam
William Morrow & Co., Inc.	Morrow
Thomas Nelson & Sons	Nelson

New Directions .... New Directions
W. W. Norton & Company, Inc............. Norton
L. C. Page & Company................... Page
Prentice-Hall, Inc. .... Prentice-Hall
G. P. Putnam's Sons..................... Putnam
Rand McNally & Company................ Rand McNally
Random House, Inc....................... Random
Rinehart & Company..................... Rinehart
Scott, Foresman & Company.............. Scott
Charles Scribner's Sons................... Scribner
Simon & Schuster, Inc.................... Simon & Schuster
United States Government Printing Office ... U. S. Govt. Print. Off.
D. Van Nostrand Company, Inc............ Van Nostrand
The Viking Press, Inc..................... Viking
Albert Whitman & Company............. Whitman
Wilcox & Follett Company................ Wilcox & Follett
John Wiley & Sons, Inc................... Wiley
The H. W. Wilson Company.............. Wilson
The World Publishing Co................. World Pub.

Definitions of technical terms

Accession. To record books and other similar material added to a library in the order of acquisition. (*A.L.A. Glossary*)[1]

Accession number. The number given to a volume in the order of its acquisition. (*A.L.A. Glossary*)

Accession record. The business record of books, etc., added to a library in the order of receipt, giving a condensed description of the book and the essential facts in its library history. (Cutter)[2]

Adaptation. A rewritten form of a literary work modified for a purpose or use other than that for which the original work was intended (*A.L.A. Glossary*), e.g., Lamb's *Tales from Shakespeare.*

Added entry. A secondary entry, i.e., any other than the main entry... [It] is a duplicate of the main entry, with the addition of a special heading... (A.L.A. 1949)[3]

Alternative title. A subtitle introduced by "or" or its equivalent, e.g., *Hypatia; or, New foes with an old face.* (A.L.A. 1949)

Analytical entry. The entry of some part of a work or of some article contained in a collection (volume of essays, serial, etc.). (A.L.A. 1949)

Anonymous classic. ...a work of unknown or doubtful authorship, com-

---

[1] *A.L.A. Glossary of Library Terms* (Chicago: A.L.A., 1943).
[2] C. A. Cutter, *Rules for a Dictionary Catalog* (4th ed. rewritten; Washington: Govt. Print. Off., 1904), p.13.
[3] Definitions with the source indicated in this way are from *A.L.A. Cataloging Rules for Author and Title Entries* (2d ed.; Chicago: A.L.A., 1949), p.229-35.

monly designated by title, which may have appeared in the course of time in many editions, versions, and/or translations (A.L.A. 1949)

Anonymous work. ...one in which the author's name does not appear anywhere in the book. (A.L.A. 1949)

Author entry. An entry of a work in a catalog under its author's name as heading...The author heading will consist of a personal or...an organization's name or some substitute for it, e.g., initials, pseudonym, etc....(A.L.A. 1949)

Author number. *See* Book number.

Authority list. An official list of forms selected as headings in a catalog, giving for author and corporate names and for the forms of entry of anonymous classics the sources used for establishing the forms together with the variant forms...(*A.L.A. Glossary*)

Book number. A combination of letters and figures used to arrange books in the same classification number in alphabetical order. (*A.L.A. Glossary*)

Card catalog. A catalog made on separate cards and kept in trays. (Cutter, adapted)[4]

Catalog. A list of books, maps, etc., arranged according to some definite plan. As distinguished from a bibliography it is a list which records, describes, and indexes the resources of a collection, a library, or a group of libraries. (A.L.A. 1949) *See also* Dictionary catalog.

Catchword title. A partial title consisting of some striking or easily remembered word or phrase. It may coincide with the subtitle or the alternative title. (A.L.A. 1949) *See also* Partial title.

Classification. "The putting together of like things." Book classification, as defined by C. A. Cutter, is "the grouping of books written on the same or similar subjects."[5]

Collation. That part of the catalog entry which describes the work as a material object, enumerating its volumes, pages...and the type and character of its illustrations. (*A.L.A. Glossary*)

Compiler. One who produces a work by collecting and putting together written or printed matter from the works of various authors. Also, one who chooses and combines into one work selections or quotations from one author. (A.L.A. 1949)

---

[4]Cutter, *op. cit.,* p.14.
[5]Corinne Bacon, *Classification* (rev. ed.; Chicago: A.L.A., 1925), p.1.

Compound name. A name formed from two or more proper names, often connected by a hyphen, a conjunction, or a preposition. (A.L.A. 1949)

Continuation. 1. A work issued as a supplement to one previously issued. 2. A part issued in continuance of a book, a serial, or a series. (A.L.A. 1949)

Conventional title. *See* Uniform title.

Copyright date. The date of copyright as recorded in the Copyright Office, and (as a rule) as given in the book on the back of the title page (L.C. 1949)[6]

Corporate entry. 1. An entry under the name of a society, institution, government department, bureau, or other organized body, for works issued in its name or by its authority, whether this be a main or an added heading. 2. The heading chosen for this entry. (A.L.A. 1949)

Cover title. The title printed on the original covers of a book or pamphlet, or lettered or stamped on the publisher's binding, as distinguished from the title lettered on the cover of a particular copy by a binder. (L.C. 1949)

Cross reference. *See* Reference, "See" reference, "See also" reference.

Cutter number. *See* Book number.

Dictionary catalog. A catalog, ~~usually on cards~~, in which all the entries (author, title, subject, series, etc.) and their related references are arranged together in one general alphabet. The subarrangement frequently varies from the strictly alphabetical. (A.L.A. 1949)

Edition. One of the successive forms in which a literary text is issued either by the author or by a subsequent editor. (A.L.A. 1949)

Editor. One who prepares for publication a work or collection of works or articles not his own... (A.L.A. 1949)

Entry. 1. A record of a book in a catalog or list. 2. The heading chosen for this record. (A.L.A. 1949)

Entry word. The word by which the entry is arranged in the catalog, usually the first word (other than an article) of the heading. (A.L.A. 1949)

Extension card. A catalog card that continues an entry from a preceding card. *(A.L.A. Glossary)*

Filing word. *See* Entry word.

---

[6]Definitions with the source indicated in this way are from *Rules for Descriptive Cataloging in the Library of Congress* (1949).

First indention. The eighth typewriter space from the left edge of the card.

Form division. A division of a class of books according to their form, e.g., a bibliography, periodical, outline.

Guide card. A projecting labeled card inserted in a card catalog to aid in finding a desired place or heading. (Cutter)[7]

Half title. A brief title...without imprint and usually without the author's name, printed on a separate leaf preceding the main title page...the text or introducing the sections of a work. (*A.L.A. Glossary*)

Heading. The name, word, or phrase used at the head of an entry to indicate some special aspect of the book (authorship, subject content, series, title, etc.) and thereby to bring together in the catalog associated and allied material. (A.L.A. 1949)

Illustration. A pictorial or other representation in or belonging to a book or other publication, as issued; usually designed to elucidate the text. In the narrow sense the term stands for illustrations within the text (i.e., those which form part of the text page...). (*A.L.A. Glossary*)

Imprint. The place and date of publication, and the name of the publisher or the printer (or sometimes both); ordinarily printed at the foot of the title page. (*A.L.A. Glossary*)

Imprint date. The year of publication or printing as specified on the title page. (*A.L.A. Glossary*)

Introduction date. The date of a book as given at the beginning or at the end of the introduction. (*A.L.A. Glossary*)

Joint author. A person who collaborates with one or more associates to produce a work in which the contribution of each is usually not separable from that of the others. (A.L.A. 1949)

Main entry. The basic catalog card, usually the author entry, giving all the information necessary to the complete identification of a work. This entry bears also the tracing of all the other headings under which the work in question is entered in the catalog. (A.L.A. 1949)

Name authority file. *See* Authority list.

Notation. A system of symbols, generally letters and figures, used separately or in combination, to represent the divisions of a classification scheme. (*A.L.A. Glossary*)

[7]Cutter, *op. cit.*, p.20.

Partial title. One which consists of a secondary part of the title as given on the title page. It may be a catchword title, subtitle, or alternative title. (A.L.A. 1949)

Periodical. A serial in parts which are not monographs and usually contain articles by several contributors. It generally has a distinctive title and the successive numbers or parts are intended to appear at stated or regular intervals, and, as a rule, for an indefinite period. *Newspapers,* whose chief function it is to disseminate news, and the *Memoirs, Proceedings, Journals,* etc., of societies are not considered periodicals under the rules. (A.L.A. 1949)

Preface date. The date given at the beginning or end of the preface. *(A.L.A. Glossary)*

Pseudonym. A false name assumed by an author to conceal his identity. (A.L.A. 1949)

Publisher. The person, firm, or corporate body undertaking the responsibility for the issue of a book or other printed matter to the public. ...*(A.L.A. Glossary)*

Reference. A direction from one heading to another. (A.L.A. 1949)

Second indention. The twelfth typewriter space from the left edge of the card.

Secondary entry. See Added entry.

"See also" reference. A direction in a catalog from a term or name under which entries are listed to another term or name under which additional or allied information may be found. *(A.L.A. Glossary)*

"See" reference. A direction in a catalog from a term or name under which no entries are listed to a term or name under which entries are listed....*(A.L.A. Glossary)*

Serial. A publication issued in successive parts, usually at regular intervals, and as a rule, intended to be continued indefinitely. Serials include periodicals, annuals (reports, yearbooks, etc.) and memoirs, proceedings, and transactions of societies. (A.L.A. 1949)

Series. 1. A number of separate works, usually related to one another in subject or otherwise, issued in succession, normally by the same publisher and in uniform style, with a collective title which generally appears at the head of the title page, on the half title, or on the cover. 2. Each of two or more volumes of essays, lectures, articles, or other writings, similar in character and issued in sequence, e.g., Lowell's *Among my books, second series.* 3. A separately numbered sequence of volumes within a series or serial, e.g., *Notes and queries, 1st series, 2d series, etc.* (A.L.A. 1949)

Series entry. An entry, (usually brief) of the several works in the library which belong to a series under the name of that series as a heading. (A.L.A. 1949)

Series statement. The information on a publication which names the series to which it belongs and specifies its place in the series if the series is comprised of a numbered sequence of parts. (L.C. 1949)

Shelf list. A record of the books in a library arranged in the order in which they stand on the shelves. (*A.L.A. Glossary*)

Source of a book. The dealer from whom it was purchased, or its donor.

Spine. That part of the cover or binding which conceals the sewed or bound edge of a book, usually bearing the title, and frequently the author. (*A.L.A. Glossary*)

Subject authority list. An official list of subject headings used in a given catalog and the references made to them.

Subject card. A catalog card bearing a subject entry. (*A.L.A. Glossary*)

Subject heading. A word or a group of words indicating a subject under which all material dealing with the same theme is entered in a catalog...(*A.L.A. Glossary*)

Subtitle. The explanatory part of the title following the main title, e.g., *The creative adult; self-education in the art of living.* (A.L.A. 1949)

Third indention. The fourteenth typewriter space from the left edge of the card.

Title. 1. In the broad sense, the distinguishing name of any written production as given on the title page, including the name of the author, editor, translator, the edition, etc., but excluding the imprint. 2. In the narrow sense the title does not include the name of the author, editor, etc. (A.L.A. 1949)

Title entry. The record of a work in the catalog under the title, generally beginning with the first word not an article. A title entry may be a main entry or an added entry. (A.L.A. 1949)

Title page. A page at the beginning of a book or work, bearing its full title and usually, though not necessarily, the author's (editor's, etc.) name and the imprint. (A.L.A. 1949)

Tracing. The record on the main entry card of all the additional headings under which the work is represented in the catalog. Also, the record on...an authority card of all the related references made.

The tracing may be on the face or on the back of the card... (A.L.A. 1949)

Uniform title. The distinctive title by which a work which has appeared under varying titles and in various versions is most generally known. Also called Conventional title. (*A.L.A. Glossary*)

Unit card. A basic catalog card, in the form of a main entry, which when duplicated may be used as a unit for all other entries for that work in the catalog by the addition of the appropriate heading. Library of Congress printed cards are the most commonly used unit cards. (A.L.A. 1949)

Withdrawal. The process of removing from library records all entries for a book no longer in the library. (*A.L.A. Glossary*)

Aids in the cataloging
of a small library

The following list was selected with reference to the availability of the material and its probable usefulness to the librarian of the small library.

A.L.A. Rules for Filing Catalog Cards, prepared by a special committee, Sophie K. Hiss, chairman. Chicago: A.L.A., 1942. 109p.

American Library Association. Division of Cataloging and Classification. *A.L.A. Cataloging Rules for Author and Title Entries.* 2d ed., edited by Clara Beetle. Chicago: A.L.A., 1949. 265p.

Barden, B. R. *Book Numbers; a Manual for Students with a Basic Code of Rules.* Chicago: A.L.A., 1937. 31p.

Bishop, W. W. *Practical Handbook of Modern Library Cataloging.* 2d ed. Baltimore: Williams & Wilkins, 1927. 152p.

The Booklist; a Guide to Current Books. Chicago: A.L.A., 1905– . Gives the Dewey Decimal Classification number and subject headings for all books listed.

Columbia University. School of Library Service. *Sample Catalog Cards.* 2d ed. N. Y.: The School, 1950. Unnumbered pages.

Current Biography; Who's News and Why. N. Y.: Wilson, 1940– .

Cutter, C. A. *Alphabetic Order Table, Altered and Fitted With Three Figures by Kate E. Sanborn.*

Daughtry, B. M. *Cataloging and Classifying Audio-Visual Materials.* Tallahassee, Fla.: Florida State Univ., 1950. 20p.

Dewey, Melvil. *Abridged Decimal Classification and Relativ Index.* Ed. 6. Lake Placid Club, N. Y.: Forest Pr., 1945. 343p.

Dewey, Melvil. *Decimal Classification and Relativ Index.* Ed. 14, rev. and enl. Lake Placid Club, N. Y.: Forest Pr., 1942. 2v. in 1.

Dewey, Melvil. *Dewey Decimal Classification & Relative Index.* Standard (15th) ed., rev. Lake Placid Club, N. Y.: Forest Pr., 1952. 872p.

Douglas, M. P. *The Teacher-Librarian's Handbook.* 2d ed. Chicago: A.L.A., 1949. 166p.

Douglass, R. R., comp. *Handbook of Card Forms for Use in Cataloging.* Rev. ed. Chicago: Wilcox & Follett, 1950. 47p.

Eaton, Thelma. *Cataloging and Classification; an Introductory Manual.* Champaign, Ill.: Distributed by The Illini Union Bookstore, 1951. 113p.

Frick, B. M. *Sears List of Subject Headings, with Practical Suggestions for the Beginner in Subject Headings Work by M. E. Sears.* 6th ed. N. Y.: Wilson, 1950. 558p.

Haykin, D. J. *Subject Headings, a Practical Guide.* Washington: Govt. Print. Off., 1951. 140p.

Herdman, M. M. *Classification; an Introductory Manual.* 2d ed. Chicago: A.L.A., 1947. 50p.

Johnson, M. F., and Cook, D. E. *Manual of Cataloging and Classification for Small School and Public Libraries.* 4th ed. N. Y.: Wilson, 1950. 71p.

Kunitz, S. J., and Haycraft, Howard. *The Junior Book of Authors.* N. Y.: Wilson, 1934. 400p.

Kunitz, S. J., and Haycraft, Howard. *Twentieth Century Authors, a Biographical Dictionary.* N. Y.: Wilson, 1942. 1577p.

Mann, Margaret. *Introduction to Cataloging and the Classification of Books.* 2d ed. Chicago: A.L.A., 1943. 276p.

Merrill, W. S. *Code for Classifiers.* 2d ed. Chicago: A.L.A., 1939. 190p.

Pittsburgh. Carnegie Library. *Rules for Filing Cards.* 5th ed. Pittsburgh: The Library, 1932. 34p.

Readers' Guide to Periodical Literature. N. Y.: Wilson, 1900– . The *Readers' Guide* and the *Abridged Readers' Guide,* published from 1935 to date, are useful for authors' full names (they do not include authors' dates) as well as for new subject headings.

Rue, Eloise and LaPlante, Effie. *Subject Headings for Children's Materials.* Chicago: A.L.A., 1952. 149p.

Rufsvold, M. I. *Audio-Visual School Library Service: a Handbook for Libraries.* Chicago: A.L.A., 1949. 116p.

Sayers, W. C. B. *An Introduction to Library Classification*. 8th ed. London: Grafton, 1950. 314p.

U. S. Library of Congress. Descriptive Cataloging Division. *Rules for Descriptive Cataloging in the Library of Congress*. Washington: Govt. Print. Off., 1949. 141p. Also its *Supplement, 1949–51; Phonorecords,* 1952; and *Motion Pictures and Filmstrips,* 1953.

Webster's Biographical Dictionary, Springfield, Mass.: Merriam, 1943. 1697p.

Who's Who; an Annual Biographical Dictionary. London: Black, 1849– .

Who's Who in America, a Biographical Dictionary. Chicago: Marquis, 1899– .

Wilson (H. W.) Company, New York. *Children's Catalog.* 8th ed., rev. N. Y.: Wilson, 1951. 919p.

Wilson (H. W.) Company, New York. *Standard Catalog for High School Libraries.* 6th ed. N. Y.: Wilson, 1952. 1128p.

Wilson (H. W.) Company, New York. *Standard Catalog for Public Libraries.* 1949 ed. N. Y.: Wilson, 1950. 2057p.

The A.L.A. *Catalogs* are very useful aids for authors' full names, suggestive classification numbers, and subject entries. The Special Libraries Association, 31 East Tenth Street, New York 3, New York, maintains a file of special classification schemes. Lists of subject headings for special subjects will be found in books, periodicals, and as printed and mimeographed lists issued by governmental and other organizations. Besides these specially prepared lists the headings used in periodical indexes in particular fields, e.g., the *Industrial Arts Index,* the *Education Index,* are useful.

Index